Cécile Armand
Madmen in Shanghai

Cécile Armand

Madmen in Shanghai

A Social History of Advertising in Modern China (1914–1956)

DE GRUYTER
OLDENBOURG

ISBN 978-3-11-138824-3
e-ISBN (PDF) 978-3-11-139000-0
e-ISBN (EPUB) 978-3-11-139029-1

Library of Congress Control Number: 2024930629

Bibliographic information published by the Deutsche Nationalbibliothek
The Deutsche Nationalbibliothek lists this publication in the Deutsche Nationalbibliografie;
detailed bibliographic data are available on the internet at http://dnb.dnb.de.

© 2024 Walter de Gruyter GmbH, Berlin/Boston
Cover image: Billboards being erected or maintained near the race course, 1948,
© Virtual Shanghai Platform
Typesetting: Integra Software Services Pvt. Ltd.
Printing and binding: CPI books GmbH, Leck

www.degruyter.com

FSC
www.fsc.org

MIX
Papier | Fördert
gute Waldnutzung
FSC® C083411

Contents

Part One: **The Birth of a Profession**

List of Maps and Figures

https://doi.org/10.1515/9783111390000-203

List of Tables

https://doi.org/10.1515/9783111390000-204

Key Abbreviations

ACC   Advertising Club of China (Zhongguo guanggao gonghui)
AAA   Association of Advertising Agencies
ACAA   Association for Chinese Advertising Agencies (Zhonghua guanggao shanghui)
BAT   British-American Tobacco Company
CCAA   China Commercial Advertising Agency (Huashang guanggao gongsi)
CP   *China Press*
CWR   *China Weekly Review*
FC   French Concession
MRFE   *Millard's Review of the Far East*
NCH   *North China Herald*
SB   *Shenbao*
SCMP   *South China Morning Post*
SMA   Shanghai Municipal Archives
SMC   Shanghai Municipal Council
WRFE   *Weekly Review of the Far East*
YMCA   Young Men's Christian Association
LMS   Lu Meiseng
LSL   Lu Shoulun
WYB   Wang Yingbin
YJW   Yao Junwei
ZYN   Zheng Yaonan
ZZP   Zhang Zhuping

https://doi.org/10.1515/9783111390000-205

We extend our heartfelt gratitude to the Chiang Ching-kuo Foundation for International Scholarly Exchange for their generous support and unwavering trust in this research endeavour.

Introduction

Shanghai, 1 September 1936. Two hundred and fifty distinguished guests were gathered at the Park Hotel to celebrate the tenth anniversary of the China Commercial Advertising Agency (CCAA) (Huashang guanggao gongsi). As a sign of the importance that advertising had earned under the Republic, the most influential figures in the economic and political world participated in the celebrations. The small company that Lin Zhenbin – a Fuzhou merchant's American-educated son – had opened ten years earlier with a single assistant had become one of China's most powerful advertising agencies. Its 60 employees worked relentlessly to serve 100 clients, including large American multinationals like Ford Motors, Colgate, Kodak and National City Bank. Headquartered in Shanghai, the agency included offices throughout China, a branch office in Hong Kong and associates worldwide. CCAA's success is only the tip of the iceberg in the history of Chinese advertising. On the eve of the Sino-Japanese War (1937–1945), more than 100 independent agencies were active in Shanghai alone.

The advertising industry in China has been a blind spot in historical knowledge, though studied abundantly in Europe and the United States.[1] Business historians began to take interest in this topic in the late 1980s. Drawing on the archives of Nanyang Brothers and British-American Tobacco companies, Sherman Cochran demonstrated the significance of advertising in the competition between these two tobacco giants.[2] The American historian analysed with equal finesse the marketing strategies of Huang Chujiu, the founder of the International Dispensary (Wuzhou dayaofang). More recently, Eugenia Lean focused on the case of Chen Diexian, a vernacular industrialist and cosmetics magnate with multifaceted activities.[3] However, these major companies with their own advertising depart-

---

1 On the history of the advertising industry in Western countries, see in particular: Marie-Emmanuelle Chessel, *La publicité: naissance d'une profession, 1900–1940* (Paris: CNRS Éditions, 1998); Marc Martin, *Trois siècles de publicité en France* (Paris: Éditions Odile Jacob, 1992); Roland Marchand, *Advertising the American Dream: Making Way for Modernity, 1920–1940* (Berkeley: University of California Press, 1985); Véronique Pouillard, of the Lettres and des Beaux-Arts of Belgium (Brussels) Académie Royale des Sciences, and Classe des Lettres, *La publicité en Belgique, 1850–1975: des courtiers aux agences internationales* (Brussels: Académie Royale de Belgique, 2005); Shelley Baranowski et al., *Selling Modernity: Advertising in Twentieth-Century Germany* (Durham: Duke University Press, 2007); Robert Crawford and Jacqueline Dickenson, *Behind Glass Doors: The World of Australian Advertising Agencies, 1959–1989*, 2016.
2 Sherman Cochran, *Big Business in China: Sino-Foreign Rivalry in the Cigarette Industry, 1890–1930* (Cambridge, Mass.; London: Harvard University Press, 1980).
3 Eugenia Lean, *Vernacular industrialism in China: local Innovation and translated technologies in the making of a cosmetics empire, 1900–1940* (New York: Columbia University Press, 2020).

https://doi.org/10.1515/9783111390000-001

ments were the exception rather than the rule. Since advertising was not their core business, it does not constitute the central focus of historians' narratives. Apart from these exceptionally well-documented cases, the work of specialised agencies remains largely unknown.

In the 1990s, the renewed interest in historical press and the digitisation of extensive collections of periodicals directed researchers towards the study of print advertisements in newspapers. Dedicated databases focusing solely on advertising emerged, facilitating the exploration of this material that had long been overlooked by press scholars.[4] While early works tended to interpret advertisements as a mirror of society,[5] more recent studies have taken a more critical approach, highlighting the complex relationship between commercial images and the social reality that inspires them.[6] The flourishing historiography in the Chinese language has focused on the best-preserved and easily accessible periodicals, notably the *Shenbao*, one of the leading national newspapers until 1949, and illustrated magazines such as *Liangyou* (Young Companion). The majority of these works have concentrated on cigarettes and medicines, as their advertisements were the most numerous and visible on newspaper pages. These two sectors have also been favoured because they lend themselves to the examination of topics dear to historians, such as tensions between tradition/modernity, nationalism/individualism, gender issues and the role of women in society. A smaller body of work has explored commercial calendars (yuefenpai), tracing the paths of renowned artists like Zhang Zhiying or Zheng Mantuo from the perspective of social art history.[7] However, these illustrated calendars occupied a marginal position in the advertising industry during the Republican era.

---

4 See in particular: "Chinese Commercial Advertisement Archive", consulted January 15, 2018, https://scholarship.rice.edu/handle/1911/69922; "Chinese Women's Magazine", consulted January 15, 2018, http://kjc-sv013.kjc.uni-heidelberg.de/frauenzeitschriften/index.php.

5 Huang Kewu, "Cong Shenbao yiyao guanggao kan minchu Shanghai de yiliao wenhua yu shehui shenghuo (1912~1926) (Medical Culture and Social Life Seen Through Medical Advertisements in *Shenbao*, 1912–1926)", *Quarterly journal of the Modern History Institute, Academia Sinica Zhongyang yanjiu yuan Jindai shi yanjiu suo jikan* 17 (1988): 141–94.

6 Laikwan Pang, *The Distorting Mirror: Visual Modernity in China* (Honolulu: University of Hawai'i Press, 2007); Barbara Mittler, "Imagined Communities Divided: Reading Visual Regimes in Shanghai's Newspaper Advertising (1860s–1910s)", in *Visualising China, 1845–1965: Moving and Still Images in Historical Narratives*, ed. Christian Henriot and Wen-hsin Yeh (Leiden: Brill, 2013), 267–378.

7 Ellen Johnston Laing, *Selling Happiness: Calendar Posters and Visual Culture in Early Twentieth-Century Shanghai* (Honolulu: University of Hawai'i Press, 2004); Russell W. Belk Xin Zhao, "Advertising Consumer Culture in 1930s Shanghai: Globalization and Localization in Yuefenpai", *Journal of Advertising* 37, n° 2 (2008): 45–56; Song Jialin, *Lao yuefenpai* (Old Calendar Posters) (Shanghai: Shanghai huabao chubanshe, 1997), 11; Cheng Chaonan and Feng Yiyou, *Lao guanggao* (Old Advertising) (Shanghai: Shanghai huabao chubanshe, 1998).

Despite their abundance, studies focused on print advertisements in the press often fall short by merely scratching the surface of the images, leading to a number of interpretative pitfalls. Traditionally, advertisements have been approached as gateways into the imagination of consumers and the collective unconscious of Chinese society. However, the lack of comprehensive supporting archives has limited the scope of these studies, resulting in speculative conclusions. Influenced by semiotics and the linguistic turn, the analysis of advertisements has largely become an exercise in hermeneutic virtuosity.[8] In the absence of campaign plans, many of these works tend to overlook a crucial aspect: the primary objective of advertisements, which is to sell products. How and by whom were they designed? What commands and social demands did they respond to? Who were the publicists and copywriters? How were they trained? What strategies did they pursue? What worldview(s) motivated them? These crucial questions concerning the materiality of advertisements, the actors involved and the historical conditions of their production are rarely addressed.

The overall neglect of the advertising industry stems from the fact that most agencies have disappeared without leaving any archives behind. Alternative sources had to be found to support this research. The Shanghai Municipal Archives (SMA) have been particularly invaluable, having preserved extensive correspondence between municipal administrations and advertising agencies, charters of professional associations, municipal regulations and various surveys on the advertising industry. The United States National Archives and Records Administration (NARA), especially the records of the Department of Commerce and the Department of State, also held several reports on advertising, including monthly trade reports compiled by American consulates in China, as well as other investigations conducted by the Office of the Commercial Attaché. The personal papers of journalist Carl Crow, held at the State Historical Association of Missouri, along with those of lawyer Norwood Allman, commercial attaché Julean Arnold and his successor Alonzo Calder, preserved at the Hoover Institution at Stanford, provided valuable testimonies as well. Lastly, the series of professional textbooks collected during our research, whether translated from American sources or written directly by Chinese authors, shed light on the gradual

---

8 One of the most influential semiological analysis is Roland Barthes' "Rhétorique de l'image", *Communications* 4 (1964): 41–42. On the linguistic turn, see in particular: Richard Rorty, *The Linguistic Turn: Recent Essays in Philosophical Method* (Chicago: University of Chicago Press, 1967); Christian Delacroix, "Linguistic turn", in *Historiographies: concepts and débats*, ed. Christian Delacroix, Patrick Garcia and Nicolas Offenstadt, vol. 1 (Paris: Gallimard, 2010), 476–90; Gabrielle Spiegel, *Practicing History: New Directions in Historical Writing after the Linguistic Turn* (Taylor & Francis, 2005).

codification of advertising practices. By drawing upon this rich and previously untapped documentation, we were able to undertake, for the first time, a social history of Chinese advertising, restoring its actors and production conditions to their rightful place. By unveiling the unexplored world of specialised agencies, this study complements previous works dedicated to in-house advertising services within companies and to prominent figures of vernacular industrialists such as Huang Chujiu or Chen Diexian.[9] It also enriches the research conducted by Tani Barlow, Barbara Mittler and other scholars on advertising images and consumer imaginaries, by giving a face to the actors who shaped them from the outset.[10]

The purpose of this book is not merely to fill a gap or catch up with Western historiography, but to shift the focus of the predominantly North American and European academic literature. By situating the development of Chinese advertising within the specific context of pre-communist China, this study offers to re-examine some themes central to the historiography of the Republican period, particularly the "golden age" of Chinese capitalism and the issue of "Westernisation", which, in the context of post-imperial China, are two inseparable elements of "modernization".[11] To understand the context which Chinese advertising emerged in, it is necessary to go further back in time. The Opium Wars (1839–1860) marked the beginning of a century of significant political and social upheavals in China, characterised by a series of wars, crises, regime changes and the country's forced entry into the global order through the so-called "unequal treaties". While these treaties did not establish a strictly colonial system, China was compelled to concede commercial and territorial privileges to some foreign powers, along with extraterritorial rights for their nationals. In practice, there was no segregation, as foreigners never represented more than a minority in the population (less than 4% in Shanghai). In treaty ports like Shanghai, Canton, or Tianjin, Chinese and foreigners interacted daily, although tensions occasionally erupted, such as the May Thirtieth Incident (1925) or the series of protests following the Treaty of Versailles (1919) and

---

9 Cochran Sherman, "Marketing Medicine and Advertising Dreams in China, 1900–1950", in *Becoming Chinese: Passages to Modernity and Beyond*, ed. Wen-Hsin Yeh (Berkeley: University of California Press, 2000), 62–97; Eugenia Lean, *Vernacular Industrialism in China: Local Innovation and Translated Technologies in the Making of a Cosmetics Empire, 1900–1940* (New York: Columbia University Press, 2020).

10 Tani Barlow, "Advertising Ephemera and the Angel of History", *Positions: East Asia Cultures Critique* 20, n° 1 (2012): 111–58; Barbara Mittler, "Gendered Advertising in China: What History Do Images Tell?", *European Journal of East Asian Studies* 6, n° 1 (2007): 13–41.

11 Marie-Claire Bergère, *L'âge d'or de la bourgeoisie chinoise, 1911–1937* (Paris: Flammarion, 1986).

the Japanese invasion of Manchuria in 1931.[12] In this critical context, Chinese elites began to think that it was necessary to learn from the West to reverse their country's perceived decline. The abolition of the imperial examinations in 1905, which had ensured the stability of the imperial system and the reproduction of scholar-officials since the Song dynasty (960–1279), gave a decisive impetus to this idea while the foundation of the Republic in 1912 opened up new career opportunities for foreign-educated elites.[13] Between the mid-nineteenth and mid-twentieth centuries, some 200,000 young Chinese went to study overseas, primarily to Japan and the United States, intending to return after their studies to apply the knowledge they had acquired abroad to rebuild their country. While North American advertising emerged as a central reference point in the first half of the twentieth century, with influential agencies such as J. Walter Thompson and Ayer & Sons, the theme of Westernisation, within the specific domain of advertising, was predominantly expressed in terms of Americanisation.[14] Although other sources of inspiration were available locally (British, German, French, Japanese), American influence had no equal impact on the development of Chinese advertising. This influence was rooted in the thousands of students who travelled to the United States (liumei) to

---

12 On May 30, 1925, several Chinese demonstrators were shot dead by the municipal police of the Shanghai International Settlement. The incident triggered a vast movement of strikes and anti-foreign riots that lasted several months and spread to other cities, including Tianjin, Canton and Hong Kong.

13 Ping-ti Ho, *The Ladder of Success in Imperial China: Aspects of Social Mobility, 1368–1911* (New York: Columbia University Press, 1962); Y.C. Wang, *Chinese intellectuals and the West, 1872–1949* (Chapel Hill: University of North Carolina Press, 1966); Benjamin A. Elman, *Civil Examinations and Meritocracy in Late Imperial China* (Harvard University Press, 2013).

14 On the influence of American advertising in Europe, Latin America and, more recently, Australia, see: Marie-Emmanuelle Chessel, "Une méthode publicitaire américaine ? Cadum dans la France de l'entre-deux-guerres", *Entreprises et Histoire*, n° 11 (1996): 61–76; Marie-Emmanuelle Chessel, "From America to Europe: Educating Consumer", *Contemporary European History* 11, n° 1 (2002): 165–75; R. Crawford, "Opening for Business: A Comparison of J. Walter Thompson and McCann Erickson's Entries into the Australian Market", *Journal of Historical Research in Marketing* 8, n° 3 (2016): 452–72; Victoria De Grazia, *Irresistible Empire: America's Advance through Twentieth-Century Europe* (Cambridge, Mass.: Belknap Press of Harvard University Press, 2005); Simona De Iulio and Carlo Vinti, "The Americanization of Italian Advertising during the 1950s and the 1960s Mediations, Conflicts, and Appropriations", *Journal of Historical Research in Marketing* 1, n° 2 (2009): 270–94; Richard F. Kuisel, *Seducing the French: The Dilemma of Americanization* (Berkeley: University of California Press, 1997); Nixon, "Apostles of Americanization?"; Véronique Pouillard, "American Advertising Agencies in Europe: J. Walter Thompson's Belgian Business in the Inter-War Years", *Business History* 47, n° 1 (January 2005): 44–58; Thomas A. Schwartz, "Coca-Cola and Pax Americana: The limits of americanization in postwar Europe", *Contemporary Austrian Studies* 3 (January 1995): 262–72; James P. Woodard, "Marketing Modernity: The J. Walter Thompson Company and North American Advertising in Brazil, 1929–1939", *Hispanic American Historical Review* 82, n° 2 (May 2002): 257.

acquire first-hand knowledge. Recent research has demonstrated that this unprecedented intellectual migration, often overlooked in earlier studies, had a decisive impact on the development of capitalism and modern professions in China. Advertising serves as an excellent illustration of this phenomenon.[15]

Aligned with the rhythms specific to the advertising industry, the chronological framework adopted for this study (1914–1956) shifts the conventional boundaries defining the Republican period (1912–1949). In 1914, the Oriental Advertising Agency, originating from the publishing world (Oriental Press), emerged as the first agency specialising in advertising. This coincided with the onset of the First World War, which facilitated Chinese industrialisation and served as a catalyst for American-inspired agencies. In 1956, the advertising industry underwent complete state control under the Communist Party, as the sector was nationalised, leading to the demise of commercial advertising and the "enlightened capitalism" that relied upon it. Between these chronological endpoints, a politically uncertain but productive period fostered the growth of the Chinese industry (1914–1927). The subsequent Nationalist regime established in Nanjing (1927–1937) brought some political stability to the vernacular industry, despite challenging economic circumstances and escalating tensions with Japan in the 1930s. The Sino-Japanese War (1937–1945) and the ensuing civil war (1945–1949), by eliminating foreign competition, allowed influential agencies to flourish until the mid-1950s. In terms of spatial focus, Shanghai occupies a central position in this narrative due to its historical and documentary significance. Functioning as an unparalleled financial and commercial centre, as well as a national hub for the press and publishing industry, Shanghai became the capital of the advertising industry, leaving behind an exceptional collection of primary materials (municipal archives, newspapers, professional literature). Although this book primarily centres on Shanghai, it extends its scope by exploring the national impact of certain agencies, the multinational nature of their clientele, advertising professionals' international training and their numerous overseas connections.

Advertising became indispensable during the Republican era and played a direct role in the profound transformations of Chinese society since the late Qing dynasty. Its pervasive presence encompassed newspaper front pages, product packaging, urban landscapes, transportation routes, industrial exhibitions and official events. By the late 1920s, advertising professionals had established themselves as

---

15 Weili Ye, *Seeking Modernity in China's Name: Chinese Students in the United States, 1900–1927* (Stanford: Stanford Univ. Press, 2001); Peter E. Hamilton, "The American-Returned Students: Educational Networks and New Forms of Business in Early Republican China", in *Knowledge, Power, and Networks. Elites in Transition in Modern China*, ed. Cécile Armand, Christian Henriot and Huei-min Sun (Leiden: Brill, 2022), 258–88; Liang Chen, Ren Yunzhu, and Li Zhongqing, *Qi shanlin zhe: Zhongguo xiandai zhishi jieceng de xingcheng* (Beijing: Beijing shehuikexue wenxian chubanshe, 2023).

indispensable actors. Not only were they directly involved in China's initial economic "miracle", which commenced during the First World War, but they also contributed to the reshaping of urban spaces and the establishment of a new economic model for the press.[16] Leveraging the ubiquity and multifaceted nature of advertising, this research aims to provide a fresh perspective on the extensively studied paths explored by modern Chinese historians. Due to its comprehensive scope, this study has been divided into two volumes. The first volume traces the development of the advertising industry and highlights its contribution to the first "golden age" of Chinese capitalism. The second volume will focus on the impact of advertising on urban transformations and the growth of the modern press.

This first book is composed of three main parts, each subdivided into three chapters. The first part analyses the process by which advertising became an autonomous profession during the Republican era. The first chapter focuses on the professional organisations that emerged in Shanghai after the First World War (Advertising Club of China, Association of Advertising Agencies, Association for Chinese Advertising Agencies), dissecting their strategies for legitimisation in response to the amateurism of "charlatans" and the abuses of predatory advertising. The second chapter documents the development and functioning of the first independent agencies, which became the driving force behind professionalisation. This chapter relies on a series of case studies representing three successive generations of agencies, marking the transition from a family business model dominated by the press industry until the 1920s (Oriental Press, Carl Crow, China Commercial Advertising Agency) to the era of conglomerates in the 1930s (Millington, Consolidated National Advertising Company). The third chapter traces their founders' diverse paths: the American journalist Carl Crow, the self-taught British Francis Millington and the two Chinese professionals trained in the United States, Lin Zhenbin and Liu Meiseng. This first part concludes that advertising professionals in China constituted a diverse and multinational group characterised by a more fluid and open structure in comparison to state-regulated professions like lawyers, doctors and accountants. While less standardised, this dynamic and organised group exhibited similar levels of dynamism and organisation when compared to their counterparts in Europe and the United States.

The second part focuses on understanding how advertising professionals gradually conquered, or more accurately constructed, their markets. The fourth chapter meticulously examines the range of products displayed in the press and streets of Shanghai. Drawing on the *Shenbao* newspaper, the Shanghai Municipal Archives

---

16 On the "economic miracle" in Republican China, see: Marie-Claire Bergère, *L'âge d'or de la bourgeoisie chinoise, 1911–1937* (Paris: Flammarion, 1986).

and street photographs, this study shows that the product offering underwent profound changes in the first half of the twentieth century. While medicines and cigarettes dominated the sector until the First World War, post-war advertisements introduced previously unknown products such as cosmetics, electrical appliances, soft drinks and dairy products, which dramatically renewed material culture and consumption patterns. The fifth chapter traces the gradual appropriation of advertising by Chinese advertisers. While foreign multinational corporations were the primary consumers of advertising until the First World War, Chinese enterprises formed under the nationalist regime quickly embraced advertising and came to dominate the clientele of professional agencies during the Sino-Japanese War. The sixth chapter analyses the creation of commercial brands and the specific translation problems they posed for market professionals in China. Originally intended to address the absence of legal protection for industrial property, commercial brands played a pivotal role in facilitating more refined market segmentation by incorporating the social attributes and cultural preferences of Chinese consumers. The second part of this study concludes that advertising played a significant role in propelling the growth of consumer industries, which, in turn, became the primary driving force behind the development of the advertising industry until the early 1950s.

What constituted an effective advertisement? To address this question, the final section delves into the realm of professional literature, examining theorists' viewpoints (Chapter 7) and juxtaposing them with tangible advertisements found in newspapers and throughout the streets of Shanghai (Chapter 8). While North American advertising remained a prominent reference point, Chinese practitioners endeavoured to adapt foreign techniques while considering the unique aspects of Chinese society. The last chapter critically examines the myth of the "four hundred million customers" and explores how early advertising professionals contemplated the prospect of a mass consumer society in China, long before the initiation of the Reform Era under Deng Xiaoping in 1978.

This publication is accompanied by a digital platform (MADSpace) which includes all the primary documents and secondary data referenced, as well as other valuable resources that readers can freely access.[17]

---

17 MADSpace (Mapping Advertising Spaces in China), https://madspace.org/ (last consulted on July 29, 2022). Regarding the development of this platform and its methodological stakes, see: Cécile Armand, "MADSpace: a Janus-faced digital companion to a PhD dissertation in Chinese history", in *Shaping the Digital Dissertation: Knowledge Production in the Arts and Humanities*, ed. Virginia Kuhn and Anke Finger (Open Book Publishers, 2021), 119–28, https://doi.org/10.11647/OBP.0239.08.

Part One: **The Birth of a Profession**

Chapter 1
In Search of Legitimacy

In its early days, advertising had a poor reputation in China. In the 1920s, pioneers in the field faced three major prejudices. To most Chinese, advertisements were considered nothing more than a fabric of lies and exaggerations. Few people bothered to read them, let alone remember their content. Chinese consumers firmly believed that a good product did not need advertising, as its reputation was established through word-of-mouth. On the contrary, advertising aroused suspicion, indicating a product of inferior quality that relied on tricks to sell. Chinese entrepreneurs, on their part, viewed advertising as an unnecessary expense or, at best, a risky investment whose effectiveness remained unproven.[18] Few considered it as a rational means to promote their products. Misguided and ill-advised, those who attempted advertising were discouraged by unfortunate experiences.[19]

Advertising pioneers recognised that the lack of awareness and adoption of modern sales techniques posed a significant hindrance to the development of the Chinese economy. Lin Zhenbin, a notable figure who received training in the United States, pointed out that the advancement of modern advertising encountered a deep-rooted culture of secrecy that had permeated the business landscape for centuries. He specifically criticised the prevailing practice among merchants of keeping their most valuable products hidden in the back storerooms, only revealing them to select clients deemed worthy.[20] Guo Bingwen and Dong Xianguang, two influential intellectuals of their time, shared similar concerns about the state of advertising in China. Dong expressed his dismay at the prevalence of misleading advertisements in the press, while Guo lamented the relatively low level of advertising expenditures in China compared to Europe and the United States.[21]

The third set of prejudices specifically concerned outdoor advertising, which was deemed detrimental to the appearance of cities. Criticism was primarily di-

---

18 S.P. Westaway and P.S. Chow (Chu Seng-shuo), "The Three Ideas I would use for Wall Calendars or Novelties for the North China Trade", *North China Herald* (NCH), February 14, 1920.

19 "Report on the first meeting of the Advertising Association of China (Copy of minutes of the meeting)", Shanghai, January 15, 1924, SMA (SMC), U1-14-3267 (General Buildings Advertisements – General).

20 C.P. Ling (Lin Zhenbin), "Advertising in China Fast Becoming Essential Part of Merchandising", *China Press* (CP), August 29, 1931; Ling, "Recording a decade of service and progress", *CP*, September 1, 1936.

21 Hollington Kong Tong, "Newspapers as an Advertising Medium in China", *CP*, September 1, 1936, 30; P.W. Kuo, "Foreign Trade and Advertising", *CP*, September 1, 1936, 28.

https://doi.org/10.1515/9783111390000-002

rected towards illegal billposting, or *sniping*, which involved covering every available space on walls, doors and facades of public and private buildings. These practices, fought against in Europe and the United States since the nineteenth century, had reached alarming proportions in post-war China, as noted by contemporary observers.[22] American journalist C.A. Bacon observed that even temples, cemeteries and utility poles were not spared.[23] In the 1920s, American-inspired billboards, which had multiplied since the war, became the target of urban elites who protested against the "defacement" of residential neighbourhoods and scenic landscapes outside the city.[24] The more conservative pointed out the obscenity of certain posters, which they argued threaten the moral integrity of women and children.[25]

In the face of these criticisms, how did advertising pioneers react? What arguments did they put forward to gain the public's trust? How did they organise themselves to legitimise their activities with consumers, businesses and public authorities? The next two sections examine the discursive strategies deployed by advertisers to combat the prejudices they faced. The final part explores the collective organisations they created to amplify their messages and defend their interests.

Three Guiding Principles: Moralise, Rationalise, Serve

Moralising Discourses

To gain the public's trust, the early self-proclaimed professionals strove to break away from the "charlatan" reputation associated with advertising. Drawing inspiration from the truth-in-advertising movement initiated in the United States around 1911, pioneers advocated an ethical advertising that was free from lies and exagger-

---

22 Regarding the issue of illegal billposting in the United States and Europe, see: Catherine Gudis, *Buyways: Billboards, Automobiles, and the American Landscape* (New York: Routledge, 2004), 9–34; Stefen Haas, "Visual Discourse and the Metropolis: The Importance of Mental Models of Cities for the Emergence of Commercial Advertising", in *Advertising and the European City: Historical Perspectives*, ed. Clemens Wischermann (Aldershot, Hants, England; Burlington, Vt.: Ashgate Pub., 2000), 64–78; Hazel Hahn, "Furnishing the Street: Urban Rationalization and Its Limits", in *Scenes of Parisian Modernity: Culture and Consumption in the Nineteenth Century* (New York: Palgrave Macmillan, 2009), 144–60.

23 C.A. Bacon, "Advertising in China", *Chinese Economic Journal and Bulletin* 5, n° 3 (September 1929): 754–67.

24 Letter from the Automobile Club of China to the Shanghai Municipal Council (SMC), May 27, 1924, SMA (SMC), U1-3-583.

25 "Victim of the 'Chinese Dracula': Girl Declared to Have died from fright on Seeing Huge Figure", *Shanghai Times*, March 11, 1937.

ations.[26] These calls for self-censorship, however, were largely individual initiatives and did not lead to an organised movement. The "unequal treaties" regime further complicated the situation. Treaty ports with foreign concessions juxtaposed multiple legal systems relying on different conceptions of morality and truth. Foreign administrations lacked sufficient authority to punish Chinese newspapers that published advertisements deemed indecent. Furthermore, national legislations, such as the Pure Food and Drug Act adopted in 1907 by the U.S. federal government to ensure the safety of American consumers, did not cross borders. Multinational companies prohibited from advertising in their home countries could find refuge in China. For example, until the Sino-Japanese War, advertisements for Dr. William's Pink Pills continued to appear in the Chinese press, even though they were censored in Europe and North America.

Rationalising Practices

To entrepreneurs who doubted its usefulness, professionals were eager to show that advertising was not only useful but indispensable for the prosperity of their businesses. In an expanded market economy where anonymity prevailed, Guo Bingwen asserted that word-of-mouth, door-to-door sales and personal relationships were no longer sufficient.[27] Advertisers who wished to scale up could not do without advertising. "There is only one real, adequate means of making your product widely known in the trade fields of the vast nation of China – ADVERTISING," proclaimed a 1920 advertisement for the Chun Mei News agency [Figure 1].[28] Advertising was particularly important for Chinese exporters whose products were little known or poorly perceived abroad, such as eggs or oranges from Fuzhou, and for those facing strong international competition, such as tea or silk.[29] However, these projections from American trade commissioner J. Sanger must be approached with caution. The trade commissioner held the status of a special envoy in charge of collecting and synthesising observations for the U.S. Bureau of Foreign Commerce. Touring Japan, China and the Philippines for a few months, he only had a superficial understanding of the field, which he viewed through the lens of a representative of the U.S. administration.

---

26 "Men and Events", *Millard's Review of the Far East* (MRFE), July 20, 1918; "Advertising Club of China. Address by Mr. J. Sanger", *NCH*, May 15, 1920.

27 Kuo, "Foreign Trade and Advertising", 28.

28 Chun Mei News Agency, "Making Your Products Widely Known in China Will Open Her Markets", *MRFE*, January 17, 1920.

29 J. Sanger, *Advertising methods in Japan, China, and the Philippines* (Washington: Govt. Print. Office, 1921), 58; "Advertising Club – Dinner at Yih Ping-hsiang", *Shanghai Times*, May 12, 1920.

Making Your Products Widely Known in China Will Open Her Markets.

THIS is the advice of one of the largest foreign banking houses of the United States given to the corporations seeking to establish trade relationships in China.

There is only one real, adequate means of making your product widely known in the trade fields of the vast nation of China — ADVERTISING.

Advertising has made the large commercial corporations of the United States and the influence of such a medium has extended to Europe where it is being employed with equal force. British manufacturers are appropriating thousands of dollars for advertising in foreign fields.

Advertising in China has passed the experimental stage. It has been proven by actual use and the most widely bought articles among the Chinese people are those same articles which have been most widely advertised.

BUT to advertise in China improperly is to waste an appropriation. Every business in the country needs advertising prepared to reach a selected field by men who know China through years of experience in her commercial centers.

The Chun Mei New Agency, Advertising Department, is a thoroughly constituted service such as will be found in the agencies of the larger cities of the United States. But in addition, men who know the field of China are employed in making trade reports, and preparing campaigns that will have a direct and correct appeal to the Chinese people — men of Chinese nationality who have been especially trained in this work—copy writers, artists and investigators.

The Chun Mei service has introduced and obtained wide sales for well known products in China. Its work has the backing of successful campaigns scientifically conducted.

ADVERTISING IN CHINA CAN ONLY BE SCIENTIFICALLY PREPARED IN THE FIELD ITSELF—CALL AND LET US SHOW YOU WHAT WE HAVE DONE FOR OTHERS.

Chun Mei News Agency

Advertising Department

34 Nanking Road   Phone: Central-—2250

Figure 1: Advertisement for Chun Mei News agency (Zhongmei tongxinshe), *Millard's Review of the Far East*, January 17, 1920.

Nevertheless, his testimony is valuable for documenting American perceptions of the Chinese market in the aftermath of World War I. Furthermore, several Chinese professionals shared his viewpoint. Transcending national interests, the same arguments circulated widely in professional circles. All pioneers hammered home the point that professional advertising, far from being a waste, enabled advertisers to rationalise their expenses and achieve economies of scale.[30]

Serving Society

To win the favour of public authorities, advertisers emphasised the social utility of their activity. They argued that advertising contributed to raising the standard of living and the general well-being of the population. It guided consumers in their purchases and helped them make choices that could improve their comfort and productivity.[31] Professionals also highlighted the educational value of advertising. For example, the Bercott Advertising Company proposed using rickshaws to raise public awareness of road safety.[32] The Millington agency relied on radio advertising to educate the working class after factory shifts and sports events.[33] Taking inspiration from Colgate in the United States, the China Soap Company used new cinematic techniques to teach basic hygiene rules to schoolchildren in Shanghai.[34] In response to criticism from the Automobile Club, American advertiser Carl Crow claimed to enhance landscapes and promote artistic awareness among city dwellers, while the China Advertising Company promised to rid the city of sniping by replacing uncontrolled billposting with standardised billboards.[35]

To support their arguments, the pioneers drew from three main sources of inspiration: the liberal professions, art and science, and history and the cult of progress.

---

30 Chun Mei News Agency, "Making Your Products Widely Known in China Will Open Her Markets". See also: Wu Tiesheng and Zhu Shengyu, *Guanggaoxue* (Advertising Studies) (Shanghai: Zhonghua shuju, 1946), 46–47.

31 Kuo, 28; Ling, August 1931. The advertising textbooks reflected the same idea: Wu and Zhu, 44 (cf. chap.7).

32 "Covers Encasing Hood. Bercott Advertising Agency (Formerly International Advertising Corporation)", SMA (SMC), U1-3-2992 (1930).

33 "Advertising Radio Broadcasting Vans, Millington, Limited", SMA (SMC), U1-3-2992 (1934).

34 "Advertising by Means of Cinematograph Displays. W.H. Jansen Cinema exhibitions in Markets, Schools, etc.", SMA (SMC), U1-4-3820 (1935); "Cinema Street Advertising – China Soap Company, Limited", SMA (SMC), U1-14-3271 (1936).

35 "China Advertising Company. Licensing Street advertising", SMA (SMC), U1-2-371 (1905–1910); "Rural Beauties Marred by Ugly Hoardings. Auto Club's Protest. Should the Council Prohibit Erection Boards Around Rubicon?", *Shanghai Sunday Times*, July 13, 1924, SMA (SMC), U1-14-5775.

Three Sources of Inspiration

The Model of Liberal Professions: Expertise and Service

The first paradigm embraced by advertising professionals was rooted in the principles of the liberal professions, which asserted their ability to offer clients a service grounded in certified expertise. However, this conception of advertising activity faced limited acceptance during the 1920s. In the aftermath of the war, the industry was largely dominated by space brokers, a group criticised for their alleged focus on personal financial gain rather than serving their clients. Consequently, these brokers were held accountable for the disrepute that plagued the advertising field. In 1936, Lin Zhenbin succinctly summarised the conditions prevalent when he embarked on his advertising career a decade earlier. He noted that "SERVICE in advertising was not generally understood at the time we started. Space-brokers were numerous, soliciting business mostly on rebates. Trained men in copy and artwork were hard to find. People were not so advertising-minded as they are today. Despite prejudices and difficulties, we determined to develop a service based on our intimate knowledge of the market and the people."[36] While Lin and his peers often portrayed a somewhat bleak picture of the industry to emphasise their pioneering efforts, it remains indisputable that they were the first practitioners to recognise advertising as a distinct service that required specialised expertise.

The term "service" found in early professionals' writings exhibited a certain linguistic flexibility, being employed both in the singular and plural forms. This notion encompassed three primary meanings that were elucidated in their texts: the protection of client interests, the range of activities offered and the expertise tailored to the local market. With a desire to distinguish themselves from unscrupulous "charlatans", these self-proclaimed professionals positioned themselves as consultants who acted in the best interest of their clients. This argument coincided with a novel conceptualisation of the market, which was perceived as a collection of business problems to which advertisers provided tangible solutions. In their advertisements, agencies prominently highlighted the diverse array of services they provided to address the growing complexity of markets. These services included placement, translation, copywriting, layout design, market research and impact analysis.[37] By showcasing this breadth of offerings, these specialised agencies sought to distance themselves from the perceived amateurism associated with

---

36 Ling, "Recording a decade of service and progress", *CP*, September 1, 1936.
37 Carl Crow, "The Advertising Agent in China and America. The Advertising Agent – His Prospects in China", CP, August 16, 1919. "Merger formed by advertising firms in Shanghai. Five leading Chinese Companies in new combine", *CP*, August 1, 1930.

brokers. They asserted their reliance on highly qualified personnel who possessed not only the general skills expected of any publicist but also specific attributes crucial for effective engagement in the Chinese context. Language proficiency, familiarity with the local culture and the ability to tailor messages to resonate with Chinese consumers were particularly emphasised by professionals active in China.[38]

While the liberal professions initially served as a model for the advertising industry, it is important to note that not all professions held the same level of appeal. While medicine served as a central reference for French publicists, it faced a different reception in China, where it remained intertwined with negative connotations of "charlatans" and quack advertisements.[39] On the other hand, the architectural profession emerged as a more appealing reference for Chinese admen, allowing them to reconcile two fundamental values in their activity: art and science.

Balancing Art and Science

To address accusations of vulgarity and landscape defacement, advertising professionals drew upon a wide range of artistic references. While Western art initially served as the primary reference, pioneers also drew inspiration from Chinese painting. Presenting late nineteenth-century French poster artists as role models, A.C. Row credited them with legitimising commercial art by reconciling it with fine art. According to the American publicist, Chinese posters would gain in quality if they drew more inspiration from masters of Chinese painting.[40] During the early years of the Republic, major cigarette and pharmaceutical manufacturers sought the services of renowned Chinese painters, with the most talented individuals such as Zheng Mantuo (1888–1961) and Hang Zhiying (1900–1947) establishing their own commercial studios.[41] Starting from the 1920s, professional manuals all included at least one section dedicated to commercial art, describing its principles and techniques. As subsequent chapters will reveal, the most influential agencies were

---

38 Chun Mei News Agency, "Making Your Products Widely Known . . .".

39 Bacon, 1929, 755–56. Regarding the advertising profession in France, see: Marie-Emmanuelle Chessel, *La publicité: naissance d'une profession, 1900–1940* (Paris: CNRS Éditions, 1998).

40 A.C. Row, "The Art of the Poster", *NCH*, February 14, 1920.

41 Cochran Sherman, "Marketing Medicine and Advertising Dreams in China, 1900–1950", in *Becoming Chinese: Passages to Modernity and Beyond*, ed. Wen-Hsin Yeh (Berkeley: University of California Press, 2000), 62–97. Ellen Johnston Laing, Selling Happiness: Calendar Posters and Visual Culture in Early Twentieth-Century Shanghai (Honolulu: University of Hawai'i Press, 2004).

equipped with an art department and strove to attract renowned artists of their time. In response to accusations of landscape "defacement", outdoor advertising promoters emphasised the artistic nature of their billboards and their contribution to the beautification of cities.[42]

To distinguish themselves from the amateurism of brokers, early professionals asserted that advertising must not only be artistic but also "scientific". References to science abounded in their discourse, although the notion of science remained somewhat vague. Coming out of the First World War, Chun Mei News agency was one of the first to propose "scientific campaigns", without providing further details: "The Chun Mei News Service has introduced and obtained wide sales for well-known products in China. Its work has the backing of successful campaigns scientifically conducted. (. . .) Advertising in China can only be scientifically prepared in the field itself" [Figure 1].[43] A decade later, Lu Meiseng justified the creation of the Consolidated National Advertising Company (Lianhe guanggao gongsi) by the "urgent need for scientific and modern advertising", but without specifying the nature of this advertising science.[44] In the mid-1930s, Lin Zhenbin divided the history of advertising into two successive ages: a "pre-scientific" age embodied by "charlatans" and a "scientific" age, in which he presented himself as a pioneer.[45] These appeals to science were not without tensions. While proclaiming the scientific nature of their activity, practitioners acknowledged that advertising remained a matter of intuition. The scientist discourse clashed with the intimate awareness that advertising was a form of "tinkering" and could never claim the status of an exact science.[46] By the end of the Second World War, scepticism began to affect the "founding fathers" such as Carl Crow, who struggled to adapt to the changes in the profession.[47] With the development of marketing, the rhetorical magic of science was no longer working. For the new generation of publicists trained in economics and cognitive sciences, scientific advertising referred to a set of cutting-edge techniques that were incompatible with the approximation of the pioneers.

---

42 Wu and Zhu, 34.
43 Chun Mei News Agency, "Making Your Products Widely Known . . .".
44 "Merger formed by advertising firms in Shanghai".
45 Ling, "Advertising in China Fast Becoming Essential Part of Merchandising".
46 Row, "The Art of the Poster".
47 Carl Crow, *Four Hundred Million Customers: The Experiences, Some Happy, Some Sad, of an American in China, and What They Taught Him* (New York; London: Harper, 1937), 315.

Reconciling the Past with Modernity

To strengthen their legitimacy, the early professionals were keen on rooting their activity in the long timeline of Chinese history and humanity. American publicist A.C. Row drew a direct lineage between Chinese posters and medieval Japanese theatre, even tracing it back to the official placards of the Zhou dynasty around 517 BCE. Equating commercial advertising with imperial propaganda, he asserted that advertising had always existed in China and that historical research would better illuminate the specificity of contemporary forms.[48] While foreign experts strove to sinicise the narrative of origins, their Chinese counterparts chose to anchor it in Western history. Guo Bingwen turned to ancient Rome, seeing in the commercial inscriptions and posters announcing gladiator fights the precursors of the modern poster.[49] Despite their divergences, these teleological discourses shared a common point. The historical continuity they established between the past and the present tended to downplay the profound shift taking place at the turn of the twentieth century with the professionalisation of advertising. While asserting this continuity, Chinese-language textbooks all began with a historical introduction that sharply separated "traditional" advertising from "modern" advertising, which supposedly began with the Opium Wars and the arrival of foreigners in China.[50] To overcome this contradiction, theorists explained that the artistic and scientific aspects of advertising were constantly improving. The history of Chinese advertising, as narrated in professional literature, was a linear history oriented towards progress.[51]

To promote these discourses and advocate for the interests of the nascent profession, three organisations were established in Shanghai following the First World War.

The Limited Role of Associations

Among the three organisations representing the advertising profession in Shanghai, the Association for Chinese Advertising Agencies (ACAA) (Zhonghua guanggao gonghui), was the only purely vernacular organisation. The other two – the Advertising Club of China (ACC) and the Association of Advertising Agencies (AAA) – were initiated by foreign professionals in China. Due to the lack of pre-

---

48 Row, "The Art of the Poster".
49 Kuo, "Foreign Trade and Advertising", 27.
50 Wu and Zhu, 10–11.
51 Bacon, 762.

served archives, these organisations remain poorly understood, but valuable information about their activities, members and operational methods can be found in the local press and municipal archives.

The Advertising Club of China (ACC) (1918, 1931)

The Advertising Club of China (Zhongguo guanggao gonghui) was formed on June 4, 1918, in Shanghai by around 30 businessmen gathered at the Oriental Hotel. This club is the oldest organisation established by advertising professionals in China. It was a mixed organisation composed of Chinese and foreign members. Without a specific program, the club set three general objectives: strengthening the connections between the business, advertising and publishing sectors; facilitating exchanges between Chinese and foreign members; and defending the common interests of the entire profession. The imprint of the First World War heavily influenced the membership conditions. Only nationals of neutral or allied countries were allowed to join, while professionals of German and Japanese nationalities were excluded.[52]

Like most associations, the ACC had a board of directors responsible for strategic decisions, a bureau handling day-to-day affairs and specialised committees. At the time of its foundation, the club elected a president (American journalist J.B. Powell), a vice president (a certain D.K. Wong), two secretaries (Chinese C.F. Lin and American A.N. Lethin), a treasurer (Kuang Fuzhuo, also known as Fong Foo Sec) and an assistant treasurer (John A. Dissmeyer). The board of directors, initially composed of five Chinese and foreign members (S.C. Wong, H.H. Wong, John S. Potter, A.G. Loehr and E. Strassman), was replaced the following year by an executive committee of about ten members elected for one year. Board members were also renewed annually. From 1920 onwards, the executive committee was divided into six specialised committees dedicated to membership, premises, communication, education, organisation and supervision. Each committee consisted of two elected members, one Chinese and one foreign, with annual renewal.[53] Apart from annual general meetings, the ACC held regular meetings.[54] By December 1919, it had already met six times in less than a year of existence.[55]

Among its members, the ACC had representatives from multinational corporations such as British-American Tobacco and Andersen Meyer & Company, as well as members from international organisations like the Pan-Pacific Association

---

52 "First Advertising Club in Orient Formed in Shanghai", *MRFE*, June 8, 1919.
53 "Advertising Club of China. Annual General Meeting and Dinner", *NCH*, June 1919.
54 *Millard's Review*, April 24, 1921.
55 *Shenbao* (SB), December 13, 1919; *Millard's Review*, December 13, 1919.

and the Young Men's Christian Association. Journalists and press figures such as J.B. Powell and C.F. Lin were also part of the club. To strengthen its legitimacy, the ACC secured the support of influential personalities, including the Chinese Commissioner for Foreign Affairs (Yang Zhang), the American Consul in Shanghai (A.G. Loehr), the Chinese Consul General in London (Cao Yunxiang, also known as Y.S. Tsao) and the American Trade Commissioner (J. Sanger).[56] The membership of the club remained relatively stable, with some members, such as C.F. Lin and J.B. Powell, remaining loyal to the club until its dissolution in 1931. However, significant changes occurred from 1920 onwards with the rise of independent advertising agencies. The founders of agencies like Carl Crow, Lin Zhenbin (China Commercial Advertising Agency), Zhang Zhuping (Consolidated National Advertising Company) and J.A.E. Bates (Oriental Advertising Agency, Millington) began to join the club. By November 1923, the ACC had more than 50 members who gathered at the premises of the Union Club to enjoy recently introduced American products in China, such as Campbell's Soup, Sun-Maid Raisins and George Washington Coffee.[57]

The ACC was heavily influenced by foreign presence and operated like most expatriate clubs. The choice of meeting venues, usually luxury hotels – Carlton Cafe (1918–1919), Columbia Country Club (1919), Union Club (1919–1920), Great Western Hotel (1929), Astor House Hotel (1931), American International Underwriters Building (1931) – reinforced this Western inclination. Nevertheless, the ACC was less exclusive than British-inspired clubs. Among the 30 founding members, there were about 20 Chinese members. The effort for integration was also evident in the diversity of the board and executive committees, which strove to maintain parity between Chinese and foreign members. For example, in 1919, J.B. Powell and H.H. Wong shared the surveillance committee, while Lin and Loehr jointly managed the organisation committee. That same year, the secretariat was shared between the American S.P. Westaway and the Chinese Thomas H. Yu.[58]

Despite its ambition to legitimise the emerging profession, the club was not a professional organisation in the strict sense. Unlike associations of doctors, journalists and lawyers, the ACC did not have a militant program aimed at obtaining official recognition. The club was simply a group for reflection and discussion among peers, relaying ideas from Europe and the United States and reflecting on

---

56 "The Art of Advertising. Advertising Club of China Hold Annual Meeting and Discuss Advertising Projects in China," *Shanghai Times*, June 18, 1919; *Millard's Review*, May 8, 1920; *NCH*, May 15, 1920; *Shanghai Times*, May 12, 1920. *SB*, May 12, 1920.
57 *China Weekly Review* (CWR), November 17, 1923.
58 *NCH*, June 21, 1919.

their applicability in China. The mission of the ACC was primarily to inform about the latest advancements in the profession and to facilitate socialisation among its members. At its establishment in 1918, the club planned to publish a bilingual newsletter reporting on its activities.[59] The following year, the organising committee announced a program of lectures covering a wide range of topics: newspapers and magazines, the art of advertising, postal advertising, Chinese "superstitions" and a comparison of agencies in China and the United States.[60] Similar to the Rotary Club founded at the same time, the lectures were often led by club members such as journalist Jabin Hsu (Xu Jianbin) and publicists Carl Crow, C.F. Lin and A.C. Row. Like the Rotary Club, the ACC also invited external experts, such as Emil Scholz, the representative of the *New York Evening News*, who visited Shanghai in June 1919.[61]

While press advertising was initially the main concern of the founders who came from journalism, during the 1920s, the ACC began to take an interest in new subjects such as posters, calendars, the marketing of dairy products, brand protection and the issue of counterfeiting.[62] Some lectures were accompanied by exhibitions, photographs and samples, demonstrating an effort to innovate in communication methods.[63] The meetings usually took place in the late afternoon and sometimes late in the evening to allow professionals to attend without encroaching on their working days. Taking inspiration from other elite clubs in Shanghai, the meetings were generally concluded with a dinner. The ACC also organised receptions at the homes of members who were willing to open their residences and outdoor activities such as walks in the Bansong Gardens.[64]

The ACC had relatively strong connections within local networks, thanks to its institutional alliances and the personal relationships of its members. Between 1918 and 1921, the Young Men's Christian Association (YMCA) regularly provided

---

59 *Shanghai Times*, August 22, 1918. It seems that this publication remained in the project stage and was never published.

60 "Advertising Club of China Announces Year's Program of Lectures", *Millard's Review*, August 9, 1919.

61 *Shanghai Times*, June 18, 1919; *Millard's China National Review*, June 21, 1919; *NCH*, June 21, 1919. Initially founded in Chicago in 1905, the Rotary Club is a transnational organisation aimed at fostering socialisation among business and professional elites in modern cities. On the Rotary Club in China, see: Cécile Armand, "Foreign Clubs with Chinese Flavor: The Rotary Club of Shanghai and the Politics of Language", In Cécile Armand, Christian Henriot and Huei-min Sung (ed.), Knowledge, Power, and Networks: Elites in Transition in Modern China, Brill, Leiden, 2022, 233–259.

62 "Advertising Club of China Has Novel Program", *Millard's Review*, September 25, 1920; "Trade Marks in China", *NCH*, August 2, 1919.

63 *Shanghai Times*, June 18, 1919.

64 *SB*, June 23, 1921; *Weekly Review of the Far East* (WRFE), June 25, 1921, October 1, 1921.

its premises for the club's meetings. Through the multiple affiliations of its members, the ACC was linked to other clubs such as the Rotary Club or the Union Club, which sometimes organised joint events. On an international level, the ACC was officially affiliated with the Associated Advertising Clubs of the World (1918) and the Advertising Association of New York (1920).[65] However, the ACC's position within global professional networks remained somewhat marginal. In 1920, the proposal made by its president, A.R. Hager, to host the next annual congress of the Associated Advertising Clubs of the World in Shanghai was rejected. Although Hager managed to secure the creation of a special section for the Far East as compensation, he bitterly regretted the lack of interest that American professionals showed towards this region of the world.[66]

The ACC disappeared from the sources after the farewell ceremony of its president, Kuang Fuzhuo, in January 1929.[67] Two years later, in June 1931, a representative from the American Asiatic Underwriters, A.E. Lucey, attempted to revive the club.[68] Among his supporters were former loyal members (A.R. Hager, Lin Zhenbin, J.B. Powell), as well as new members such as J.A.E. Bates (Oriental Advertising-Millington), A. Hill-Reid (Millington) and Bruno Perme, the director of the eponymous agency. However, due to a lack of resources, the attempt failed the following year, and the remaining funds were donated to a charity supporting rickshaw pullers.[69] Several reasons may explain the disappearance of the ACC. Focused on its foreign and journalistic origins, it is possible that the club failed to adapt to the rapid changes in the profession, particularly the development of outdoor advertising and the growing influence of Chinese professionals (see Chapter 2). Furthermore, the ACC faced competition from two new organisations formed in the early 1920s, the Association for Chinese Advertising Agencies (1923) and the Association of Advertising Agencies (1924).

The Association of Advertising Agencies (AAA) (1924)

The Association of Advertising Agencies (AAA) was founded on January 15, 1924, when representatives from six advertising agencies gathered at the premises of the Union Club in Shanghai. Unfortunately, there is limited information available about the AAA, with only the minutes of its inaugural meeting preserved in the

---

65 *Shanghai Times*, August 22, 1918; "Sanger Talk At Club Dinner", *Millard's Review*, May 8, 1920.
66 *Millard's Review*, November 13, 1920.
67 *NCH*, January 26, 1929. *China Press*, January 27, 1929.
68 *CWR*, June 13, 1931.
69 *CWR*, October 15, 1932.

Shanghai Municipal Archives. The founding members included branches of three publishing companies: China Publicity Company, affiliated with the Commercial Press (Shangwu yinshuguan); Morning Society, affiliated with Chenshe Publishing House; and the Oriental Advertising Agency, affiliated with the French Oriental Press (Presse Orientale). There were also four agencies founded by expatriates: Carl Crow, Incorporated (American), North China Advertising Company and Harvey Billposting Company (British). In his inaugural speech, President N.N. Leashin presented a rather bleak picture of outdoor advertising in China. He described it as discredited, lagging behind Western countries, and plagued by amateurism, sniping practices and real estate speculation. The new association set out to combat these three challenges as part of its mission.[70]

Less exclusive than a club, the AAA welcomed any professional who committed to abide by collectively defined rules. The association aimed to be more inclusive and less hierarchical than the ACC. Instead of establishing an executive committee and specialised offices, the founders preferred decisions to be made collegially, by all members gathered in plenary assembly. From its inception, the AAA was a defensive organisation driven by the desire to safeguard against the three threats described by its president. More assertive than the club, it set forth a binding action program, which contrasted with the playful nature of the ACC. Its priority was to develop regulations for outdoor advertising, establish common rules for the entire profession and ensure their enforcement. However, it appears that the inaugural meeting did not lead to further progress. Why did the initiative not receive the expected support? Did the idea of imposing sanctions and binding rules deter potential members? Was the AAA too narrowly focused on outdoor advertising in a country where the daily press constituted the main medium? In the absence of archival evidence, these questions remain unanswered.

The Association for Chinese Advertising Agencies (ACAA) (1923)

The Association for Chinese Advertising Agencies (ACAA) (Zhonghua guanggao shanghui) was founded in 1923 by a group of Chinese entrepreneurs who believed it necessary to establish a special organisation to defend the interests of the "Chinese people" (Huaren gongzhong).[71] Its first meeting took place in November 1923, and

---

70 "Report on the first meeting of the Advertising Association of China (Copy of minutes of the meeting)", Shanghai, January 15, 1924, SMA (SMC), U1-14-3267 (General Buildings Advertisements – General).
71 *SB*, November 24, 1923. The founding members included: Wang Zilian 王梓濂 (president), Ren Jinping 任矜蘋 (secretary), Yan Xigui 嚴錫圭, Zheng Yaonan 鄭耀南 and Yao Junwei 姚君偉 (cf. chapter 3).

its founding charter was approved by the new Chinese municipality in July 1927. Although the ACAA was born in response to the ACC, its founders were not inherently hostile to the foreign club. In fact, some of them were members of both organisations. The two entities had very similar names in the Chinese language (Zhongguo/Zhonghua guanggao gonghui) and operated in a similar manner. Like the ACC, the Chinese association annually elected an executive board, an executive committee and specialised committees. It held regular meetings and organised lecture series to inform its members about the state of the profession. With no premises of their own, the ACAA gathered in the same type of establishment as the foreign club. Each meeting was followed by a closing tea, which, in a sinicised form, recalled the dinners of the ACC.

Despite leaving little trace, the ACAA proved to be the most active and enduring of the three organisations. It gained significance in the 1930s, just as the foreign organisations were starting to decline. By 1929, the ACAA boasted an impressive membership of approximately 50 individuals, and this number further expanded to encompass 30 collective entities, including advertising agencies and advertisers, by 1930. The association's growth in membership paralleled its development of a more structured and organised framework. In 1929, recognising the need for administrative support and oversight, a secretariat and a vigilance committee were established to assist the expanding executive committee. During this period, the executive committee witnessed a membership increase from seven to nine individuals between 1927 and 1930. Notably, the ACAA's membership predominantly consisted of individuals from the press industry, indicating a sense of stability and continuity within the association. In 1930, the ACAA underwent a name change and became known as the *Shanghai tebieshi guanggao tongye gonghui* (上海特別是廣告同業公會) to comply with the new law on associations introduced by the Ministry of Industry and Commerce.[72] This new name emphasised the professional nature of the association and its local roots, rather than focusing on its national identity. Despite this alteration in name and legal status, the ACAA's activism remained unwavering. In June 1930, for instance, it vehemently protested against a new police regulation that banned parades and the use of "sandwich men" within the International Settlement. The association felt this was an unfair restriction and voiced its opposition.[73] In 1931, the ACAA challenged a decision made by the Shanghai Municipal Council to impose a discriminatory tax on rooftop advertisements, which targeted Chinese advertisers unfairly.

---

72 Shanghai guanggao shangye lishi yange ji huiwu baogao (History of the advertising industry in Shanghai and minutes of meetings of the association), SMA, S315-1-1 (1945).
73 Letter from Shanghai Advertisers' Guild to SMC, June 26, 1930, SMA (SMC), U1-3-3917.

Through its efforts, the association succeeded in having the new tax abolished the following year.[74]

The ACAA vanished from historical records until the end of the concessions. However, in June 1943, it resurfaced amidst a wave of administrative changes, undergoing yet another name change. As part of the municipal reorganisation, the ACAA was rechristened as the *Shanghaishi guanggao shangye tongye gonghui* (上海市廣告同業公會). By 1947, the association had adopted a new charter and internal regulations. At this point, it boasted around 100 members, predominantly comprising Chinese agencies. Unlike the voluntary nature of membership in the pre-war clubs, joining the association had become a legal obligation due to the new association law. Professionals in the industry were now required to adhere to certain conditions: being over 20 years old, possessing full civic rights, paying an entrance fee and a monthly membership fee proportionate to their income level. The regulations governing the association were more stringent than those of the previous organisations. They outlined the rights and responsibilities of members, established procedures for elections and outlined the protocols for convening general assemblies. Any member had the opportunity to run as a candidate during elections, but once elected they were bound to their commitment and could not retract their involvement. Each agency was required to send at least one representative to every regular assembly, with any absences needing to be justified in writing. To maintain professional standards and protect the reputation of the industry, the regulations included provisions for imposing sanctions, including the possibility of expulsion, in cases of rule violations or actions detrimental to the profession's standing. The newly adopted charter encompassed both general principles common to all professional associations, such as serving the public interest and promoting social progress, as well as specific objectives related to the field of advertising. These objectives included conducting market surveys, generating statistical data and facilitating the exchange of information within the industry.[75]

After the Communist revolution, the new regime embarked on stricter regulation of professional corporations, and the advertising industry was not exempt. During the 1950s, advertising professionals lost their autonomy and gradually came under the control of the Party-State. In 1956, agencies were forced to merge and form a large semi-public enterprise known as *gongsi heying* (公司合營). Following the merger, only six agencies remained, each specialising in a specific domain:

---

74 Letter from the Association for Chinese Advertising Agencies to SMC Secretary, July 27, 1931, SMA (SMC), U1-14-3267.

75 Shanghaishi guanggao shangye tongye gonghui, SMA, S315-1-5, S315-1-7 (June 3, 1947).

press advertising (Lianhe guanggao gongsi 聯合廣告公司), print advertising (Daxin guanggao gongsi 大新廣告公司), billboards (Rongchangxiang guanggao gongsi 榮昌祥廣告公司), shop window displays (Gongnong bingmeishu gongchang 工農兵美術工場), films (Yinxing guanggao gongsi 銀星廣告公司) and photography (Lianhui guanggao meishu she 聯揮廣告美術社). With a capital exceeding four million yuan, the new organisation employed over 400 staff members. In 1959, another merger took place, resulting in the establishment of a single organisation. In Shanghai, as in other cities, this organisation became a local branch of the national advertising enterprise (Zhongguo guanggao gongsi 中國廣告公司), headquartered in the capital city of Beijing. Thus, the profession was reorganised on a territorial basis, becoming more centralised and hierarchically distributed. Shanghai, once hailed as the capital of the advertising industry, lost its status and was marginalised by the communist regime, which viewed it as a residue of imperialism and Western capitalism.[76]

Conclusion

In the aftermath of World War I, the emergence of self-proclaimed advertising professionals led to their concerted efforts to combat the prevailing prejudices associated with the field. Drawing inspiration from other liberal professions, these advertising pioneers sought to emphasise the ideals of professionalism, independence and public service as a means to legitimise their activities. However, unlike the legal and medical professions, the state played a relatively minor role in asserting and regulating the advertising profession. Even during the nationalist regime that followed in 1927, advertising professionals primarily relied on self-regulation, largely evading direct state control. It was only under the People's Republic of China that the advertising industry came under the control of the Party-State. This limited state involvement in the advertising profession underscored its hybrid nature. Structurally, advertising experts formed an open interprofessional group, intersecting with multiple areas of expertise.

Moreover, national identities held a secondary position in the ideological construction of the profession. Rather than being defined by nationalism, it was the language barrier that created a divide between the Advertising Club of China and the Association for Chinese Advertising Agencies.[77] The ACC, by predominantly

---

76 Sun Shunhua, *Zhongguo guanggao shi* (History of advertising in China) (Jinan: Shandong daxue chuban she, 2007), 116.

77 The situation was very similar to that of the Rotary Club, which was established around the same time (1919). On this subject, see: Cécile Armand, "Foreign Clubs with Chinese Flavor: The

using English as its *lingua franca,* inadvertently excluded non-English-speaking professionals. In response, the ACAA adopted the use of the vernacular language to integrate Chinese professionals who did not have a strong command of English.

Although less numerous than in the United States, advertising associations in China played a pivotal role in structuring the profession in its nascent stage. These organisations provided a platform for pioneers to gather, exchange information, socialise and collectively advocate for their interests. However, as the industry matured, their significance declined in the 1930s with the rise of independent agencies.

Rotary Club of Shanghai and the Politics of Language", in *Knowledge, Power, and Networks: Elites in Transition in Modern China*, ed. Cécile Armand, Christian Henriot and Huei-min Sun (Leiden: Brill, 2022), 233–59.

Chapter 2
The Rise of Independent Agencies

The emergence of the first specialised advertising agencies in Shanghai at the conclusion of the First World War marked a significant turning point in the realm of advertising. These novel agencies, established in response to the amateurism of pre-war brokers, played a crucial role in the professionalisation of the advertising industry, propelling it towards becoming a distinct and independent field. Unlike in-house departments found within corporations such as British-American Tobacco or the International Dispensary (Wuzhou dayaofang), which exclusively catered to the needs of their respective advertisers, independent agencies operated on behalf of diverse clients, occasionally even serving rival companies. Inquiring into the origins, organisation and evolution of these agencies during the Republic, the first section of this chapter examines their rapid growth from the 1920s onward, with particular emphasis on the remarkable progress achieved by Chinese agencies during the nationalist regime. The subsequent three sections offer a series of meticulously investigated case studies, each representing a distinctive phase in the development of the advertising industry: its early roots within the realm of publishing (Oriental Press, Oriental Advertising Agency), the pioneering American-inspired agencies (Carl Crow, China Commercial Advertising Agency) and, finally, the formation of conglomerates in the early 1930s (Millington, Consolidated National Advertising Company).

Professionalisation, Growth and Sinicisation

Several distinctive features distinguished the independent advertising agencies from both "amateurs" and in-house advertising departments. Unlike mere brokers with no legal existence and business offices, advertising agencies were registered with the official authorities (ministry, consulate or local administration) and listed in professional directories. To further strengthen their legal existence, each agency adopted a distinctive name, a motto and a logo, which gave them their own identity and set them apart from their competitors. In order to limit risk and increase their capital, most of them opted for the status of a limited liability company, which made them accountable to their shareholders. Many of them had their headquarters located in Shanghai, which was asserting itself as the capital of the advertising industry under the Republic. The larger agencies also opened branches in other cities such as Beijing, Tianjin, Hankou, Hangzhou, Guangzhou and Hong Kong.

https://doi.org/10.1515/9783111390000-003

Starting from the 1920s, independent agencies embarked on a process of integration, aiming to expand their range of activities and gain control over the entire production chain. This encompassed various aspects, including ad placement, translation, copywriting, typesetting, campaign planning and market surveys. The growing complexity of advertising techniques necessitated highly skilled personnel and a more strategic division of labour. Consequently, in the 1920s, independent agencies initiated the structuring of specialised departments within their organisations. Notably, the most well-equipped agencies, such as the Oriental Advertising Agency, the China Publicity Company and Millington, Ltd., also extended their services to assist other agencies with fewer resources.[78] In the late 1920s, the first artistic departments were established, complemented by the inclusion of outdoor advertising and market research departments in the 1930s.[79] This simultaneous process of integration and division of skills allowed agencies to cater to diverse needs while maintaining a focus on specific areas. For instance, the Acme agency exclusively dedicated itself to outdoor advertising, while Claude Neon Lights specialised in neon lights, and the Shanghai Ricsha Advertising Company specialised in placing advertisements on rickshaw vehicles and pullers.

Prior to the outbreak of the First World War, three prominent advertising agencies held a dominant position in Shanghai's advertising sector. These included the Oriental Advertising Agency (Faxing guanggao gongsi), which operated as a subsidiary of the (French) Oriental Press; the Harvey Advertising & Billposting Agency (Hawei gaobai jingli), representing British interests; and the China Publicity Company (Zhongguo shangwu guanggao gongsi), a subsidiary of the Commercial Press (Shangwu yinshuguan).[80] While Harvey Advertising & Billposting Agency ceased its operations during the war, both the Oriental Advertising Agency and China Publicity Company continued to thrive until the 1930s, despite facing increasing competition from American-inspired agencies that emerged following the model established by American journalist Carl Crow in 1918. The subsequent decades witnessed a proliferation of independent agencies. In 1919, there were approximately 30 agencies, which grew to 76 between 1919 and 1929. By the 1930s, the

---

78 Carl Crow, *Four Hundred Million Customers; the Experiences – Some Happy, Some Sad, of an American in China, and What They Taught Him* (New York; London: Harper, 1937), 98.

79 *CP*, February 15, 1930.

80 John A. Fowles, "Memorandum by John A. Fowles, American Trade Commissioner, to Grosvenor M. Jones, Assistant Chief, Bureau of Foreign and Domestic Commerce, Department of Commerce, Washington, D.C., 4 December 1918", Memorandum, Records of the Bureau of Foreign and Domestic Commerce, General Records, 1914–1958. Trade Promotion, File 470, "Advertising (Strait Settlements) – Publicity." 471.1, News & Trade Papers, Box 2252 (Washington, D.C.: National Archives and Records Administration (NARA), 1918).

number further escalated to 105 agencies. However, the onset of the Sino-Japanese War in 1937 slowed down the establishment of new agencies. Despite this, Shanghai still accommodated 76 agencies at the onset of the war. However, following the abolition of foreign concessions in 1943, the number significantly dwindled to only 11 agencies remaining in the city (as shown in Table 1).[81]

Until the establishment of the Nationalist regime in 1927, foreign agencies held a dominant position in the advertising sector. However, following this period, there was a significant proliferation of vernacular agencies, which eventually surpassed their foreign counterparts in number during the Sino-Japanese War. The presence of European and American agencies declined from 65% prior to 1919 to 35% after 1937, while Chinese agencies experienced substantial growth, increasing from 30% to 60% during the same period. In contrast, Japanese agencies remained a minority, comprising less than 15% of the total agencies. In 1915, there was only one Japanese agency associated with the Japanese newspaper Shanghai Nippo Sha (Shanghai ribao she), which increased to 25 in the 1920s and subsequently decreased to less than 10 in the 1930s. The sporadic nature of the war and the Japanese occupation hindered the long-term establishment of Japanese advertising in Shanghai. It is worth noting that all agencies of foreign origin were locally established. Despite the interest and fascination with China in American business circles, no agencies based in the United States established a presence in the Republic of China.[82] Factors such as geographical distance, political instability, and a focus on other markets, particularly Europe, Latin America, and Australia, may have deterred the establishment of U.S.-based agencies in China.

Behind the general statistics, a wide range of situations existed within the advertising industry. Until the 1930s, there were self-proclaimed agencies that functioned merely as brokers, while others provided limited services.[83] The complete eradication of amateurism by professional agencies was not achieved, as occasional resurgence of amateur practices occurred. The economic depression of the 1930s and the Sino-Japanese War attracted many unemployed individuals seeking livelihoods and emigrants who had fled war and persecution in Eastern Europe.[84]

---

81 The figures presented are derived from a comprehensive compilation of agency data obtained from multiple sources, including the directory of the Bankers' Cooperative Credit Service (Zhongguo zhengxinsuo), the Shanghai telephone directory (honglist) from 1941, as well as various files sourced from the Shanghai Municipal Archives.

82 J. Sanger, *Advertising methods in Japan, China, and the Philippines* (Washington: Govt. Print. Office, 1921), 74.

83 Sanger, *Advertising methods in Japan, China, and the Philippines*, 74.

84 C.P. Ling, "Recording a decade of service and progress", *CP*, September 1936. "Advertisements on Footpaths. K. Mondenach", SMA (SMC), U1-14-3257 (1940); "Alfred Gherart – Painting Advertisements on pavements", SMA (SMC), U1-3822 (1940); "Oskar Gross & Jaques Reti – Offering Service

As competition intensified and the level of demand increased, the process of professionalisation varied in its degree of success.[85] Several criteria can be employed to assess the level of professionalism exhibited by agencies. These include their longevity, geographical reach, the diversity and reputation of their clientele, the size and qualifications of their staff, as well as their equipment, capital, and financial stability. According to American reporter C.A. Bacon, in the late 1920s, only six agencies held significant influence in Shanghai. Aside from the Oriental Press, which was in its final days, there were two American agencies (Carl Crow, Acme), one British agency (Millington), and two Chinese agencies (China Commercial Advertising Agency, United Advertising Advisers) that set the standard for the industry.[86] Throughout the Republican period, three of these agencies – Carl Crow, China Commercial Advertising Agency, and Millington, Ltd. – maintained their presence. These agencies boasted substantial capital, employed dozens of staff members, and served numerous clients. Trailing behind these leading agencies, there were around forty medium-sized agencies with shorter lifespans (less than ten years) and a more volatile economic standing. The majority of agencies were small and short-lived, established during the optimistic period following the establishment of the Nationalist regime in 1927 (constituting 70% of agencies). While there was a trend towards the development of larger agencies in the 1930s, few Chinese agencies reached the scale to rival those on New York's Madison Avenue.[87]

The development of the advertising industry in Shanghai can be summarized into three key phases: its roots in the publishing industry (Presse Orientale, Oriental Advertising Agency), the emergence of American-inspired agencies after WWI (Carl Crow, CCAA), and the era of conglomerates from the 1930s onwards (Millington, Consolidated National Advertising).

---

in connection with promotion of scheme for posting advertising placards on Municipal property and buildings and on streets", SMA (SMC), U1-3822 (1941).

85 Bacon, 765–66.

86 Bacon, 755.

87 For the record, the two American giants J.W. Thompson and W. Ayer & Son employed up to 500 people in the early 1920s, five times as many as Millington, ten times as many as China Commercial Advertising Agency (CCAA) and 20 times as many as Carl Crow. Margaret E Brown, "Advertising to the Elite: The Role of Innovation of Fine Art in Advertising in the Development of the Advertising Industry" (M.A. Department of History, Indianapolis, Indiana University-Purdue University, 2015), 26–27.

The Oriental Press & Oriental Advertising Agency (1914)

The Oriental Advertising Agency (OAA), the first known agency in Shanghai, was established as a subsidiary of the French publishing company Oriental Press (Presse Orientale). The Oriental Press, founded in Shanghai in 1897, began with an initial capital of 100,000 Chinese dollars.[88] It was registered in Hong Kong but headquartered in the French Concession of Shanghai. Initially located on Rue du Consulat, it later moved to Edward VII Avenue in 1907. One of the main founders of the Oriental Press was Joseph-Julien Chollot (1861–1938), the chief engineer of the French Concession, who remained a board member until 1927.[89] During the Republican era, the leadership of the Oriental Press took on a more international outlook. From 1911 onwards, an Italian businessman named Matteo Bos assumed leadership until his death in 1928. The board of directors comprised not only the French founders J.J. Chollot, E.J. Burgoyne, F. Lefon, and Rev. F. Morin but also British and American businessmen such as B. Rozenbaum and J.R. Moodie, as recorded in the 1927 general meeting minutes. The Oriental Press also implemented an international recruitment policy for its advertising experts. James L. Cowen, co-founder of the Chester, Cowen Company advertising agency, joined the team in 1920, while Philip L. Bickel (1895–1924), Carl Crow's former partner, served as the assistant director from 1921 until his passing in 1924.

Initially, the Oriental Press primarily focused on publishing, producing a diverse range of printed materials including magazines like *The Review* and *L'Echo de Chine*, as well as catalogs, brochures, and circulars.[90] In 1909, the company established a comprehensive advertising department, equipped with an art studio and a workshop for billboard production. Additionally, in partnership with Philips Neon Tubes, they formed a specialized department for neon lighting. This advertising department later evolved into an independent agency, giving rise to the Oriental Advertising Agency (OAA) in 1914. In 1923, the Oriental Advertising Agency (OAA) merged with Chester, Cowen & Company and the Asia Advertising Agency, forming a new agency.[91] To better align with the local landscape, the agency adopted a Chinese-style arch, known as a pailou, as its logo. The agency also translated its name into the vernacular, becoming known as the Shanghai

---

88 SMA (SMC), U1-14-3258.
89 *CP*, August 18, 1927.
90 Bacon, 759.
91 Letter from the Oriental Advertising Agency to the Shanghai Municipal Council (SMC). Shanghai, 14 November 1923. SMA (SMC), U1-14-3258.

Faxin guanggao gongsi.[92] The agency's slogan, "Oriental Advertising Agency – Publicity Service," coupled with the widely recognized business maxim "It pays to advertise," firmly positioned advertising as a professional service with unquestionable effectiveness.[93]

The Oriental Advertising Agency (OAA) operated in both foreign concessions in Shanghai and left a significant imprint on the advertising landscape. The agency's extensive correspondence with the municipal administration, documented in over fifty-five files in the municipal archives, dwarfed that of other agencies, underscoring its prominence and level of engagement with local authorities. According to journalist C.A. Bacon, OAA was a trailblazer in the use of modern billboards in China. As early as 1912, OAA applied for a municipal permit to install these innovative boards near the George Dallas Stables, situated west of the International Settlement.[94] In the first large-scale survey conducted by the Shanghai Municipal Council in 1914, OAA greatly surpassed its competitors, owning more than 150 billboards in the settlement.[95] The agency also demonstrated a penchant for experimenting with cutting-edge media, including illuminated kiosks, neon signs, stereoscopic lanterns, and even air balloons. In the early 1920s, OAA secured exclusive rights for displaying advertisements on the tramcars operating within the two foreign concessions.[96]

The influence of the Oriental Advertising Agency (OAA) extended beyond Shanghai, encompassing both national and international reach. The map attached herewith (Figure 2), highlights the locations of OAA's relay offices across Chinese territory, indicating a concentration of activities in economically developed areas along the east coast. Notably, OAA exercised direct control over offices situated along the Yangtze River near Shanghai (Jiangsu) and Hangzhou (Zhejiang), while its associate, the North China Advertising Company in Tianjin, oversaw the northern offices. However, OAA had limited representation in the southern regions of

---

92 Letter from the Oriental Advertising Agency to the SMC, Shanghai, March 30, 1930. SMA (SMC), U1-3-584 (1737).

93 Bacon, 759.

94 "Oriental Advertising Agency, Advertising Boards, George Dallas' Stables, 1912–1913", SMA (SMC), U1-2-898 (1912). General Buildings Advertisements – Taxation of Street Advertising. Measuring Advertising Space. 1914, SMA (SMC), U1-14-3267.

95 General Buildings Advertisements – Taxation of Street Advertising. Measuring Advertising Space, SMA (SMC), U1-14-3267 (1914).

96 "Advertising on Trams – Oriental Press", SMA (SMC), U1-3-1284 (1921); "Oriental Press, Advertising kiosks on the Bund Foreshore and Public Gardens", SMA (SMC), U1-14-3387 (1921); "Stereoscopic lantern Advertisements. Thibet Road, Oriental Press", SMA (SMC), U1-3-1081 (1922); "Oriental Advertising Agency & Toa Kuchiu Sendensha (Tokyo Japanese Company), Advertising balloon", SMA, French Concession (FC), U38-4-1112 (1930).

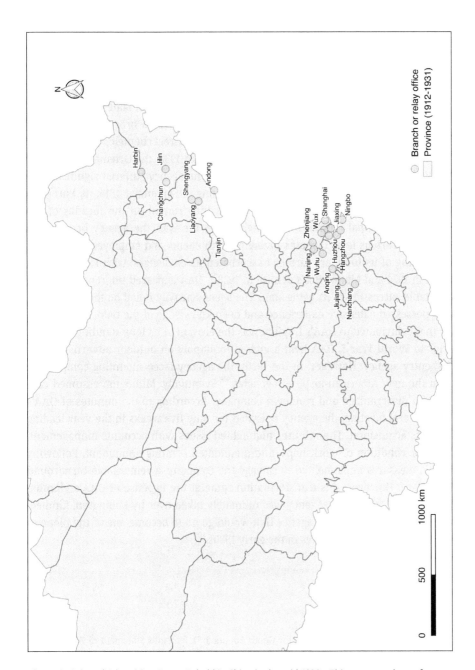

Figure 2: Oriental Advertising Agency's hold in China in the mid-1920s. This map was drawn from the agency's letterheads dated March 1924. SMA (SMC), U1-14-3258 (2381–2384). Interactive map: https://madspace.org/cooked/Maps?ID=217.

Guangzhou and Hong Kong, as well as in the interior provinces of Sichuan and Mongolia. Internationally, OAA's main clients were based in Europe and Asia, particularly Japan. Notably, OAA did not have any clients in North America. However, the agency was affiliated with the New York-based agency J. Roland Kay, which maintained offices in multiple countries, including the United States, Great Britain, France, and Australia. This association provided OAA with a broader network and expanded reach in international markets beyond its direct clientele.

On the brink of its acquisition by Millington in 1930, the Oriental Advertising Agency (OAA) displayed signs of vulnerability. The agency suffered significant repercussions from the First World War. Beginning in September 1914, its European clients gradually withdrew from the spaces they rented on the façades of the Shanghai Municipal Council's building.[97] After the war, the agency became entangled in various legal disputes involving both clients and employees. Tragically, the passing of its founders further exacerbated its challenges, with Philip Bickel's death in 1924 and Matteo Bos's demise in 1928.[98] OAA appeared unprepared for the inevitable succession of its aging staff. The agency heavily relied on these pioneers, who possessed extensive experience and deep knowledge of the field. Another factor that contributed to OAA's fragility was the erosion of its long-standing network. Prior to World War I, OAA held a virtual monopoly on outdoor advertising as a first-entry agency. However, in the 1920s, the agency faced mounting competition from the new American-inspired agencies.[99] Eventually, Millington assumed control of a disorganized and rundown company. According to the minutes of OAA's final general meeting, the agency operated for only five weeks in the year leading up to its acquisition. The minutes highlighted issues with accounts management, the poor condition of workshops, and dilapidated printing equipment. Following drastic measures implemented to salvage the company, a remarkable turnaround took place. However, this transformation came at the expense of OAA's identity. The Oriental Advertising Agency was ultimately taken over by Millington, Limited, a newly established British agency that would go on to become one of the pioneering advertising conglomerates in the early 1930s.[100]

---

97 SMA (SMC), U1-14-3251, U1-14-3267.

98 "A Venture in Journalism: Claim for Goods Supplied: Defendant's Statement of Alleged Partnership", *North China Herald*, December 1923; "An Average Man's Debts", *NCH*, February 1926; "Mr. Matteo Bos. Monday's Funeral at Pahsienjao Cemetery", *NCH*, March 31, 1928. See also: *CP*, March 28, 1928.

99 Bacon, 759.

100 *NCH*, February 24, 1931.

The First American-inspired Agencies

Carl Crow, Incorporated (Carl Crow, Inc.) and the China Commercial Advertising Agency (CCAA) epitomize the post-World War I era of independent agencies. Their extensive historical documentation and remarkable longevity serve as testaments to the profound influence of American practices on the development of Chinese advertising.[101]

Carl Crow, Incorporated (1918)

Founded in 1918, Carl Crow, Incorporated (Kelao guanggao gongsi) took its name from its founder, American journalist Carl Crow (Kelao). The agency originated from a split with the Chun Mei News agency (Zhongmei tongxinshe), which served as the local relay for the Committee of Public Information (ComPub), an American intelligence service led by Carl Crow during World War I.[102] Chun Mei primarily focused on translating and placing articles in the local press to promote a pro-U.S. viewpoint. With headquarters in Shanghai and branches in Beijing and Tianjin, the agency faced a diplomatic scandal that led to Carl Crow's departure and the establishment of his independent company, shifting its focus from war

---

101 Both Carl Crow, Incorporated (Carl Crow, Inc.) and the China Commercial Advertising Agency (CCAA) are extensively documented in the archives of the Shanghai municipal authorities, benefiting from surveys conducted between 1930 and 1941. The local press also serves as a valuable source, regularly featuring their advertisements, reporting on their activities and publishing articles authored by their founders. Notably, CCAA received special coverage in a dedicated issue of the periodical *China Press* on its tenth anniversary in September 1936. Additional insights into Carl Crow can be gleaned from his personal papers, housed at the State Historical Society of Missouri, and the archives of the U.S. Department of State at the National Archives and Record Administration (NARA). Carl Crow himself authored around 15 books during his lifetime, some of which continue to be republished today. His renowned work, *Four Hundred Million Customers* (1937), provides a unique first-hand account of the early days of advertising in China, although historical analysis must carefully navigate the author's narrative strategies. It is also worthwhile to consult secondary literature, such as Paul French's book *Carl Crow, a tough old China hand: the life, times and adventures of an American in Shanghai* (Hong Kong: Hong Kong University Press, 2006). While French's work exhibits a lively narrative style, it draws on solid documentation. *Carl Crow, a tough old China hand: the life, times and adventures of an American in Shanghai* (Hong Kong: Hong Kong University Press, 2006).
102 National Archives and Records Administration (NARA), General records of the Department of State, RG59, CDF 1910–1929, Box 948.

propaganda to commercial advertising.[103] Embracing the motto "Advertising and Merchandising Agents," the agency distanced itself from the publishing industry and aligned advertising with the marketing of goods. The choice of a Chinese junk ship as its logo highlighted the agency's location in Shanghai and its global perspective. Legally, the agency operated as a limited liability company with Carl Crow as the sole proprietor. For tax purposes, the company was initially incorporated in the State of Delaware and later in Alaska. By the 1920s, its capital amounted to U.S.$25,000, and the agency held multiple bank accounts with prominent Chinese and Sino-foreign banks, including the Hongkong & Shanghai Banking Corporation (HSBC), the Shanghai Commercial & Savings Bank, the Shanghai Bank, and the International Banking Corporation.[104]

The agency's operations were primarily focused on three key areas: publishing, outdoor advertising, and postal advertising.[105] Building upon its journalistic roots, Carl Crow, Inc. maintained a robust editorial presence. In the early 1920s, Crow established The Trade Journals Publishing Company, which produced *The Chinese Engineer and Contractor*, a magazine catering to Chinese engineers working abroad.[106] In addition to translating and placing advertisements in the local press, Crow played a pivotal role in creating the first press directory in China. Published between 1931 and 1937, the *Newspaper Directory of China* series became an authoritative reference work on the periodical press in China and Hong Kong, offering valuable insights and reliable data during a time when such information was challenging to obtain.[107] Carl Crow also maintained close connections with the American evening daily, the *Shanghai Evening Post*, where he served as the manager until 1930. The newspaper provided essential support to the advertising agency, as it shared its printing equipment when the agency did not have its own facilities. This collaboration facilitated the agency's ability to produce printed materials and expand its reach.[108]

During its early stages, Carl Crow, Inc. had a relatively simple structure and employed around a dozen people. Carl Crow himself described his agency as a family-like organization based on trust. In his autobiographical account, he hu-

---

103 French, *Carl Crow, a tough old China hand*, 89–92. In 1919, the Tokyo Mainichi newspaper accused Carl Crow and his agency of harbouring anti-Japanese sentiments. See on this subject the letter from the American ambassador in Peking (Paul S. Reinsch) to the American Secretary of State, Washington, D.C., dated May 1, 1919. NARA, RG59, CDF 1910–1929, Box 948.

104 SMA, Q275-1-1840-37.

105 Carl Crow, Inc., "Merchandising in China", *China Journal of Science and Art*, November 1924.

106 *MRFE*, Shanghai, July 2, 1921.

107 Carl Crow, Inc., "Merchandising in China".

108 *CWR*, April 21, 1928, January 3, 1931; *NCH*, December 25, 1930. SMA, Q275-1-1840-37.

morously recounted an encounter with a millionaire visitor who, in an attempt to offer advice, stressed the significance of departmentalization for efficient functioning of an advertising agency:

> Just after the close of the War, we had a lot of strange American visitors in Shanghai. They were the new millionaires who had been created by the War, and most them gave me the impression that they were taking a trip round the world to see whether or not they wanted to buy it. One of these millionaires spent a good deal of time in my office, because he had once been in the advertising business and liked to talk shop, and as I was just getting my business started, he gave me a lot of advice. For one thing, he told me that an advertising agency, in order to function efficiently, should be "highly departmentalized". As I had about a dozen employees, including coolies, at the time, I couldn't do very much about following his advice, as there were already more departments than there were men on the staff.[109]

Carl Crow portrayed himself as a paternalistic manager who showed empathy towards his Chinese staff. He respected their beliefs, even allowing a visit from a geomancer, and refrained from introducing new working methods or altering the office decor.[110] In return, he claimed his employees were completely devoted to him. Crow found amusement in their enthusiasm for their work, their desire to appear busy at all times and their efforts to convey the agency's prosperity through constant activity, especially when an esteemed client was expected. The local press, however, presents a different perspective. Despite its small size, Carl Crow's agency was not exempt from social tensions. In 1933, for example, a court case pitted the manager against one of his employees, Bruno Perme, over unpaid wages. Following his dismissal, Perme established his own agency (Beimei guang-gao gongsi), which directly competed with his former employer.[111]

Despite its relatively modest level of compartmentalisation, Carl Crow, Inc. was among the pioneers in establishing an art department. The agency employed renowned artists, including the Russian cartoonist Georgii Avksent'ievich Sapoj-nikoff, known by the pseudonym Sapajou.[112] Besides his involvement in the press, Carl Crow played a significant role in shaping outdoor advertising in Shanghai.[113] He claimed to have introduced the city's first modern billboards based on American standards. However, he recognised the unique characteristics of Chinese cities, with their narrow and winding streets, and advocated for the use of smaller

---

109 Crow, *Four Hundred Million Customers*, 98.
110 Crow, *Four Hundred Million Customers*, 114.
111 *CP*, July 11, 1933.
112 Bacon, 759; Crow, *Four Hundred Million Customers*, 112.
113 Carl Crow, Inc., "Merchandising in China".

boards that he deemed more suitable.[114] It is likely that Carl Crow, Inc. relied on its own workshops to manufacture these billboards, which were then rented out to clients.[115] Furthermore, Carl Crow actively participated in the development of the first special regulations on advertising in the International Settlement. He collaborated with the Shanghai Municipal Council and other advertising agencies to draft these regulations, emphasising his dedication to advancing the advertising industry in Shanghai.[116]

Carl Crow's innovative approach extended to postal advertising. Recognising the untapped potential of the Chinese Post Office's high-quality services, he calculated that the literate population in China, approximately 20 million people, received an average of one letter per month, while the total population of 400 million received about one letter per year.[117] Understanding the significant opportunity, Carl Crow compiled an extensive address book containing over 100,000 names from across China. This comprehensive directory not only included customers' names and addresses but also provided details on their income levels and occupations. Recognising its value, Crow made this address book available to clients for a fee, enabling them to target specific niche markets effectively.[118]

Despite its modest size, Carl Crow, Inc. had a strong presence within local and international networks. It was a member of the Advertising Club of China (1919) and the Advertising Association of China (1924), showcasing its active engagement within the advertising community. The agency also had an association with N.W. Ayer and Son, an American agency based in Philadelphia, further expanding its network and resources.[119] To broaden its reach beyond Shanghai, Carl Crow, Inc. established outlets in Guangzhou, Ningbo, Hankou and Peking (Beijing) during the 1920s, as indicated on the attached map (Figure 3).[120] As the decade progressed, the agency expanded its operations to other regions, including India, Siam (Thailand), Java (Indonesia), Singapore, Japan and the Philippines. The agency's portfolio boasted more than 25 Chinese and foreign clients spanning various industries, including cigarettes, food, automobiles, pharmaceuticals, hygiene and cosmetics. While it catered to a diverse client base, a significant portion of its

---

114 Carl Crow, Inc., "Posters in Outports", *CWR*, September 16, 1922. See also: Bacon, 759.

115 Crow, *Four Hundred Million Customers*, 132.

116 SMA (SMC), U1-5-584.

117 Carl Crow, Inc., *Newspaper Directory of China (Including Hongkong)* (Shanghai: Carl Crow, Inc., 1931).

118 Sanger, *Advertising methods in Japan, China, and the Philippines*, 91.

119 *CWR*, September 17, 1932.

120 Sanger, 1921: 74. Carl Crow, Inc., "Merchandising in China". See also: Crow, *Four Hundred Million Customers*, 132–33.

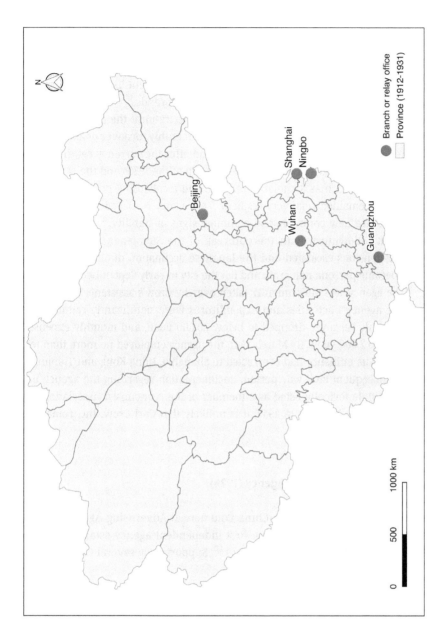

Figure 3: Carl Crow's *hold* in China in the interwar years. Based on: J. Sanger, *Advertising methods in Japan, China, and the Philippines* (Washington: Govt. Print. Office, 1921), 74; Carl Crow, *Four Hundred Million Customers: the Experiences – Some Happy, Some Sad, of an American in China, and What They Taught Him* (New York; London: Harper, 1937), 132–33. Interactive map: https://madspace.org/cooked/Maps?ID=218.

business came from American companies. In 1930, major multinational corporations such as Liggett & Myers Tobacco, Eastman Kodak, Sun-Maid Raisin, Pond's Cold Cream and General Motors entrusted their advertising campaigns in China to Carl Crow, Inc. By the following decade, the agency's client list had grown substantially, encompassing nearly 100 world-renowned brands.[121]

Carl Crow, Inc. experienced a period of prosperity until the outbreak of the Sino-Japanese War. In 1930, the agency achieved a monthly turnover of 40,000 Mexican dollars, which later decreased to 30,000 yuan after the currency reform in the early 1930s. Despite the global economic depression of the 1930s and the challenges faced by Shanghai, such as a cholera epidemic and a collapsing property market, Carl Crow, Inc. remained relatively resilient. The agency managed to maintain its client base, secure new contracts and exhibited signs of stability.[122] However, the situation took a downturn with the outbreak of the Sino-Japanese War in August 1937. As tensions escalated and the Japanese occupation of Shanghai began, Carl Crow became persona non grata and left the city in early September 1937 (chapter 3).[123] The agency was subsequently taken over by Crow's assistant. Throughout the war, the agency's activities and expenditures were significantly reduced. By 1940, the monthly turnover dropped to below 20,000 yuan, and monthly expenses were reduced to 2,000 yuan. By March 1941, the agency employed no more than ten individuals and its influence had contracted to Shanghai, Hong Kong and Tianjin.[124] During the subsequent civil war period, documentation regarding the agency became scarce. While formally listed as a member of the reorganised Association for Chinese Advertising Agencies in 1947, it is unlikely that Carl Crow, Inc. remained active at that time.

China Commercial Advertising Agency (1926)

Founded in Shanghai in 1926, the China Commercial Advertising Agency (CCAA) (Huashang guanggao gongsi) was the first independent agency established by a Chinese individual, Lin Zhenbin (C.P. Ling).[125] Supported by several Chinese busi-

---

121 SMA, Q275-1-1840-37.
122 Crow, *Four Hundred Million Customers*, 114.
123 French, *Carl Crow, a tough old China hand*, 210.
124 SMA, Q275-1-1840-37.
125 Sources on CCAA are less plentiful than for Carl Crow. Our account is based mainly on the series of audits conducted by various Chinese and foreign banks between 1929 and 1939, a special issue compiled on the occasion of CCAA's tenth anniversary (1936) and various articles in the local press documenting the agency's daily activities.

nessmen, Lin started his company with a capital of $10,000 or $15,000. In 1928, he bought out his partners' shares and remained the managing director for the rest of his life. Unlike Carl Crow, CCAA did not bear its founder's name. More impersonal, the name of the agency simply reflected its area of expertise (*guanggao*, advertising) and its geographical location (*Zhongguo*, China). From the outset, Lin was eager to place his expertise at the service of his clients to make Chinese advertising more effective. He set two main missions to his agency: to place his clients' advertisements, whatever their origin, in the vernacular press, and to act as an intermediary for Chinese entrepreneurs wishing to expand their market in the United States. His motto "Service and Progress" summarised both the founder's personal ambitions and the ethos of the profession as a whole. Like the Oriental agency, Lin chose a *pailou* as his agency's logo, signalling its roots in Chinese culture.[126]

Building on its founder's experience, CCAA specialised in press advertising. Before setting up his own company, Lin Zhenbin had worked for the China Publicity Company (Zhongguo shangwu guanggao gongsi) in Hankou.[127] CCAA worked closely with Shanghai's two major daily newspapers, the *Shenbao* and the *Xinwenbao*. These two newspapers were the agency's major shareholders and two prime outlets for the placement of its advertisements. In addition, CCAA contracted with about 100 publications across China.[128] The agency itself was the source of an intense editorial production directly linked to its advertising activity. In the early 1930s, Lin Zhenbin founded the Pagoda Printing Company (Tayinshua gongsi), specialising in the printing of high-quality colour illustrations.[129] In 1934, he published *A Practical Guide to Newspapers and Periodicals for China Advertisers* which competed with Carl Crow's *Newspapers Directory of China*.[130] He also cooperated with the Japanese-run Zen Sing Brothers Printing Company, which he contemplated buying in 1932 while it was struggling financially.[131] To expand its services beyond print advertising, CCAA teamed up in 1926 with the Acme Adver-

---

126 "More Effective Advertising and Better Agency Work in China", *CWR*, April 27, 1929.

127 Based in Shanghai, the Commercial Press was one of the largest Chinese publishing houses at the time. Around 1929, it published two-thirds of the books sold in China and employed some 5,000 people. Bacon, 760. On the Commercial Press, see: Jean Pierre Drège, *La Commercial Press de Shanghai (1897–1949)* (Paris: PUF, 1978); Robert Joseph Culp, *The Power of Print in Modern China: Intellectuals and Industrial Publishing from the End of Empire to Maoist State Socialism* (New York: Columbia University Press, 2019).

128 *CWR*, April 27, 1929.

129 SMA, Q275-1-1840-37.

130 *CP*, December 9, 1934. *North China Herald* (NCH), January 1, 1935.

131 "Haskins & Sells (Certified Public Accountants). Audit of China Commercial Advertising Agency, Shanghai, 1 April 1932", SMA, Q275-1-1840-37.

tising Agency, an American agency specialising in outdoor advertising. In addition to Lin Zhenbin's sitting on the board of directors of the two agencies, the physical proximity of their offices, both located in the central district of the International Settlement, greatly facilitated their collaboration.[132]

To commemorate its tenth anniversary in 1936, the China Commercial Advertising Agency (CCAA) published a special issue that celebrated its remarkable expansion. The brochure highlighted the agency's challenging beginnings, facing both the lack of legitimacy that plagued the entire advertising profession and competition from foreign pioneers.[133] Although the account of its origins was intentionally romanticised to glorify its founder's role, there was truth to its modest start. Initially, Lin Zhenbin operated from a small office with only one assistant. In 1926, his main client was the Bakerite Company (Chocolate Shop). However, the agency's fortunes rapidly changed the following year when it secured a prestigious account with the American multinational Ford Motor Exports Company, marking its first major advertising campaign in China.

From there, CCAA experienced an extraordinary ascent. By 1935, the agency boasted a staff of 40 employees, which further increased to 60 in 1936, making it one of the largest Chinese agencies at the time. While CCAA initially had only five clients in 1926, a decade later it held contracts with 100 clients representing 200 different brands, predominantly foreign. During the early 1930s, the agency's portfolio encompassed prominent American, British and German companies across various sectors. These included automobile manufacturers such as Ford Motor Company and Bills Motors, food product companies like Bakerite, Wrigley's Gum, Quaker Oats and Welch's Grape Juice, pharmaceutical brands including Colgate, Pro-phy-lac-tic, Gillette, Listerine, Santal Midy and Kofa American Drug, as well as real estate, finance, cultural devices and energy and transportation industries. The agency's versatility and the multilingualism of its employees enabled its success and diverse clientele. Notably, CCAA's commercial achievements also led to its involvement with public institutions. For instance, in 1933, the agency was commissioned to promote the National Athletic Games held in Nanjing.[134] In 1936, it was hired by the Ministry of Transportation (Guomin zhengfu hangkong gonglu jianshe jiangquan banshi) to promote its national road network construction campaign.[135]

CCAA's operations extended throughout China, as depicted on the attached map (Figure 4). The agency had a strong presence in the Jiangnan region in the

---

132 *CWR*, April 27, 1929.
133 Ling, "Recording a decade of service and progress".
134 "China Commercial Advertising Agency To Compile Program", *CP*, August 1933.
135 SMA, Q275-1-1840-37.

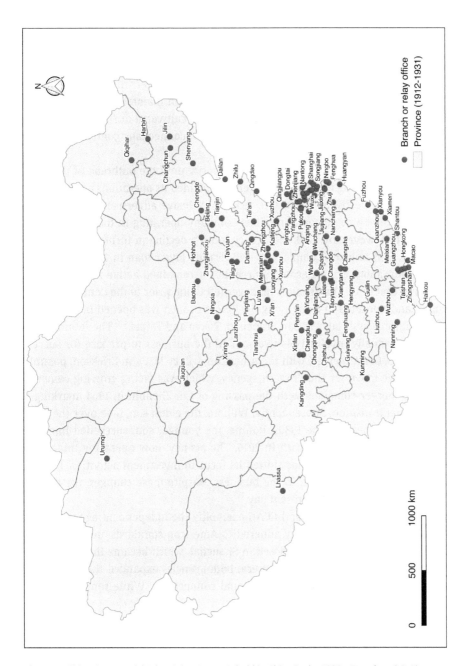

Figure 4: China Commercial Advertising Agency's hold in China in the 1930s. Based on C.P. Ling, "Recording a decade of service and progress", *China Press*, September 1, 1936. Interactive map: https://madspace.org/cooked/Maps?ID=214.

south, as well as in the northern cities of Beijing and Tianjin. It also established outposts in Manchuria, including Harbin and Shenyang, as well as in Sichuan and Tibet. In 1938, CCAA expanded its reach by opening new offices in Hong Kong. Furthermore, CCAA's influence transcended national borders through its multinational clientele and connections abroad. Lin Zhenbin maintained close ties with the American business community, which he had cultivated during his studies in the United States (chapter 3). These international connections contributed to the agency's broader reach and global impact.

CCAA, like Carl Crow, experienced prosperity until the outbreak of the Sino-Japanese War. During the 1930s, the agency expanded its operations and ventured into outdoor advertising. In 1938, it secured exclusive advertising rights on the vehicles of the China General Omnibus Company operating in the International Settlement. However, by 1939, the agency faced a decline in turnover and had to reduce its staff to just 20 employees, significantly fewer than in 1936. After 1948, information about CCAA became scarce, but it remained active in Shanghai at least until that time. The agency's manager left China prior to the Communist revolution and relocated to Hong Kong. In 1957, a branch was opened in New York, with additional associates in San Francisco, Tokyo and Taipei.[136] The founder, Lin Zhenbin, gradually involved his two sons in the business to prepare for succession. In 1963, CCAA merged with the American agency McCann-Erickson, possibly as a strategic move for the Chinese agency, which was facing growing competition. This merger coincided with the passing of Lin Zhenbin in 1964, marking a generational transition. Subsequently, William, the eldest son, took over the company's management. In the 1980s, Ronnie, the younger son, succeeded him and remained active until his death in 2015. The agency, now operating under the name Adling Holdings, Ltd, has shifted its focus to investment activities. The Lin family is no longer involved in the business. Despite these changes, the agency continues to operate in the present day.[137]

In summary, Carl Crow and CCAA exemplify the independent agency model shaped by their founders. They adhered to American standards and focused on press and outdoor advertising. Based in Shanghai, which became the advertising industry hub during the Republican era, both agencies expanded their influence across China and established international connections. While remaining rela-

---

136 *SCMP*, September 20, 1957.

137 Ronnie Lin made a final public appearance in 2014 at the Kam Fan Awards ceremony organised by the Association of Accredited Advertising Agencies of Hong Kong (HK4As) (https://cdn.i.hay marketmedia.asia/?n=campaign-asia%2fcontent%2f20141201095734-Photo+4.JPG, last accessed July 21, 2022). I am grateful to the Lin family and the current managers for opening the doors of their company in Hong Kong and for kindly sharing the documents they have kept.

tively modest in size, these early agencies emphasised individual ownership and a paternalistic approach. However, during the Nanjing decade, a new generation of joint-stock companies emerged, adopting more rational management practices and paving the way for conglomerates in the 1930s.

The Era of Conglomerates

Millington, Limited (1927)

Established in 1927, Millington, Limited became the first major British agency in China.[138] Its founder, Francis Charles Millington, initially operated as an "Incorporated Advertising Consultant", and served as the sole proprietor. The agency experienced rapid growth, leading to its reorganisation as a limited liability company registered in Hong Kong under the Companies Ordinances regime in 1930.[139] The shareholders primarily consisted of British businessmen who had achieved success in commerce, finance and construction. Liu Hongsheng, a prominent Chinese industrialist, also joined the board of directors in 1930.[140] While the board underwent several renewals, the profiles of its members remained relatively unchanged. New additions came from high finance, insurance and real estate sectors.[141] Following the acquisition of the Oriental Press in 1930, Millington was handed over to top ex-

---

138 Although corporate archives are lacking, the Millington agency benefits from relatively extensive documentation. The Shanghai Municipal Archives house a wealth of materials, including correspondence with municipal administrations, audits and minutes of annual general meetings spanning from 1933 to 1941. Additionally, the local press regularly featured articles on the agency and its manager, providing further insight into its activities and operations.

139 SMA, Q275-1-1840-37. Established in 1865, the Companies Ordinance aimed to provide a legal framework for conducting business and protecting the rights and interests of shareholders and stakeholders.

140 Liu Hongsheng, also known as O.S. Lieu, was a prominent figure in various industries and earned nicknames such as the "King of Matches" and the "King of Wool". He established several companies in diverse sectors, including cement (Shanghai Portland Cement Co.), textiles (China Wool Co.), matches (China Match Co.) and transportation. One of Liu Hongsheng's notable ventures, the match company, has been the subject of an in-depth study by historian Sherman Cochran, *Encountering Chinese Networks: Western, Japanese, and Chinese Corporations in China, 1880–1937* (Berkeley, Calif.: University of California Press, 2000), 147.

141 The initial board of directors comprised S.A. Seth, N.C. MacGregor and D.W. Kau in the years 1928–1929. T.G. Drakeford and N.L. Sparke were appointed in 1930, and they were joined by O.S. Lieu, Col. M.H. Logan and J.A.E. Bates in 1932. In response to a significant crisis, the board underwent a restructuring in 1934, with E.F. Harris, A.P. Nazer, N.W. Hickling, S.A. Seth and F.C. Millington assuming key directorial positions. This board composition remained unchanged

ecutives J.A.E. Bates and B. Rozenbaum. The agency fostered expertise transfers through personnel continuity while also bringing in new recruits to introduce innovations. In 1928, F.H. Hindle, a renowned painter and professor at the Royal College of Art in London, was recruited to head Millington's art department and establish a new school of commercial art. Subsequently, the sales department was placed under the direction of J. Heymann, and L.H.W. Jones held the positions of secretary and accountant concurrently in 1930.

Subsequently, Millington's agency underwent a process of specialisation and departmentalisation, distinguishing it from Carl Crow's more loosely structured organisation. By 1930, the agency had established four distinct departments. In addition to its art studio, there were dedicated departments for copywriting, display and sales. The role of advertising manager was assumed by A. Hill-Reid in 1932, followed by B. Rozenbaum in 1934, who later became the head of the newly formed outdoor advertising department. The agency also ventured into box-making in 1936 but discontinued the department the following year due to lack of profitability.[142] Alongside the division of labour, a regional division was established between the Shanghai headquarters and branches in Hong Kong and Singapore. Initially, Millington's offices were located on Nanking Road in the central district of the International Settlement in Shanghai. As the agency expanded, an adjacent building at No. 106 Nanking Road was acquired to accommodate its growing operations.[143] Seizing upon its rapid success, Millington established a branch in Hong Kong in the early 1930s, which was managed by Elma Kelly, an Australian-born career woman (see chapter 3).[144] With the outbreak of the Sino-Japanese War in September 1937, Millington opened a second branch in Singapore, led by A. Hill-Reid, the former advertising director in Shanghai.[145]

At the core of Millington's business operations was publishing and print advertising. In 1927, Millington and his partner B.L. Gabbott established the Willow Pattern Press (Liuyin yinshua gongsi), which later merged with the Oriental Press after its takeover in 1930. Willow Pattern Press specialised in artistic printing, while the Oriental Press focused on traditional editorial work.[146] These press companies

until 1941, except for the replacement of S.A. Seth, who had been with the agency since its inception, by W. Massey in 1938. SMA (SMC), U1-14-3255.

142 SMA (SMC), U1-14-3255; "Millington Limited: Advertising and Depression Explained", *NCH*, June 3, 1936; *CWR*, May 29, 1937; *NCH*, June 2, 1937.

143 *CWR*, January 8, 1927. *CP*, July 1, 1930.

144 *CP*, February 3, 1930.

145 "Trade in South Good, Millington Declares", *China Press*, March 15, 1938.

146 Until 1934, the Oriental Press operated its workshops on Avenue Edward VII, while the Willow Pattern Press relocated to Nanking Road, in close proximity to the Millington agency. In 1934, a consolidation took place, bringing the two operations together under one roof in the Gallia

served as crucial platforms for printing not only advertising materials but also magazines and reference publications. One notable publication was the *Hongs & Homes* directory, which provided a comprehensive listing of businesses, professionals, and individuals residing in Shanghai.[147] Among the prominent magazines produced by Millington were *Safety First* and *Shanghai Defence League Magazine*. These publications advocated for a stronger British military presence in Shanghai following the May Thirtieth Incident in 1925 and gained popularity among the English-speaking community in the city.[148] Starting from 1931, Millington took on the role of editor for the official newsletter of the Rotary Club of Shanghai, called *The Pagoda*, of which he had been a member since February 1927.[149] In 1934, Millington had plans to publish a guidebook on Shanghai with the goal of enhancing the city's image and promoting tourism, which had been affected by the economic crisis and the Sino-Japanese War of 1932.[150] In 1938, Millington expanded his publishing endeavors by launching two new magazines: *Far Eastern Engineering* and *Indian and Eastern Engineer* which targeted English-speaking engineers working in the Far East and the Indian peninsula.[151]

In addition to its publishing endeavours, Millington actively fostered artistic creation. In 1928, the agency established its own art studio, which swiftly gained recognition as one of the premier creative hubs in China.[152] Recognising the importance of nurturing talent, Francis Millington took a visionary step in 1930 by founding the first integrated art school, aimed at training a new generation of commercial artists. This strategic move not only fulfilled the agency's artistic needs but also served as a talent pool for recruitment, with exceptional students being offered positions within the agency upon completing their training. Alongside its emphasis on print advertis-

---

Building on Szechuen Road, in the central district of the International Settlement. Bacon, 760; Millington, Ltd., "The Willow Pattern Press", *Distinctive Printing*, 1937. SMA, Q275-1-1840-37; *NCH*, February 24, 1931.

147 Following in the footsteps of Rosenstock's Directory, the *Hong & Homes* was regularly enriched and updated. In 1927, it introduced a special section devoted to women's hygiene. In 1929, it expanded further by incorporating a staff directory of the Shanghai Power Company and the Shanghai Municipal Council's Electricity Department. Bacon, 759; *CWR*, February 16, 1929. "Hongs & Homes", *CP*, July 14, 1929; SMA (SMC), U1-4-246.

148 *CWR*, May 21, 1927.

149 *The Pagoda* (Official Organ of the Rotary Club of Shanghai), n° 613 (September 1931): 1; "Shanghai Rotary Club Roster, July 1, 1930", Alonzo Bland Calder Papers, 1911–1956, Hoover Institution Archives, Stanford, Calif., Box 19, f. 1.

150 "Publicity for Shanghai Said Mostly Bad. Book of Information on this city planned to popularize us abroad. Millington tells Rotary all about Advertising", *CP*, May 11, 1934.

151 *CP*, March 15, 1938.

152 "Millington's Has New Art Director Brought From Home", *CP*, October 28, 1928. "Annual General Meeting of Millington Limited", *CP*, June 21, 1929.

ing, Millington actively engaged in outdoor advertising. In 1928, Francis Millington assumed the role of advertising consultant to the Shanghai Municipal Council (SMC) and played a vital role in facilitating discussions surrounding the formulation of the initial advertising regulations within the International Settlement.[153] Over the course of 1928 to 1939, Millington corresponded with the municipal authorities on more than 30 occasions, seeking permission to install hoardings and billboards throughout the concessions. Recognising the significance of a robust poster service, the agency acquired Star Photo Engraving Photography in 1930, a company specialising in the making of colour posters.[154] As the agency's outdoor advertising activities continued to flourish, the need for a dedicated department became apparent, leading to the establishment of a specialised division in 1934. This expansion further solidified Millington's position as a prominent player in the field of advertising, offering comprehensive services encompassing both print and outdoor advertising.[155]

Confronted with intensifying competition and challenging economic conditions during the 1930s, Millington sought new avenues to expand its reach. In the late 1920s, he successfully persuaded municipal authorities to permit commercial advertising on public transportation, which had previously been reserved for official announcements and charitable campaigns.[156] Embracing emerging technologies, Millington was an early advocate for radio advertising in the early 1930s. Francis Millington played a pivotal role in the establishment of the China Broadcast Association (CBA) and was instrumental in setting up the first radio station in Shanghai (XCBL).[157] To deepen his understanding of the radio industry, he embarked on an extensive trip to Great Britain and the United States in 1932, where he studied the operations of national channels such as the BBC and NBC. Upon his return to China, Millington was widely recognised as an expert in the field.[158] In 1933, he assumed the role of the head of the organising committee for the Shanghai Radio and Industry Exhibition, drawing inspiration from similar events held in London and New York.[159] Furthermore, in 1935, he was appointed as an advisor to the Chinese

---

153 General Buildings Advertisements – Taxation of Street Advertising. Special Regulations with Respect to Advertisement Structures & Boards, SMA (SMC), U1-14-3267 (1928–1932).
154 Shanghai Bank, Audit of Millington, Ltd., April 14–16, 1934, SMA, Q275-1-1840-37.
155 Letter from Millington to the SMC, September 11, 1934. SMA (SMC), U1-14-3255.
156 "Suggested Revenue from Advertising on Trams, Buses and Lorries (Letter from Millington to SMC, Shanghai, 2 August 1928)", SMA (SMC), U1-3-1284. Millington certainly inherited this monopoly from the Oriental agency, which was the first to receive such exclusivity. *NCH*, June 3, 1936.
157 "XCBL Broadcast A Success. Many Congratulations on First Radio Programme", *NCH*, May 19, 1931; "China Broadcast Association to Convene May 28", *CP*, May 22, 1931.
158 "Millington To Get New Radio Ideas. China Broadcast Official Leaves for tour of U.S., England", *CP*, June 7, 1932.
159 *CP*, November 5, 1933.

government for the establishment of the nation's first national radio station, XQCH. Housed in the Sassoon House adjacent to Millington's offices in Shanghai, the radio station operated under the auspices of the Ministry of Communications. This collaboration between public authorities and a private advertising agency signalled a shift in political communication, with advertising techniques developed in the commercial sector being embraced for political purposes. The Nationalist regime, facing financial difficulties, recognised the potential revenue that could be generated through radio advertising and enthusiastically embraced this opportunity.[160]

The Millington agency demonstrated its prowess in organising trade exhibitions as well. In November 1935 and June 1937, the agency successfully orchestrated two editions of the Better Homes Exhibition (Xiandai jiating zhanlanhui), which aimed to stimulate industrial growth and consumer spending amidst the economic depression. Millington spared no effort in ensuring the exhibitions' success. Over the course of a week, the racecourse was transformed into a bustling venue accommodating around 100 exhibitors from various sectors. According to reports in the local press, the events were resounding triumphs. The May-June 1937 exhibition alone attracted over 100,000 visitors, five times more than the previous edition.[161] In addition to the exhibitors' booths, visitors were treated to a range of attractions designed to entertain and captivate them. The program included theatrical performances, film screenings, fireworks display, dragon boat races and even dog and baby shows. The presence of esteemed individuals such as Wu Tiecheng, the mayor of the Chinese municipality, who served as the guest of honour at the inaugural ceremony, added to the event's prestige. It is highly likely that the exhibition would have been repeated in subsequent years if it had not been for the outbreak of war in August 1937, which abruptly halted further editions.[162]

Millington's history can be divided into three major phases. The initial phase from 1927 to 1933 was marked by rapid growth and success. However, the agency encountered a series of crises during the second phase from 1934 to 1938. Despite these difficulties, there was a brief period of recovery before the final collapse of the agency in 1952. In February 1930, the Millington agency celebrated its third

---

160 "New Radio Station in Shanghai. Chinese Government to run Station XQHC", *NCH*, March 13, 1935.

161 These exhibitions were inspired by the Better Homes national campaign launched in the United States in the early 1920s to facilitate access to property and improve household comfort. On this subject, see: Catherine Gudis, *Buyways: Billboards, Automobiles, and the American Landscape* (New York: Routledge, 2004), 137.

162 *CP*, February 3 and 11, April 11, May 18, 1937; *NCH*, June 12 and 13, 1937; "Publicity – Propositions from Advertising Agent. Millington, Ltd.: Better Homes Exhibition", SMA (SMC), U1-4-246 (1935).

anniversary in a warm and congenial atmosphere.[163] The gathering took place at the Eddie Cafe on Broadway, where the agency's 80 staff members from both the Millington agency and the Willow Pattern Press came together to commemorate the occasion. This celebration served as a culmination of three years of continuous achievements since the agency's establishment in 1927. Like Lin Zhenbin of CCAA, F.C. Millington emphasised the challenges faced in the early days in order to highlight the significant progress that had been made. He sought to cultivate a sense of sacrifice and dedication among his employees towards the company. In his inaugural speech, Millington outlined what he considered to be the five pillars of success: to look ahead, save as much as possible for investment, hard work, determination to win and loyal supporters. Humbly, he attributed his success to the strong bonds of trust and solidarity within his team, expressing gratitude to the salesmen whom he regarded as the "lifeblood" of the agency.[164] The agency boasted excellent financial health at the time. Its turnover and staff have more than doubled in two years, reaching 25,000 taels and 200 employees.[165] Outdoor advertising played a large part in this success. The number of its billboards doubled on Shanghai's streets, resulting in a commensurate increase in derived revenue. The roster of clients continued to grow and diversify: Bovril, Kruschen, Sanatogen, Cuticura pharmaceuticals, Viyella textile, Johnny Walker whisky, General Electric and Morris Car.[166] In 1930, several big names in finance and communications enriched its portfolio (Shanghai Telephone Company, Dollar Steamship, Asia Realty, American-Oriental Banking Corporation).[167]

However, the period of growth and prosperity for Millington was abruptly halted as it encountered various challenges. The agency began to feel the adverse effects of the 1929 global economic crisis and the Japanese attack on Shanghai in early 1932. The impact of the worldwide depression became increasingly severe from 1933 onwards, significantly affecting Millington's operations. Many clients in Shanghai cancelled their orders or faced difficulties in fulfilling previously agreed contracts, exacerbated by the banking crisis. The agency's financial troubles were further compounded by the bankruptcy of its primary financial partner, the

---

163 "Third Anniversary Of Millington Limited is Celebrated in Dinner. Head of successful Advertising Organization delivers Inspiring Speech of his early Struggle against hardships", *CP*, February 3, 1930.

164 "Annual General Meeting of Millington Limited", *CP*, June 21, 1929.

165 *CP*, June 21, 1929.

166 Bacon, 759.

167 "Clients, Friends Are Met by Millington, Directors, Staff at Firm's New Home. C.M. Bain, Outlining Aims of Company. Says it is out to provide Shanghai with a first-class advertising agency", *CP*, October 2, 1930.

American-Oriental Banking Corporation, which resulted in a doubling of its debts. The following year brought even more challenges, with the Hong Kong branch facing the possibility of closure unless immediate financial adjustments were made. In response, the Board of Directors convened an extraordinary general meeting and made the difficult decision to implement drastic measures.[168] These measures included a restructuring of the agency's capital, shareholders forgoing their dividends and salary reductions for employees. To mitigate the financial strain, Millington was compelled to sell the former premises of the Oriental Press on Avenue Edward VII and consolidate its operations into the Gallia Building. Additionally, F.C. Millington sold a plot of land he owned on Edinburgh Street and disposed of outdated printing equipment inherited from the Oriental Press. Beyond the tangible financial losses, the crisis also eroded internal confidence within the agency. In 1935, Millington was forced to take legal action against an employee who was accused of stealing a typewriter. More significantly, two young salesmen, previously praised for their loyalty, were accused of embezzling funds, further exacerbating the agency's difficulties.[169]

The restructured company, combined with improving economic conditions, began to show positive results in the following year, 1935. Although the initial profits were modest, they doubled in the subsequent year.[170] Just as Millington was beginning to regain stability, the outbreak of war in August 1937 dealt a severe blow to the agency. The first half of 1938 marked the most challenging period in the company's history. However, the crisis proved to be short-lived, and the recovery in the second half of 1938 exceeded all expectations.[171] The agency not only returned to profitability but was also able to resume paying dividends to its shareholders. Additionally, the Hong Kong branch fully recovered and experienced its most prosperous period to date. After the departure of founder Francis Charles in 1939, his partner B. Rozenbaum assumed the role of managing director. The preserved annual balance sheets from the municipal archives indicate that

---

168 SMA, Q275-1-1840-37. "Millington & Co. Suffer from Sino-Japanese Conflict", *CWR*, June 17, 1933; "Company Meetings. Millington Ltd.", *NCH*, June 14, 1933. "Millington's Holds Annual General Meet. Advertising Agency has $41,003.94 loss for 1933: New Home Costly", *NCH*, June 14, 1933. "Company to reduce its capital: Extraordinary General Meeting of Shareholders of Millington, Limited", *NCH*, July 4, 1934.

169 *CP*, June 26, 1934.

170 "Millington, Ltd. Makes $1,059 profit in '35", *CP*, May 29, 1936; "Millington Limited. Advertising and Depressions Explained", *NCH*, June 3, 1936; "No Dividend To be Declared for 1936 by Millington Ltd.", *CP*, May 26, 1937.

171 "Millington's Show Debit Balance: Position healthier than for Some Years: Increase of Business Foreshadowed", *NCH*, June 2, 1937.

the agency continued to thrive until 1941, further reinforcing its post-crisis recovery and sustained success during this period.[172]

During the war, the cohesiveness of the Millington group was significantly disrupted. Starting from 1941, the parent company in Shanghai and its two branches began to operate independently. The Hong Kong branch gained recognition at the beginning of the war for its support of donation campaigns for war prisoners. However, its activities came to a halt following the arrest of its manager, Elma Kelly, in January 1942. Kelly remained detained in the Japanese prison of Stanley Camp for over three years. Upon her release in August 1945, she established her own company, Cathay Advertising Agency.[173] The Singapore branch, on the other hand, remained active until at least 1946, primarily engaging with Australian companies.[174] As the war came to an end, the Shanghai agency shifted its focus back to its editorial endeavours. In October 1945, it took over the publication of the British newspaper *North China Herald and Daily News*, which had been suspended during the war. However, declining subscriber numbers and advertising revenues plagued the publication, and the century-old newspaper was ultimately shut down in March 1952. The agency also assumed control of the periodical *China Weekly/Monthly Review* until its discontinuation in October 1952. These post-war developments signified a shift in the agency's activities, as it navigated the challenges of the era and adapted to the changing landscape of the advertising and publishing industries.[175]

In conclusion, Millington marked the transition between two generations of independent agencies. Originally a one-man operation, the agency began modestly and grew by leaps and bounds. When it reached the proportions of a conglomerate in the mid-1930s, its founder nonetheless continued to nurture the family mythology to overcome crises. The last generation, embodied by Consolidated National Advertising Company, differed from its predecessors in that from the outset it assumed the stature of a giant.

---

172 SMA Q5-3-3098; *NCH*, April 22, 1939; *NCH*, May 21, 1941.

173 *SCMP*, February 4, November 28, 1941. *SCMP*, October 14, 1945; January 17, 1947. About this atypical advertising woman, see the work of Jacqueline Dickenson, *Australian Women in Advertising in the Twentieth Century*, 2015, 40–49.

174 *SCMP*, November 7, 1946.

175 *Printed for the Proprietors, the North China Daily News & Herald, Ltd. by Millington Ltd. (Willow Pattern Press), 117 Hongkong Road. North China Daily News*, January 1, 1946, 8; *SCMP*, November 11, 1957. *CWR*, January 1, 1950; *CMR*, October 1, 1952.

The Consolidated National Advertising Company (Lianhe) (1930)

The Consolidated National Advertising Company, referred to as Lianhe, was created through the merger of five existing agencies owned by three prominent Chinese businessmen [Figure 5]. Among them, Yao Junwei (Yao Chunwei) owned three agencies: the Commercial Advertising Agency (Shangye guanggao she or Shangye guanggao gongsi), established in 1924 and specialising in press advertising; the United Advertising Advisers (Lianhe guanggao guwenshe), founded in 1926 to handle advertising in the Chinese newspaper *Shenbao*; and the Ji Da (I-Tai) Advertising Company (Yida guanggao gongsi), which focused on advertising along roads and railways. Zheng Yaonan (Chen Yaonan) operated the Yaonan Advertising Company (Yaonan guanggao gongsi), which also specialised in press advertising. Additionally, Lu Meiseng (Lewis Mason) was responsible for the Great China Advertising Corporation (Dahua guanggao gongsi), which facilitated the placement of European and American advertisers' advertisements in Chinese newspapers. Leveraging this collaborative effort, Lianhe was established as a limited liability company with an initial capital of 200,000 yuan, which was 20 times the capital of CCAA or Carl Crow agencies.[176]

The Chinese name of the newly formed group, Lianhe, was partly derived from the name of the United Advertising Advisers (Lianhe guanggao guwenshe), owned by Yao Junwei, who played a significant role in the merger. The term "Lianhe" emphasised the concept of association and collaboration. However, in the English transliteration, "Consolidated National", a national dimension was added that was not present in the Chinese name, highlighting a sense of national unity and identity. The term *lianhe guanggao* had another connotation as well. It referred to a method introduced by the agency in the early 1930s, which involved bringing together advertisers from the same industry or those involved in a common project, such as the promotion of national products (guohuo). This approach, known as collective advertising, gained popularity during the nationalist regime, which encouraged Chinese companies to unite for the purpose of national salvation. During the 1930s, collective advertisements became more prevalent as a response to the economic depression, compelling advertisers to pool their resources and collaborate in order to achieve economies of scale.[177]

In an interview with the *China Press* newspaper in August 1930, manager Lu Meiseng outlined the objectives of the newly formed Lianhe agency. At a time when Chinese entrepreneurs were no longer questioning the importance of adver-

---

176 *CP*, August 1, 1930; "Tokyo Koshinjo Limited. Information No.27340". SMA, Q275-1-1840-37.
177 *SB*, September 12, 1931.

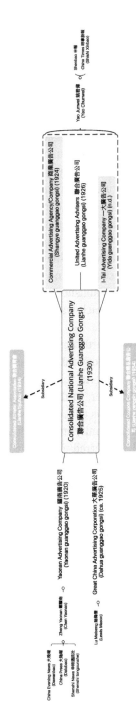

Figure 5: Genealogy of the Consolidated National Advertising Company (1930). Interactive map: https://madspace.org/cooked/Trees?ID=184.

tising but seeking ways to enhance their campaigns, Lianhe aimed to meet this demand for more strategic and effective advertising. In contrast to space brokers, Lu
positioned the agency as a consultancy firm that conducted "scientific" campaigns
for clients, grounded in thorough planning and market research. While Lianhe offered a diverse range of services, its primary focus was on print advertising. This
emphasis was largely influenced by the backgrounds of its founders, many of
whom held significant positions in the Shanghai press (chapter 3). Yao Junwei
served on the boards of major Chinese newspapers such as *Shenbao* and *China
Times* (Shishi Xinbao), both of which were shareholders in the Lianhe group.
Through Zheng Yaonan, the agency was also connected to publications like *China
Evening News* (Dawanbao) and *China Press* (Dalubao), as well as the news agency
Shenshi (Shenshi tongxunshe). Upon acquiring the United Advertising Advisers
agency, Lianhe assumed responsibility for advertising accounts in *Shenbao* and its
illustrated supplement, the *Shenbao Pictorial Supplement* (Shenbao tuhua zhoukan).
In June 1932, Lianhe further expanded its client base by acquiring the clientele of
the Commercial Press, which had suffered equipment losses during the Japanese
attack earlier that year. Under the agreement, the publishing house relinquished
all advertising activities and transferred its contracts to Lianhe. This development,
coupled with Millington's acquisition of the Oriental Press two years prior, marked
a significant turning point in the history of Chinese advertising, departing from its
origins primarily rooted in the publishing industry.[178]

Based on the records from the Shanghai municipal archives, Lianhe's involvement in outdoor advertising appears to have been relatively limited. Unlike
Carl Crow and Millington, who frequently corresponded with the administrations
of the foreign concessions, Lianhe's presence in municipal correspondence is
noted only twice. In 1938, during a cholera epidemic threatening the city, Lianhe
proposed to the Public Health Department (PHD) the publication of a Chinese-
language medical magazine at its own expense. Inspired by the American magazine *Hygenia* and the monthly newsletter of the Chinese Municipal Bureau of Public Health, the purpose of the magazine was to promote awareness of the PHD's
activities and educate the Chinese population, particularly women, about basic
public hygiene practices.[179] Although the proposal was declined by the Shanghai
Municipal Council (SMC), in 1941 Lianhe was granted permission to install a tem-

---

178 "Merger formed by advertising firms in Shanghai. Five leading Chinese Companies in new
combine", *CP*, August 1, 1930.
179 The municipal authorities rejected the proposal, which was considered redundant with the
Municipal Gazette. SMA (SMC), U1-4-246 (1158–1161).

porary billboard on a construction site located west of the International Settlement, at the junction of Bubbling Well and Moulmien Road.[180]

Alongside its advertising activities, Lianhe diversified its services to include other areas. In 1933, the agency sponsored several radio programs broadcast on the Mingyuan channel (Mingyuan guangbo diantai), although its involvement in this field was not as extensive as that of Millington. Concerned with the growing issue of unemployment during the 1930s, Lianhe also took on the role of an employment agency, advertising job opportunities in the press. The job offers ranged from services such as private tuition and restaurant waitstaff to intellectual professions such as artists and architects, as well as office workers like typists. Furthermore, Lianhe acted as a travel agency and ticket office, providing services for shows, exhibitions and other cultural events.[181]

The Lianhe agency also ventured into innovative techniques to stimulate purchases, including the use of coupons and samples. Unlike Carl Crow's approach, which discouraged their use due to high poverty levels in China, Lianhe began distributing coupons for the Eagle brand of electric torches (Fengpai diantong) in the early 1930s. The success of this experiment led to other prominent brands such as Palmolive and various pharmaceutical, food and tobacco companies adopting the coupon method as well.[182] To engage readers and maintain their interest, Lianhe's managers introduced interactive elements such as riddles, puzzles, drawing competitions and writing contests within their advertisements. These games became immensely popular among *Shenbao* readers. In August 1934, recognising the enthusiasm generated by these activities, the agency established a specialised subsidiary called Consolidated Coupon Company (Lianhe zengpin gufen youxian gongsi). This subsidiary was responsible for evaluating the numerous responses received and awarding prizes to the winners. The creation of the subsidiary allowed advertisers to combine their coupon orders, resulting in cost savings. The initiative received support from various entities, including the Shanghai Bankers' Club as the main investor, the Shanghai municipal government's Social Affairs Bureau, which viewed it as a means to boost consumption, and Sincere (Xianshi) department stores, which provided prizes and hosted prize-giving ceremonies. Outside of Shanghai, the China

---

180 Letter from Y. Lewis Mason (Consolidated National Advertising Company) to Wilfried S.B. Wong, General Manager of the American Engineering Corporation, Shanghai, September 8, 1941, SMA, Q459-1-233.
181 *SB*, August 15, and October 15, 1930, August 7, 1932, August 28, 1934, July 14, 1939.
182 *SB*, June 4 and 26 1932, August 24 1933.

Travel Service acted as a relay until Lianhe established its own offices in Tianjin, Hankou and Guangzhou.[183]

Lianhe enjoyed a prosperous period until the mid-1950s. Despite the challenges posed by the economic depression, the agency consistently maintained profitable accounts, achieving annual sales of over one million yuan in the 1930s.[184] Its international reputation allowed Lianhe to serve as an intermediary for foreign agencies seeking to place advertisements in the Chinese press, including the Far Eastern Advertising Agency based in London and the Foreign Advertising & Service Bureau in New York. Although there are gaps in available documentation, Lianhe's remarkable longevity suggests its ability to weather crises that severely impacted its competitors. The conglomerate may have benefited from the Sino-Japanese War, which eliminated foreign competition and provided an opportunity for the agency to establish itself through national mobilisation campaigns.[185] By the mid-1950s, Lianhe emerged as one of the few surviving agencies after undergoing the drastic sector restructuring imposed by the Communist State-Party.

Conclusion

While professional organisations provided a platform for pioneers to socialise, exchange information and defend their shared interests, it was the independent agencies that truly embodied the emerging profession's ethical principles. The earliest agencies had their origins in the in-house advertising departments of publishing companies, such as the Oriental Advertising Agency and the China Publicity Company. Prior to the First World War, these departments became independent entities separate from their parent companies, the Oriental Press and the Commercial Press, respectively. After the war, the first agencies emerged at the intersection of two influences. American journalists, like Carl Crow, who had engaged in propaganda activities during the war (ComPub, Chun Mei News), redirected their efforts towards commercial advertising. Simultaneously, a new generation of young Chinese individuals who had studied commercial sciences in the United States, such as Lin Zhenbin and Lu Meiseng, returned to establish their own companies (China

---

183 *CP*, February 19, 1934. *SB*, October 3, 1931, 14. *SB*, June 4 and 26, 1932, August 24, 1933. *CP*, August 17, 1934. *CP*, May 25 and August 17, 1934. Regarding the China Travel Service, see: Yajun Mo, *Touring China: A History of Travel Culture, 1912–1949* (Ithaca: Cornell University Press, 2021).
184 Lianhe had several accounts in three major Chinese banks: Bank of Communications (Jiaotong yinhang 交通銀行), Zhejiang Commercial Bank (Zhejiang shiye yinhang 浙江實業銀行) and South China Bank (Zhongnan yinhang 中南銀行). SMA, Q275-1-1840-27 (37).
185 *SB*, December 12, 1938, January 6, and August 5–8, 1945.

Commercial Advertising Agency, Great China Advertising Corporation). In the 1930s, the formation of advertising conglomerates (Millington, Lianhe) marked a new chapter in the profession's history. The previous in-house departments of publishing companies were assimilated by these new agencies, signifying the end of the era of "founding fathers" operating individual companies with a familial spirit. By the early 1930s, advertising had developed into an independent industry.

While the initial agencies were established by foreign expatriates, vernacular agencies proliferated during the Nanjing decade and eventually came to dominate the industry from the Sino-Japanese War onward. Prior to the war, the sector was relatively evenly distributed. Foreign agencies held sway over the English-language press and the foreign concessions, while their Chinese counterparts dominated the Chinese-language press and territories under Chinese administration. Only the most influential agencies had the capacity to transcend these divisions by joining forces (CCAA and Acme), relying on their multicultural staff and leveraging their relationships with the press and local authorities. The war resulted in the disappearance of most foreign agencies (Carl Crow) and significantly weakened those that remained (Millington). On the eve of the Communist revolution, Chinese agencies had unrivaled dominance across all sectors.

Although independent agencies did not encompass the entirety of advertising activities, they played a crucial part in the professionalisation of the field. While they did not replace the in-house services of large companies such as British-American Tobacco, Five Continents Drugstore, or Household Industries, they facilitated the scaling up of advertising, attracting smaller advertisers and expanding into sectors beyond pharmaceuticals and cigarettes. The case of Lianhe illustrates how the two influences could converge and reinforce each other. Formed in 1930 through the collaboration of various vernacular industrialists, the Lianhe agency benefited from the infusion of new expertise brought in by the younger generation trained in the United States. It was this cross-pollination of experiences that ultimately propelled Lianhe to become one of the industry's leaders and endure until the waves of nationalisation in the mid-1950s.

Chapter 3
Biographical Trajectories

Who were the first advertising professionals in China? Where were they trained? How did they work on a daily basis? How did they navigate the crises that shook the Republic? What set them apart from their counterparts in Europe and the United States? To shed light on these questions, this chapter presents a series of portraits that complement the study of agencies presented in the previous chapter. Carl Crow (1883–1945) and Lin Zhenbin (1896–1964) represent the first generation of professionals trained in American universities. Francis Charles Millington (1888–1985) embodies the transition to the era of conglomerates, which, in the case of the Lianhe agency, necessitates a collective biography. These portraits illustrate the three major models of cultural entrepreneurs identified by historian Christopher Rea.[186] Highlighting their professional and geographical mobility, their propensity to invest and experiment, and their particular sensitivity to both culture and market dynamics, the concept of cultural entrepreneur proves particularly effective in analysing the trajectories of advertising professionals. Carl Crow epitomises the cultural personality, creating his own products, style and brand image. Lin Zhenbin and F.C. Millington represent two tycoon figures who used various modes of cultural production to extend their influence. Unlike the cultural personality, who creates their own works and assigns intrinsic value to culture, the tycoon places economic value above cultural value and delegates production to employees or associates. Lastly, the Lianhe agency provides an example of a collective enterprise pursuing the same economic objectives as the tycoon but distributing power more equitably among partners. In conclusion, this chapter will strive to give voice to women and anonymous employees who remain in the shadow of the advertising industry.

Portraits of Two Pioneers: Carl Crow and Lin Zhenbin

Origins and Education

Carl Crow and Lin Zhenbin had notable differences in their backgrounds and career paths [Figures 6 and 7]. Born in Highland, Missouri in 1883, Carl Crow grew

---

186 Christopher G Rea, "Enter the Cultural Entrepreneur" in *The Business of Culture: Cultural Entrepreneurs in China and Southeast Asia, 1900–65*, ed. Nicolai Volland and Christopher G. Rea (Vancouver: University of British Columbia Press, 2014), 9–34.

https://doi.org/10.1515/9783111390000-004

up in the United States. His move to Shanghai in 1911 was an unexpected opportunity, which he embraced as an exciting adventure. He settled in China permanently and would have likely remained there if not for the outbreak of the Sino-Japanese War in 1937, which forced him to leave Shanghai. On the other hand, Lin Zhenbin, born in Fujian province, China, initially left for the United States to pursue his studies. He was part of the Boxer Indemnity Scholarship Program, which sent thousands of young Chinese students to study abroad with the intention of returning to contribute to their country's development.[187] The 13-year age difference between Crow and Lin had a significant impact on their academic training, with Lin benefiting from the evolving field of advertising education, while Crow pursued journalism studies instead.

In an unpublished text, Carl Crow revealed that his passion for advertising began during his childhood while flipping through the pages of the magazine *Printers' Ink*.[188] His journey into the field started as an apprentice in a print shop, where he gained hands-on experience. In 1908, he enrolled in the newly established School of Journalism at the University of Missouri, simultaneously working as a columnist for the local newspaper, the *Columbia Missourian*. During his free time, Crow immersed himself in learning advertising techniques and began creating his own advertisements. Initially, his work involved formatting the ads submitted by local shopkeepers, drawing inspiration from the typography used in the local press. While his customers were satisfied with his work, Crow felt that his talent was not being fully recognised. In 1911, an opportunity arose for Crow to escape the routine of the American Midwest when journalist Thomas F. Millard invited him to join him in Shanghai to launch the first American newspaper in China, initially known as *Millard's Review of the Far East* and later renamed *China Weekly Review* in 1917. The outbreak of World War I played a significant role in shaping Crow's career trajectory, propelling him from a newspaperman to an intelligence agent and ultimately an advertising agent. In 1917, he was appointed as a representative of the Committee of Public Information (ComPub) and went on to establish the Chun Mei News agency. This venture provided him with

---

187 In 1908, the American government decided to waive the indemnities imposed on China in compensation for the losses suffered during the Boxer Rebellion (1900) and to convert them into scholarships. The Boxer Indemnity Scholarship Program created the conditions that sent growing waves of students to the United States until the early 1950s and supported multiple cultural and scientific exchanges programs between the two countries. On this subject, see: Michael H. Hunt, "The American Remission of the Boxer Indemnity: A Reappraisal", *The Journal of Asian Studies* 31, no. 3 (1972): 539–59; Yang Tsui-hua, *Patronage of Science: The China Foundation for the Promotion of Education and Culture* (Taipei: Institute of Modern History, Academia Sinica, 1991).
188 Carl Crow, "The Advertising Bulk Pile", Crow, Carl (1883–1945), Papers, 1913–1945. Compositions and Notes Series, f.12 (Columbia, MO: State Historical Society of Missouri, s. d.), 1.

valuable experience in translating and placing advertisements in the Chinese press, further expanding his expertise in the field (Chapter 2).[189]

Figure 6: Carl Crow (1883–1945) in the 1930s. Source: Paul French, *Carl Crow, a tough old China hand: The life, times and adventures of an American in Shanghai* (Hong Kong: Hong Kong University Press, 2006).

Born in Fuzhou in 1896, Lin Zhenbin began his educational journey at the Anglo-Chinese College in his hometown. In 1910, he successfully passed a highly competitive examination organised by the provincial authorities, earning a scholarship to pursue further studies at the prestigious Qinghua University (Tsinghua College) in Beijing. Established the previous year, Qinghua aimed to prepare talented individuals for advanced studies in the United States. With the support of university president Zhou Yichun (Y.T. Tsur), Lin was admitted to Rochester University and subsequently Columbia University in New York, where he completed his degree in 1919. Seeking to enhance his education in the field of advertising, Lin chose to pursue a specialised program at Columbia Business School. Concurrently, he took sociology courses at New York University and gained practical experience by working for a local advertising agency. In 1922, upon returning to China, he was recruited by the China Publicity Company to manage its branch in Hankou. However, in 1926, Lin decided to resign from his position and establish his own

---

189 French, 75; National Archives and Records (NARA), General records of the Department of State, RG59, Box 736; *Millard's Review of the Far East* (MRFE), September 13, 1919.

agency, the China Commercial Advertising Agency (CCAA), which he helmed until his passing (Chapter 2).[190]

Figure 7: Lin Zhenbin (1896–1964), around 1936. From Kyatang Woo, "Catchy Slogans, Ambition Carry C.P. Ling to Success", *China Press*, September 1, 1936, 3.

Two Figures of Educators

Both Carl Crow and Lin Zhenbin shared a pedagogical ambition, but their approaches differed in terms of target audience and methods. Lin, one of China's pioneering advertising professors, taught the discipline at various universities in Shanghai. Although he did not leave behind any written works, his teachings played a significant role in training the new generation of Chinese advertising professionals and establishing advertising as an academic discipline in its own right.[191] On the other hand, Crow, as an "Old China Hand", was determined to challenge the prejudices held by his fellow Americans against the Chinese. He was considered an authority on both China and advertising, and his expertise made him a sought-after speaker for lectures, interviews and contributions to collective publications. For in-

---

190 SMA, Q275-1-1840/37-1. K. Woo, "Catchy Slogans, Ambition Carry C.P. Ling to Success", *CP*, September 1936; John Benjamin Powell, *Who's Who in China* (Shanghai: China Weekly Review, 1936), 161.
191 *CP*, September 20, 1933.

stance, in 1919, the Advertising Club of China invited him to give a lecture on the prospects of advertising agencies in China.[192] In 1926, the American commercial attaché Julean Arnold asked Crow to contribute the chapter on advertising in his comprehensive *Commercial Handbook of China*.[193] Throughout his life, Crow maintained prolific writing output. In addition to articles aimed at introducing China to the American public, he published a popular tourist guide to China, an anthology of President Wilson's speeches translated into Chinese, a poker handbook in Chinese, a bilingual automobile dictionary and the first fashion catalogue in Chinese.[194] Some of his editorials in the press were polemical and occasionally aggressively anti-Japanese, which garnered him both admirers and adversaries.[195]

Two Men of Networks

Both Carl Crow and Lin Zhenbin were actively engaged in professional organisations and cultivated their alumni networks. In 1920, Crow was elected as a member of the executive committee and the educational affairs committee of the Advertising Club of China. He also attended the inaugural meeting of the Association of Advertising Agencies in January 1924.[196] Lin, on the other hand, was elected as the Chinese secretary of the Advertising Club of China in 1923 and later became its vice-president in 1931.[197] Crow played a significant role in facilitating exchanges between China and the Missouri School of Journalism, which served as a significant source of recruitment for advertising agencies.[198] Lin, during his

---

192 Carl Crow, "The Advertising Agent in China and America. The Advertising Agent – His Prospects in China", *CP*, August 1919.

193 Crow, "Advertising and Merchandising".

194 Carl Crow, *The Travelers' Handbook for China* (San Francisco, Calif.: San Francisco News Company, 1913). Carl Crow, "When You Advertise to Orientals", *Printers' Ink Monthly*, December 1927, 39–40, 116–23; Carl Crow, "Advertising Meets War and Survives", *Printers' Ink Monthly*, April 1937; Carl Crow, "Team-Work in The Flowery Republic", *Semi-Monthly Magazine, Chinese Guides for American Business*, 1945. *MRFE*, December 14, 1928; French, 80.

195 In 1930, for example, Colonel Yuan Liang of the Shanghai Public Security Bureau took legal action against Crow following an offensive article published by the journalist in the *Shanghai Evening Post*, which led to his resignation (*NCH*, February 4, 1930). Crow was also known for his anti-Japanese views in the *St. Louis Post Dispatch*, which were echoed in Shanghai by the *China Weekly Review* and *China Press*.

196 *MRFE*, April 24, 1921.

197 *CWR*, November 17, 1923.

198 The "Missouri Colony", established around 1910 by two students, had dual objectives. Firstly, it aimed to provide young American journalists with practical experience abroad, with the expectation that upon their return, these journalists would contribute to raising American awareness

studies in the United States, gained admission to selective student fraternities, notably Phi Beta Kappa, and eventually became the head of the Asian branch in 1941. Upon his return to Shanghai, he actively participated in various alumni associations, including the Tsing Hua Alumni Club, the American Returned Students' Association and the American University Club.[199]

Both Crow and Lin were esteemed members of Shanghai's elite clubs. Crow was a charter member of the Rotary Club, while Lin was affiliated with prestigious clubs such as the Chinese Jockey Club, the Shanghai Bankers' Club, the International Recreation Club and the Royal Asiatic Society. Lin also demonstrated a commitment to international peace by involving himself in organisations such as the Pan-Pacific Association and the Institute of Pacific Relations, which provided platforms for discussions on trans-Pacific issues.[200] Reflecting the philanthropic spirit that had been prominent among the Chinese elite since the late Qing dynasty, Lin engaged in a wide range of charitable activities, making regular donations to child protection charities.[201]

Carl Crow's social life included hosting receptions and dinners to commemorate significant events or honour notable figures. For example, in December 1923, he held a grand reception at his home to celebrate the release of American hostages in Shandong province.[202] In August 1931, he organised a lavish dinner in honour of Senator Harry B. Hawkes from Missouri, who was visiting China at the time. Crow's personal wealth, estimated at 30,000 taels, allowed him to become the primary shareholder in his agency and pursue his ambitions.[203] Similarly, Lin

---

of international political issues. Secondly, the founders sought to offer new perspectives to young Chinese and Japanese journalists. However, the exchange of journalists remained largely one-sided. By 1928, while 25 American students had been sent to China and Japan to work for various newspapers and press agencies, the number of Chinese and Japanese journalists who had the opportunity to study journalism at the University of Missouri could be counted on one hand. Thomas F Millard, "The Missouri 'News Monopoly' in the Far East", *China Weekly Review*, March28, 1927; John Maxwell Hamilton, "The Missouri News Monopoly and American Altruism in China: Thomas F.F. Millard, J. B. Powell, and Edgar Snow", *Pacific Historical Review* 55, n° 1 (1986): 27–48.

199 *CWR*, January 4, 1941; SMA, Q275-1-1840.

200 Regarding the Rotary Club in China, see: Cécile Armand, "Foreign Clubs with Chinese Flavor: The Rotary Club of Shanghai and the Politics of Language", in *Knowledge, Power, and Networks: Elites in Transition in Modern China*, ed. Cécile Armand, Christian Henriot and Huei-min Sun (Leiden: Brill, 2022), 233–59. Regarding the Institute of Pacific Relations, please refer to: Zhang Jing, *Zhongguo Taiping Yang guoji xuehui yanjiu, 1925–1945* (Research on the China Institute of Pacific Relations, 1925–1945) (Beijing: Shehui kexue wenxian chubanshe, 2012).

201 "Hong Kong Society for the Protection of Children", *SCMP*, April 12 and 17, 1956.

202 *CWR*, December 15, 1923.

203 *CWR*, August 15, 1931. SMA, Q275-1-1840-37; Crow, *Four Hundred Million Customers*, 102.

Zhenbin also maintained an active social life and was known to organise gatherings and events that were covered in the local press. These social engagements helped him maintain his contacts and reputation in the industry. Lin was not hesitant to put himself in the limelight to better serve his clients, as demonstrated by his posing with his new V-8 Ford Sedan.[204]

While Carl Crow and Lin Zhenbin were active in their professional lives and engaged in various social activities, details about their private lives are less widely known.

Public Life and Private Life

While there are some details available about their marriages, the private lives of both Carl Crow and Lin Zhenbin remain relatively less documented compared to their professional achievements and contributions to the advertising industry. Carl Crow was married twice. His first wife, Mildred S. Powers, had her own successful career as a journalist and later worked for Dodwell and Company, handling commercial relations with Japan.[205] She eventually started her own company, Mildred Crow, Incorporated, specialising in the trade of Chinese antiques with the United States. She also opened an art gallery in Shanghai called The Jade Tree.[206] However, their marriage ended in divorce, and Carl Crow lost custody of their adopted daughter, Mildred Elizabeth "Betty".[207] Carl Crow remarried Helen Marie Hanniger (1893–1941) in 1930, who was described as a more reserved and less publicly visible woman. It seems that she better fulfilled his expectations as a companion for a man of his standing.[208]

Lin Zhenbin's family life appeared to be relatively stable and prosperous. In March 1928, he married Annie Ying Tong, the daughter of a wealthy Shanghai broker. The wedding ceremony was held at the Majestic Hotel and was attended by over 250 guests, including notable figures from both Chinese and American communities. The guest list included former Chinese Premier Xu Shiying, Foreign Minister Guo Daiji, representatives from the U.S. Department of Commerce, colleagues

---

204 *CWR*, August 27, 1932.
205 French, 55–56.
206 French, 81.
207 French, 134. See also: "The Story of Mildred and Betty", *China Rhyming* (blog), last accessed April 26, 2020, http://www.chinarhyming.com/2009/09/15/the-story-of-mildred-and-betty/. See also: French, *Carl Crow, a tough old China hand*, 134.
208 *CWR*, November 24, 1928; April 26, 1928; August 30, 1930; September 13, 1930; *SCMP*, November 26, 1941.

from the Commercial Press and major American clients such as the representative from Ford Motor Company.[209] Lin and Annie had four children together: two daughters and two sons. The two sons, William and Ronald, later became partners in managing the agency in the mid-1950s, continuing their father's legacy. Lin's eldest daughter, Sarah Siu-Mei, married a British naval engineer named Bruce Auld and moved to Hong Kong, where she gained recognition for her artistic activities.[210] The youngest daughter, Dorothea, married William Morgan, who was British-born, and settled in New York. Although they were not extensively covered in the press, both daughters briefly appeared in the media on the occasion of their marriages.[211]

Grey Areas: The Daily Lives of Advertising Managers

The daily lives of advertising managers Carl Crow and Lin Zhenbin are not extensively documented, and historians must piece together fragments of information from various sources. Municipal archives, accounts from Crow himself and chronicles from the local press provide glimpses into their activities.[212] Crow's daily routine involved overseeing his advertising billboards in Shanghai, exploring new advertising spaces and addressing potential violations of municipal regulations. He also faced challenges related to social tensions, such as strikes by printers and coolies at the *Shanghai Evening Post and Mercury* in 1929. Lawsuits, including those with the American Newspaper Company and salary disputes with his own staff, were part of his managerial responsibilities (chapter 2).[213] Through newspaper accounts, we can follow the business travels of both men. Crow visited Beijing in 1919 and Nantong in 1921 to inspect local roads and industries. From 1928 to 1930, he embarked on an extended stay in the United States and went on a four-month global tour with a colleague from the *Shanghai Evening Post*. Lin also undertook market research trips, such as a two-week visit to southern China and Hong Kong in May 1930.[214] After the Communist revolution in 1949, Lin continued to travel to the United States, Japan and Taiwan to meet with associates, establish new contracts and strengthen the foundations of his reorganised agency in Hong Kong (Chapter 2).[215]

---

209 *CP*, March 31, 1928.
210 *South China Sunday Post-Herald*, Hong Kong, July 16, 1951.
211 *SCMP*, December 8, 1956, 12.
212 Letter from Carl Crow to the Shanghai Municipal Council, Shanghai, January 23, 1934. SMA (SMC), U1-4-3815.
213 *CP*, October 16, 1929; *CWR*, 14 March 1931.
214 *CWR*, May 10, 1930.
215 *MRFE*, September 13, 1919, March 19, 1921; *CWR*, April 26, 1928, September 13, 1930.

Divergent Paths after the War

The Sino-Japanese War had a significant impact on the lives of both Carl Crow and Lin Zhenbin, albeit in different ways. After the outbreak of the Sino-Japanese War and the events of "Black Saturday" in August 1937, Carl Crow was forced to leave Shanghai and seek refuge in New York.[216] Despite being wanted by the Japanese, he made multiple attempts to return to China, as documented in his book *Through the Back Door to China.*[217] In 1939, he managed to travel to Chongqing to collect materials for *Liberty* magazine, but he did not dare venture to Shanghai, which was still under Japanese occupation.[218] Following his time in Chongqing, Crow embarked on a two-year journey (1939–1941) that took him to various places including Burma, Mandalay, Rangoon and Kunming. During this period, he kept a diary which was later published posthumously. Despite his efforts, Crow eventually gave up on the idea of resettling in China, recognising the challenges and risks involved.[219]

Carl Crow's post-war life in the United States was marked by a sense of displacement and struggle to find his place in the advertising industry. Despite being a respected figure in Chinese advertising, he faced challenges in the highly competitive and evolving landscape of Madison Avenue. He preferred the role of a consultant rather than being employed by a traditional agency, valuing his independence and unique perspective.[220] Crow's attempts to venture into Latin America as a substitute for the lost China were not successful. While he had some involvement with the J. Walter Thompson agency and went on inspection mis-

---

216 Carl Crow, "China will wear down foe", *Seattle Daily Times*, n.d.; Carl Crow and Esther Brock Bird, *Foreign Devils in the Flowery Kingdom* (New York; London: Harper & Bros., 1940), 330; Carl Crow, *China Takes Her Place* (New York; London: Harper & Bros., 1944), 193; French, 210.

217 Carl Crow and Paul French, *The Long Road Back to China: Along the Burma Road to China's Wartime Capital in 1939* (Hong Kong: Earnshaw Books, 2009). See also: Crow, *China Takes Her Place*, 234–38; French, 223–36.

218 *CWR*, June 24, 1939.

219 "Diary of trip via the Burma Road in the summer 1941", Crow, Carl (1883–1945), Papers, 1913–1945. Compositions and Notes Series, f.55–71 (Columbia, MO: State Historical Society of Missouri, 1941). Carl Crow and Paul French, *The Long Road Back to China: Along the Burma Road to China's Wartime Capital in 1939* (Hong Kong: Earnshaw Books, 2009).

220 Letters from Frank E. Morrisson to M.F. Sletzer, Bloomer, Wisconsin, March 4, 1940; Outdoor Advertising Incorporated, New York, May 1, 1941; Advertising Club of New York, New York, June 3, 1941; Crow, Carl (1883–1945), Papers, 1913–1945. Correspondence Series, f.170, 183, 184, 202 (Columbia, MO: State Historical Society of Missouri). Letters from C.B. Larrabee (Managing Editor, Printers' Ink Publications), July 8, 1940; Harry W. Alexander, May 3, 1941; Export Advertising Agency, Inc., July 11 and 21, 1941, Crow, Carl (1883–1945), Papers, 1913–1945. Correspondence Series, f.184 (Columbia, MO: State Historical Society of Missouri, 1941).

sions to countries like Brazil and Chile, he did not secure any significant con-tracts.[221] This South American adventure can be seen as an attempt to escape or find a new purpose, reflecting the disillusionment and discomfort of an expatriate who struggled to readapt to a country he felt disconnected from. Crow's life was cut short by cancer in early 1945, just months before the Japanese defeat. His passing symbolised the end of an era and the challenges faced by those who had spent a significant part of their lives in China but struggled to regain their footing in a world that had undergone significant changes.[222]

Unlike Carl Crow, Lin Zhenbin's departure from China was not a result of the Sino-Japanese War but rather the Communist revolution. In 1948, he was still actively involved in business organisations such as the Council for the Promotion of International Trade, which aimed to protect business interests in relation to the Chinese government.[223] However, with the establishment of the People's Re-public of China in 1949, Lin was forced to flee to Hong Kong. In the preceding years, Lin had strategically laid the groundwork in Asia and North America, set-ting the stage for his future activities outside of Shanghai. As he approached re-tirement in the early 1960s, Lin began to pass on the reins of the business to his two sons.[224] In 1962, the CCAA launched a campaign in the Hong Kong press to introduce the new generation of executives, signifying the transition of leadership within the agency.[225] While Lin remained officially active, the day-to-day opera-tions were now in the hands of his eldest son, William. In 1963, Lin officially re-tired from the business he had built, and he passed away the following year.[226]

Portrait of a British Tycoon in China: Francis Charles Millington (1888–1982)

The life of Francis Charles Millington, the founder of the Millington agency, is in-deed less extensively documented compared to his agency's history. While Mill-ington did not leave behind any autobiographical works or posthumous writings,

221 Letter from J. Walter Thompson Company, New York, November 27, 1940; Moore-Mc Cor-mack (Navegação), S.A. Rio de Janeiro, Brazil, October 3, 1940, Crow, Carl (1883–1945), Papers, 1913–1945. Correspondence Series, f.177 (Columbia, MO: State Historical Society of Missouri).
222 Letter from Coveleigh Club, July 19, 1945; Letter from Carl Crow to his sister, New York, 11 April 1945, Crow, Carl (1883–1945), Papers, 1913–1945. Correspondence Series, f.210 (Columbia, MO: State Historical Society of Missouri).
223 *CWR*, May 15, 1948.
224 *SCMP*, September 20, 1957.
225 *SCMP*, June 25, July 30, 1962.
226 *SCMP*, July 18, 19, 20 1964.

historians can rely on a combination of archival materials, records from the local press and his extensive correspondence with municipal authorities to construct an impressionistic portrait of his life [Figure 8].[227]

Figure 8: Francis Charles Millington in the 1920s. Millington family archives.

The Beginnings of a Military Educator (1888–1925)

Born in 1888 in England, Francis Charles Millington had humble beginnings. At the age of ten, he joined the ranks of the Boy Scout movement under Sir Robert Baden-Powell. Alongside his interest in scouting, Millington displayed an early passion for teaching. In 1904, he enrolled in the Pupil Teachers Centre Cadet Corps, an institution specialising in teacher training. In 1909, he declined an employment offer at Boy Scout headquarters to pursue further training as a teacher at St. John's College in York. The following year, he taught at Islington Primary School near London. In 1912, Millington embarked on a new chapter of his life by joining the British Navy. Initially serving as an ordinary sailor, he later took on

---

227 This biographical study is based primarily on the recollections recorded by his daughter Andra Nelki (born in Shanghai in 1935) and on the documentary made by the BBC in 2013 as part of the programme "Who Do You Think You Are?", about Millington's granddaughter, the actress Minnie Driver. I am very grateful to the family for kindly sharing their private archives.

the role of a teacher. His primary responsibility was to teach illiterate young sailors the basics of reading and writing. During his time in the Navy, Millington had the opportunity to visit China, which ignited his fascination with the country. In November 1914, Millington secured a teaching position at the Ellis Kadoorie School, a private institution catering to young Chinese residents of the International Settlement in Shanghai. However, the outbreak of World War I prompted him to join the Royal Artillery Regiment in India in August 1915.[228]

After the conclusion of World War I, Francis Charles Millington resumed his academic pursuits at the University of Hong Kong. Subsequently, in 1920, he returned to Shanghai, where he pursued his two primary passions: scouting and teaching. In Shanghai, Millington was appointed as the commissioner of the British Scouts section. He successfully obtained a plot of land situated west of the French Concession, where he established a scout camp. During the Sino-Japanese War of 1932, Millington's scout troops demonstrated remarkable dedication by assisting refugees, sharing vital information and carrying out various administrative tasks. The efforts of the "First Known Scouters" garnered admiration, further enhancing Millington's reputation. Additionally, Millington actively participated in the Shanghai Volunteer Corps, a civilian militia responsible for safeguarding the interests and well-being of foreign residents in Shanghai. His personal involvement in this organisation certainly contributed to his later elevated standing within the community.[229]

In the field of education, Francis Millington held several notable positions that showcased his passion for teaching and artistic expression. He began his educational career as an assistant principal at the Polytechnic Public School for Chinese from 1920 to 1921. Subsequently, he served as the acting headmaster of the Ellis Kadoorie School in 1921–1922 and again in 1925–1926. During this time, Millington concurrently taught at various municipal schools in the International Concession. It was during his tenure as an educator that Millington's talent for drawing and artistry became evident. He fostered his students' artistic development by establishing an art library and actively seeking out young talent through his visits to the China Society of Science and Art. Additionally, Millington's artistic skills found an outlet in his contributions to the Shanghai Sunday Times, where he regularly produced nearly 50 caricatures between 1924 and 1926. These carica-

---

228 George F.M. Nellist, *Men of Shanghai and North China. A Standard Biographical Reference Work* (Shanghai: The Oriental Press, 1933).
229 The Shanghai Volunteer Corps (SVC) was established in 1853 following the Taiping Rebellion, a significant uprising in China that lasted from 1850 to 1864. The primary objective of the SVC was to safeguard the foreign concessions and ensure the safety of foreign residents in Shanghai. Formed on a voluntary basis, it was made up of different units, some of which were formed on a national basis. It was disbanded in 1942 when Japanese troops took control of the International Settlement.

tures, which depicted international current affairs and scenes from local life, showcased a clever blend of humorous illustrations with captions that resembled advertising slogans. In this way, Millington's drawings exemplified the ideals of visual advertising as articulated in professional literature (see chapter 7).[230]

From Artist to Businessman (1927–1938)

After his experiences in teaching, scouting and his involvement with the Shanghai Volunteer Corps, Francis Charles Millington set his sights on establishing his own advertising agency. To gather the necessary capital for this venture, he began investing in property. In 1927, Millington successfully launched his own agency, Millington, Limited. He assumed the role of manager and led the agency until 1939. While pursuing his career as an advertising agency owner, Millington had to resign from his municipal duties to avoid any potential conflicts of interest. However, he maintained a close association with the Shanghai Municipal Council. He served as an advertising consultant for the Council and took on the role of editor for various municipal literature projects.[231]

Based on the available documentation, Francis Charles Millington's daily routine as an entrepreneur was likely filled with various activities and responsibilities. His extensive correspondence indicates that he devoted a significant amount of time to writing or dictating letters, addressing a range of matters such as defending his projects, challenging municipal decisions, or persuading clients to utilise his services. Millington's frequent travels around the world reflect his active pursuit of ideas and contacts. In the early 1930s, he visited London and New York to stay updated on the latest developments in radio and seek inspiration for overcoming the crisis. During the Sino-Japanese War, he travelled to Hong Kong and Singapore to explore local markets and establish new offices. As a recognised expert in his field, Millington was frequently sought after for interviews by the press and invitations to speak at various events. Examples include his lectures at venues like the Rotary Club of Shanghai in 1934 and the Rotary Club of Hong Kong in 1937, where he likely shared insights and perspectives on advertising and related topics.[232]

---

230 Millington's drawings exhibited a critical stance towards various political entities, including the Communists, the Nationalists and, at times, even the Shanghai Municipal Council. His provocative depictions eventually provoked displeasure from the Council's Secretary. In response, Millington was allowed to continue his work as a cartoonist, under the condition that he refrained from targeting the municipal authorities in his illustrations.
231 Nellist, 288; *CP*, January 8, 1927; Bacon, 760.
232 *CP*, June 7, 1932, March 15, 1938; *NCH*, June 3, 1936, May 18, 1938.

Based on the available information, it seems that Francis Charles Millington had a complex personal life that went through significant changes during his career. Similar to Carl Crow, Millington experienced a restructured family situation. His first marriage to Arabella Victoria Henderson resulted in the birth of two children, Kathleen Isabel and Fiona Macdonald. However, their divorce in 1934 led to Millington losing custody of his children. Millington then remarried shortly after his divorce to Constance Amy Lacy, with whom he had three daughters: Andrea, Elizabeth and Gaynor. It appears that Millington maintained a separation between his family and his business ventures, suggesting a desire to keep his personal and professional lives distinct from each other. Unlike Lin Zhenbin, Millington did not seem to actively pursue a succession plan for his business, possibly because he only had female heirs.[233]

Millington's level of engagement with Chinese culture appears to have been more limited in comparison to Carl Crow. According to his daughter Elizabeth, he displayed little interest in Chinese cuisine, earning him the nickname "Meat and potato man". In Shanghai, Millington was well assimilated into the hierarchical society of British expatriates, embodying the lifestyle of a typical Shanghailander.[234] Despite his modest background, he gained entry into exclusive social clubs such as the Race Club and the Shanghai Club, providing opportunities for social interaction with peers and associates. Like many other young expatriates in Shanghai, Millington embraced various sports activities, including golf and horse-riding, which were highly popular among the British elite.

After the bombings of August 1937, Francis Millington left Shanghai with his wife and three daughters due to concerns over Japanese occupation.[235] Initially seeking refuge in Hong Kong, they later relocated to Plymouth in July 1938. Despite the risks, Millington returned to Shanghai to continue his business activities

---

233 *CWR*, January 13, 1934.
234 Robert Bickers, "Shanghailanders: The Formation and Identity of the British Settler Community in Shanghai 1843–1937", *Past & Present*, n° 159 (1998): 161–211.
235 His daughter Elizabeth remembers: "I believe my father left shortly after us in 1938–9, I know we had to leave in a hurry, people had already started to be interned, because my father was so famous we had guards stationed outside our house in Shanghai, my mother refused to leave if my father didn't so we were sent to Hong Kong where our father had an office. Our house in Shanghai was ransacked by the Japanese and destroyed, and I know my father lost a lot of papers etc." Interview with Elizabeth Millington, August 31, 2014. Her version converges with that of her sister Andra Nelki: "As far as I know, he/we left Shanghai during the bombing as my mother thought it was all too dangerous for the young family and went to London just in time for the second world war. So as far as I know, everything was left behind." Interview with Andra Nelki (born Millington), August 31, 2014. In February 1940, a letter addressed to Millington from Shanghai was intercepted by the Nazi censorship in Germany. *NCH*, February 28, 1940.

and only reunited with his family in London a year later. By February 1940, Millington had established permanent residence in London, thus avoiding internment in the Japanese camps where a significant number of British civilians were detained between January 1942 and August 1945.[236]

A Fresh Start After the War

Following the war, Francis Millington embarked on a venture to re-establish his presence in China by founding an agency in London. This agency served as a liaison between Western companies interested in the Chinese market and Chinese companies seeking to export their goods to Europe and North America.[237] Concurrently, Millington established China Trade Press, Limited, a publishing company that produced notable publications such as the bilingual magazine *China Trade & Engineering.*[238] In his pursuit of new contracts, Millington undertook several trips to Asia and America. After visiting New York, he travelled to Hong Kong in August 1947 to explore business opportunities first-hand.[239] When not personally travelling, Millington played host to the Hong Kong Economic Mission, organising a prominent reception in London in May 1949.[240]

With the Communist takeover in October 1949, Francis Millington's plans for China came to an abrupt halt. He shifted his focus to Europe and North America, where he managed to sustain his advertising activities unlike Carl Crow. In 1961, he obtained a franchise that allowed him to advertise Western products in the Soviet Union. While still involved in advertising, Millington primarily devoted his attention to publishing. In England, he owned several publishing companies, including China Trade Press and Windmill Publications. As his business thrived, he acquired a larger property in Sevenoaks, Kent, where he and his family settled. Limited information is available regarding the later years of Millington's life. The pioneering Shanghai publicist passed away on 28 November 1982 at the age of almost 100, in Dagenham, located on the outskirts of London.

---

236 *NCH*, February 28, 1940.

237 *SCMP*, July 25, 1946.

238 The *China Trade & Engineering* journal had a wide circulation across Asia, Europe and North America. It published market surveys and featured a dedicated section for young engineers to publish their curriculum vitae. Additionally, the journal played a crucial role in compiling a comprehensive professional directory that included over 400,000 names of companies seeking business partnerships. *SCMP*, August 4, 1946.

239 *SCMP*, August 30, 1946.

240 *SCMP*, May 15, 1949.

In conclusion, Millington's life and career was a colourful one. There was nothing at the outset to destine the military educator for a career in advertising, aside from his affinity for drawing. This sets him apart from both Carl Crow and Lin Zhenbin, who received formal academic training in renowned American universities and gained experience working in the press and advertising agencies before venturing into their own enterprises. These contrasting profiles emphasise the absence of a predetermined trajectory for the pioneering generation born in the late nineteenth century. The advertising profession itself served as a convergence point for individuals with diverse backgrounds and aspirations, as demonstrated by the composite portrait of the Lianhe agency. This agency ideally encapsulated the multifaceted nature of the industry and the varied paths taken by its practitioners.

The Artisans of Lianhe: A Collective Biography

The Lianhe agency, being a collective effort, necessitates a collective biography to truly capture its essence. Six individuals played key roles in the association: Zhang Zhuping (ZZP), Zheng Yaonan (ZYN), Yao Junwei (YJW), Lu Meiseng (LMS), Wang Yingbin (WYB) and Lu Shoulun (LSL). Each of these individuals contributed their unique skills and expertise to the agency, collectively shaping its identity and success.

Common Origins

The six partners of the Lianhe agency all originated from provinces located in or near the lower Yangtze valley. Four of them hailed from Jiangsu province (ZZP, ZYN, YJW, LMS), one from Zhejiang province (LSL) and one from Anhui province (WYB).[241] These provinces were characterised by their high level of urbanisation and served as economic powerhouses in China, housing a significant portion of the country's capital, industries and service sectors. Shanghai, in particular, attracted migrants from various parts of China, including those in close proximity and more distant areas, who brought with them diverse backgrounds and motivations. Urban migration waves facilitated the formation of associations that aimed to maintain

---

241 Zhang Zhuping was born in Taicang in 1885, Zheng Yaonan in Shanghai in 1892, Lu Meiseng in Yixing in 1896. Yao Junwei was from Wujin (year of birth unknown). Lu Shoulun was born in Dinghai in 1901, but his family was originally from Ningbo in the same province (Zhejiang). Wang Yingbin was born in Wuyuan, Anhui. Powell, *Who's Who in China*, 5; *Shanghai gongshangren minglu* [Shanghai Business directory] (Shanghai: Meihua shuju, 1936), 172.

solidarity among residents with shared origins. The Lianhe agency's artisans, like many other migrants, actively participated in these native-place associations (tong-xianghui), which were associated with their birthplaces or ancestral hometowns, such as Chaozhou and Guangdong for ZYN, Yixing for LMS and Dinghai for LSL.[242] These native-place associations played a crucial role in the professional and personal lives of the Lianhe partners. However, they did not hinder the development of national sentiments, as highlighted by historian Bryna Goodman, and the cultivation of an international consciousness, especially among the agency's publicists who had received education abroad.[243]

Before establishing the Lianhe agency, the six partners had already collaborated in the advertising and press industries, often working simultaneously in multiple companies. In 1926, Yao Junwei and Lu Meiseng were recruited by United Advertising Advisers to handle advertising for the *Shenbao* newspaper. This newspaper played a significant role in the future formation of the Lianhe agency as it served as an important platform for recruitment. Under the leadership of Zhang Zhuping (ZZP), the main founders of Lianhe had all worked at *Shenbao* in various capacities. Wang Yingbin (WYB) served as the deputy manager, while Yao Junwei (YJW), Lu Meiseng (LMS) and Lu Shoulun (LSL) held positions as advertising directors. Additionally, the future partners had interactions at the *China Times* newspaper, which was managed by ZZP initially and later by Zhang Zuyi (ZZY), starting from 1935. Furthermore, Zhang Zhuping (ZZP) and Zheng Yaonan (ZYN) had collaborated in the Shenshi press agency. These shared experiences and collaborations in the advertising and press industry laid the foundation for their future partnership in establishing the Lianhe agency.[244]

Two Paths to Advertising Career

Despite their shared geographical and professional backgrounds, the six partners of the Lianhe agency can be divided into two groups based on their educational experiences. Zhang Zhuping (ZZP), Zheng Yaonan (ZYN), Yao Junwei (YJW) and Lu Shoulun (LSL) did not receive formal academic education but instead gained

---

242 *SB*, August 20, 1924 (Ningbo tongxiang hui), September 11, 1932 (Chaozhou lühu tongxiang hui), February 20, 1934 (Guangdong lühu tongxiang hui), November 28, 1938 (Yixing tongxiang hui); November 11, 1936 (Dinghai lühu tongxiang hui).

243 Bryna Goodman, *Native Place, City, and Nation Regional Networks and Identities in Shanghai, 1853–1937* (Berkeley: University of California Press, 1995).

244 Powell, *Who's Who in China*, 5; Shanghai Bank (Shanghai yinhang 上海銀行), "Lianhe guang-gao gongsi" 聯合廣告公司, Shanghai, April 4–May 7, 1937, SMA, Q275-1-1840-37, 111.

practical knowledge and skills through hands-on experience in business from an early age. Although they were involved in various other activities, advertising was a central element in their entrepreneurial strategy. Each of these four partners represents a distinct embodiment of the entrepreneurial figure, as described by Christopher Rea in his classification of cultural entrepreneurs.

Zhang Zhuping began his educational journey at Chants Academy, a missionary school in Shanghai, where he likely received a foundation in Western education. Subsequently, he enrolled at St. John's University in Shanghai, which was established in 1879 by American missionaries and played a significant role in introducing Western languages and sciences to China[245] However, ZZP's academic pursuits were interrupted in 1911 when he decided to join the *Shenbao*. This marked a significant turning point in his career, as he eventually rose to become one of Shanghai's most influential newspaper figures. ZZP held key positions as the managing director of several major newspapers, including *Shenbao, China Times, China Evening News* and the Shenshi news agency, which he directed until May 1935.[246]

Zheng Yaonan came from a background connected to the advertising industry, as his father worked as an advertising broker. Due to his early involvement in advertising, ZYN did not pursue higher education. In 1916, he was appointed as the advertising manager for the *New World* newspaper (Xinshijie rikan) and later for *Shenbao*.[247] In 1920, ZYN established his own agency, the Yaonan Advertising Company (Yaonan guanggao gongsi), which specialised in press advertising. As seen earlier, this agency was one of the five agencies that formed the foundation for the establishment of the Lianhe agency (chapter 2). ZYN gained a reputation for being discreet, reliable and cautious in his business dealings, which contributed to his success. His astute business practices allowed him to amass a significant fortune, estimated to be around 200,000 yuan in 1930. With his financial resources, ZYN made investments in numerous enterprises across various sectors, including the press, food products, raw materials and the textile industry, particularly wool and cotton.[248] ZYN's influence extended beyond his advertising endeavours. He held

245 On this university, see: Wen-Hsin Yeh, *The Alienated Academy: Culture and Politics in Republican China, 1919–1937* (Cambridge, Mass.; London: Council on East Asian studies, Harvard University, 1990).

246 Powell, *Who's Who in China*, 5.

247 *SB*, November 23, 1916, October 6, 1917.

248 Notably Huafeng Raw Materials (Huafeng yuanliao gongsi), Shanghai Yarn Market (Shanghai shaxian zhengquan shichang choubei chu), *SB*, August 12, 1921; Taifeng Cotton Engineering Company (Taifeng shachang gongcheng gufenyouxian gongsi), *SB*, April 22, 1946. In the food industry, Huimin Milk Powder Company (Huimin naifen gongsi), Xinghua Machine Noodle Company (Xinghua zhimian gongsi) and Guanshengyuan Food Products Company, Ltd. (Guanshengyuan shipin

memberships in esteemed organisations such as the Chinese Ratepayers' Association and the Shanghai Chamber of Commerce, serving on the board of directors and the committee for the promotion of national products (guohuo).[249]

At the time of the formation of Lianhe, Yao Junwei possessed extensive experience in the field of advertising. He held key positions in three significant agencies that later became part of the merger (see chapter 2). Like Zheng Yaonan, YJW relied on a substantial fortune, estimated to be several tens of thousands of taels.[250] His financial resources allowed him to make strategic investments in various industries. He held shares in *Shenbao* and its competitor *Xinwenbao*, demonstrating his prominent position in the newspaper industry. Additionally, he had interests in companies operating in the food industry (Taifeng Canned Food Company) as well as the tobacco industry (Nanyang Tobacco Company).[251]

Lu Shoulun presented an intermediate profile among the six partners of Lianhe. Like his colleagues, he did not pursue higher education but instead joined the advertising departments of *Shenbao* and *China Times*. Lu's financial wealth allowed him to make significant investments in various industries, particularly the tobacco industry, taking the positions of managing director of Minsheng and Guohua tobacco companies after WWI. In addition, Lu held shares in several publishing enterprises, such as Shanghai Modern Publishing Company (Shanghai xiandai shuju) and Lianhua Book Company (Lianhua tushu gongsi). His diverse investments extended to other sectors, including the textile industry (Dingxin weaving mill), the electrical industry (Zhoushan Electric Company), trade (Lianhua Trading Company), shipping (Zhoushan Steamship Company), banking (Shanghai Industrial Bank), restaurants and music (China Gramophone Manufacturing Company). LSL, however, was younger than the three previous partners. Born in 1901, his age and his advertising skills placed him in closer alignment with the second group formed by Lu Meiseng and Wang Yinbin.[252]

Lu Meiseng and Wang Yinbin distinguished themselves from the other partners of Lianhe with their advanced academic training, educational backgrounds and international experiences. Like Lin Zhenbin, LMS was granted a scholarship

---

gufen youxian gongsi). *SB*, October 13, 1931, June 6, 1932, October 24, 1933, May 29, 1934, May 27, 1935. *SHGSML*, 172; Shanghai Bank, "Lianhe guanggao gongsi", October 15 1936, SMA, Q275-1-1840-37, 108.

249 Guohuo weiyuanhui 國貨委員會, *SB*, July 11, 1930, September 29, 1931, July 11, 1936.
250 SMA, Q275-1-1840-27, 37.
251 Taifeng Canned Foods Company (Taifeng guantoushipin gongsi), *SB*, January 30, 1935; Nanyang Tobacco Company (Nanyang cao gongsi), *SB*, October 24, 1935.
252 *Shanghai gongshangren wuzhi* [Chronicles of Shanghai Businessmen] (Shanghai: Quanguo geda shuju, 1948), 175. *Shanghaishi gongjieren wuzhi* [Chronicles of Shanghai Industrialists] (Shanghai: Zhanwang chubanshe, 1947), 149; *SB*, August 20, 1928; February 28, 1930; August 16, 1931; August 10, September 22, 1941; May 21, 1942; May 18, 1946.

to study in the United States and received his preparatory education at Tsinghua College in Beijing. After spending a year at the University of Colorado in 1921, he pursued his studies at Columbia University in New York, where he graduated in 1923. Seeking further expertise in commercial science, LMS enrolled in New York University in 1925 and gained practical experience working for the World Wide Advertising Corporation, a New York-based agency.[253] Wang Yinbin, like Zhang Zhuping, initially attended St. John's University before joining *Shenbao*. With the support of his colleagues, Wang embarked on a journey to the United States to further his journalistic training. Unlike LMS, Wang self-financed his studies by working as a correspondent for various Shanghai newspapers. After spending a year at the University of Missouri, he proceeded to Columbia University in New York, where he obtained a master's degree in journalism.[254]

Knowledge Transfer and Professionalisation

Upon returning from the United States, LMS and WYB brought back valuable first-hand knowledge, positioning themselves as leading experts in their respective fields. Their expertise and insights were highly sought after, leading to invitations to speak at various professional and student gatherings. They delivered talks at various venues such as the Overseas Chinese Students' Association, Shanghai Journalists' Association, Far Eastern News Agency, Shanghai Chamber of Commerce, Rotary Club, Young Men's Christian Association (YMCA) and Y's Men Club. Both LMS and WYB shared a commitment to nurturing the next generation of professionals. They actively engaged in teaching at several Shanghai universities, playing instrumental roles in establishing journalism and business courses at institutions such as Nanshi, Daxia and Guanghua universities. LMS, in particular, was a pioneering figure in teaching commercial psychology at Nanshi Business School (Shanghai nanshi shangke zhongxue).[255] Recognising the importance of continuing education, LMS and WYB opened their classes to a wider audience and organised evening courses and summer schools. They also facilitated the connection between universities and enterprises by arranging tours of their premises for students and offering work placements, drawing inspiration from the practices of the Ford Motor Company in the United States.[256] Furthermore, WYB founded an association specifically dedicated to vocational training (Zhonghua zhiye jiaoyu she). In 1932, he established a continuing education program at Hujiang Uni-

253 *Who's Who in China* (Shanghai: China Weekly Review, 1940), 32.
254 *SB*, December 21, 1921; *SB*, August 2, 5, 6, 22 1922; May 26, 1924.
255 *SB*, June 20, 1926. Lu Meiseng, *Guanggao* [Advertising] (Shanghai: Commercial Press, 1940).
256 *SB*, March 6, 1926; *SB*, October 25, 1924; *SB*, May 21, 1926; *SB*, April 4, 1928.

versity Business School in collaboration with the Association of Chinese Industrialists and Engineers (Zhonghua gongye zong lianhehui) and the Chinese Institute of Management (Zhongguo gongshang guanli xiehui).[257]

Although ZYN, YJW and LSL did not directly teach advertising, they shared their expertise through various professional publications and collective works. They made significant contributions to publications such as the quarterly journal *Guanggao yu tuixiao jikan* (Advertising and Promotion). Additionally, they contributed to collective works, including a monumental history of Chinese advertising published in 1948.[258] These publications served as valuable resources for professionals in the field and helped shape the understanding and development of advertising practices in China. One notable example is Lu Shoulun's contribution titled "How to make buyers satisfied" (Ruhe shimai keman), which advocated the use of coupons as an effective method to encourage purchases. This article, which appeared in *Shenbao* in August 1934, aimed to accompany the creation of the Consolidated Coupon Company.[259]

Overseas Experiences

LMS and WYB, strongly influenced by their American education, developed an international profile that set them apart from their colleagues. WYB, fresh out of St. John's University, played a crucial role as an interpreter for visiting foreign personalities in Shanghai. He assisted notable figures such as the editor of the *Times* in London (1921), the dean of the University of Missouri's School of Journalism, British writer Bertram Lenox Simpson in 1922 and representatives of the American multinational General Motors in 1929.[260] While in the United States, LMS was admitted to prestigious student fraternities, including Alpha Kappa Psi, Eta Mu Pi and Phi Lambda.[261] Upon their return, both LMS and WYB maintained strong connections with their former classmates and actively participated in alumni associations and meetings. LMS was a member of the Qinghua, New York, and Columbia University alumni associations, while WYB was involved with the World Chinese Students' Federation, St. John's Alumni Association and the Missouri Alumni Association, of which he was a founding member.

---

257 *SB*, May 22, 1926; *SB*, August 24, 1932; *CP*, July 20, October 24, 1932.
258 *SB*, May 12, 1936, November 2, 1948.
259 "Ruhe shimai keman yi Lu Shoulun" (How to make customers happy, by Lu Shoulun), *SB*, August 8, 1934, 13.
260 *SB*, November 20, 21 1921; December 13, 1921; January 22, 1922; June 21, 1929.
261 *CP*, August 1, 1930.

Throughout their lives, both LMS and WYB nurtured their connections with the American community in Shanghai and the Young Men's Christian Association (YMCA) network. WYB was a member of the Rotary Club from 1928 to 1934, representing *Shenbao* in the category of journalism.[262] LMS served as president of the Y's Men Club in 1935–1936 and regional director in 1938 and 1939.[263] Additionally, LMS was a founding member of the International Club[264] and the Rotary Club of Shanghai West, established in October 1948 to cater to non-English-speaking Chinese elites.[265] Their international awareness extended to their leisure activities as well. For example, LMS developed a fondness for tennis during his time in the United States, in contrast to ZYN who manifested his preference for martial arts.

The Division of Labour Among Partners

Each partner assumed their own specific roles and responsibilities, contributing to the overall functioning and success of the Lianhe agency. ZZP served as the CEO and ZYN as the managing director, being the two main founders of the agency. As majority shareholders, ZZP and ZYN held ex-officio positions on the board of directors. The board also included YJW as the assistant manager and LSL as the account director. In addition to their roles within the agency, ZZP and ZYN were also shareholders of the Consolidated Coupon Company and the Consolidated Sports Association.[266] LMS held the position of manager within the Lianhe agency and concurrently served as the manager of the *Shenbao Pictorial Supple-*

---

262 *SB*, July 6, 1928; "Shanghai Rotary Club Roster, July 1, 1930", Alonzo Bland Calder Papers, 1911–1956, Hoover Institution Archives, Stanford, California, Box 19, f.1; "Rotary Club of Shanghai, Roster for June 1933"; "Rotary Club of Shanghai, Roster for August 1934", Rotary International Archives, Evanston, Ill., vol. 21, 24. I am very grateful to Susan Hanf, Heritage Communications Specialist for Rotary International, for sharing these documents.

263 *CP*, December 8 and 9, 1936, August 8, 1937, December 14, 1938; *SCMP*, December 19, 1938; *NCH*, December 27, 1939. The network of Y's Men Clubs was launched in 1920 to assist the work of the YMCA organisation in Toledo, Ohio. Established in 1924, the Shanghai club was the first to be established outside the United States.

264 *CP*, December 1 and 3, 1935; *NCH*, December 4, 1935. Influenced by the internationalist spirit of the interwar years, the International Club aimed to promote mutual understanding and friendship between peoples. On this club, see: James Layton Huskey, "Americans in Shanghai: Community Formation and Response to Revolution, 1919–1928" (Doctoral Dissertation, Chapel Hill, University of North Carolina, 1985), 192–95.

265 "Rotary Club of Shanghai West, List of Charter Members", Shanghai, November 2, 1948, Rotary International Archives, Evanston, Ill., vol. 38. See Armand, "Foreign Clubs with Chinese Flavor: The Rotary Club of Shanghai and the Politics of Language".

266 *SB*, February 17, July 2, 1934; *CP*, February 19, May 28, August 17, 1934.

ment starting from 1930. Additionally, in 1934, he took on the role of manager of the Consolidated Coupon Company and became a member of the standing committee of the Consolidated Sports Association.[267] WYB, known for his artistic skills and expertise as an art critic, was appointed as the art director of the agency.[268] LSL took on the responsibility of account director, specifically focusing on advertising in the tobacco industry. His expertise and campaigns contributed to the popularity of major Chinese cigarette brands such as Golden Jade (Jinyupai) and The Brandy (Bailandi xiangyan). Notably, LSL began signing his work in 1925, distinguishing him as an exceptional copywriter in China during that time.

Beyond their roles within the Lianhe agency, the partners actively participated in professional organisations. Four of them were founding members of the Association of Chinese Advertising Agencies (ACAA). ZYN and YJW held memberships in the Advertising Club of China and served on the standing committee of the ACAA.[269] Even after the reorganisation of the association in 1930, ZYN and YJW maintained their positions on the executive committee. During the anti-Japanese campaign following the invasion of Manchuria in 1931, ZYN took on leadership roles as head of the inspection team and later as head of the propaganda committee. LMS was elected president of the association in 1926 and was re-elected in 1948. From 1930, LSL held responsibilities within the accounts and current affairs committee and served as a member of the supervisory committee and subsequently the executive committee. Following the war, LSL continued to actively participate in the reorganised association and eventually became its president in 1948.[270]

Committed Entrepreneurs

In addition to their professional pursuits, the partners of Lianhe demonstrated a commitment to serving Chinese society through their philanthropic endeavours. Reflecting the "enlightened paternalism" prevalent among the new class of industrialists during the Republican era, their philanthropic activities primarily revolved around four main areas: aid for natural disaster victims from the 1920s;

---

267 *SB*, June 20, 1926; *SB*, August 1, 1930; *CP*, August 1, 1930. *SB*, February 17, July 2, August 16, 1934; *CP*, February 19, May 28, August 17, 1934.
268 *CP*, August 1, 1930; *SB*, August 1, 1930.
269 *SB*, June 27, 1921, July 1, 1922, November 24, 1923. *SB*, October 15, 1929, June 10, 1930.
270 *SB*, May 18, 1926; *SB*, October 15, 1929, June 1 and 10, 1930, August 12, 1934. *SB*, June 10, 1946, September 20, 1948, October 3, 1948.

children welfare and public health from the 1930s; national defence and refugee relief during the Sino-Japanese War; post-war reconstruction and educational programs.[271]

From the 1920s onwards, the future partners of Lianhe agency actively supported disaster-stricken populations in various provinces that were frequently affected by floods, droughts and famines. They organised volunteer calls and fundraising campaigns through initiatives such as lotteries, exhibitions and charity balls. Additionally, they made individual donations and contributions on behalf of their agency to provide aid and support to those in need.[272] In 1936, Lu Meiseng took personal involvement in the Yangtze River Flood Relief Committee, which operated under the auspices of the China International Famine Relief Commission (CIFRC).[273]

Following the Japanese invasion of Manchuria in 1931, ZYN, YJW and LSL demonstrated increased commitment to national defence. They played key roles in advocating for the formation of a special resistance committee within the Association for Chinese Advertising Agencies. In 1933, the three partners also joined the Air Defence Movement (Huangkong jiuguo yundong), a patriotic initiative aimed at strengthening China's defence capabilities.[274] In 1936, ZYN organised a collection of gas masks to provide vital equipment for Chinese troops. Recognising the plight of the massive influx of refugees during the Sino-Japanese War, the partners actively supported the Shanghai Refugee Association (Shanghai jiuji nanmin xiehui). They made direct donations, initiated fundraising campaigns and sponsored the construction of a children's hospital in Shanghai called the Shanghai Nantong Hospital.[275] Furthermore, LMS devised a comprehensive resettlement plan in 1938 to address the refugee crisis. The plan involved allocating pristine land in Jiangxi province for the resettlement of refugees. The objectives were to enable refugees to

---

271 Wen-Hsin Yeh, *Shanghai Splendor: Economic Sentiments and the Making of Modern China, 1843–1949* (Berkeley: University of California Press, 2007).

272 Among the main disasters, the floods of 1931 resulting from exceptional high water levels in the Yangtze and Huai rivers severely affected the provinces of Anhui, Hubei, Hunan, Jiangsu, Jianxi and Zhejiang (*SB*, August 21, 1931, September 14, 1931, September 17, 1931). Other floods occurred in the 1920s and 1930s (*SB*, September 5, 1922, January 1, 1923, January 19, 1929). The associates also mobilised their resources against the severe droughts and subsequent famines that hit the Shaanxi region between 1928 and 1930 (*SB*, July 23, 1935).

273 *SB*, January 1, April 25, 1936; February 6, 19, March 15, June 20, 1937.

274 *SB*, March 18, 1933; December 4, 1936.

275 Between the summer and the end of 1937, more than a million refugees poured into the foreign concessions. Nearly 200 refugee camps were established in Shanghai, often in precarious conditions. Christian Henriot, "Shanghai and the Experience of War: The Fate of Refugees", *European Journal of East Asian Studies* 5, n° 2 (2006): 215–45. *SB*, October 29, 1938, February 24, 1945. *SB*, October 29, 1938, February 24, 1945.

support themselves, develop the underdeveloped Jiangxi region, alleviate the burden on charitable organisations and redirect the efforts of social workers to other areas of work. LMS utilised the resources of the Lianhe's agency to promote his program, which, however, remained unfulfilled.[276]

In addition to their commitment to national defense and refugee relief, the Lianhe partners actively engaged in the promotion of public health in Shanghai. They financed the construction of various hospitals, including the Hongkew Clinic, a hospital dedicated to workers, and the Shanghai Nantong Hospital for children. Meanwhile, Lu Meiseng played a prominent role in the establishment of the Zhabei Maternity Hospital, in collaboration with the Y's Men Club. He and his partners exhibited a strong dedication to children's welfare, supporting the Chinese Children Welfare Society and sponsoring the construction of a children's village in Shanghai. Lu Meiseng's involvement in child welfare led to his invitation to sit on the Children Relief Fund, under the United Nations Relief and Rehabilitation Administration (UNRRA).[277] The Lianhe associates, especially ZYN and YJW, were also concerned with the resurgence of epidemics in the city, particularly cholera. They funded the renovation of the Chinese Infectious Disease Hospital, which had been originally established by wealthy Chinese entrepreneurs at the beginning of the century.[278] On the other hand, Lu Meiseng and Lu Shoulun were active in the fight against leprosy (Zhonghua mafeng jiuji hui) and tuberculosis (Zhongguo laoyiyuan)[279] Additionally, the Lianhe agency and the *Shenbao* newspaper collaborated on hygiene education campaigns, including initiatives to eradicate public spitting in the winter of 1947.[280]

---

276 *CP*, January 12 and 13, February 18, 1938.

277 *SB*, November 6, 1932, July 12, 1939; *SB*, February 27, 1933; *SB*, November 9, 1931; *CP*, January 12, 1930, April 16, 1933, July 14, 1935; *CP*, May 8, 1936; *SB*, October 24, 1940, December 18, 1941, June 19, 1942, April 14, 1946; *SB*, April 3, 1948.

278 *SB*, September 11, 1933, July 12, 1939, July 28, 1942. Established in the early twentieth century by wealthy Chinese entrepreneurs, the Chinese Infectious Disease Hospital (CIDH) was originally a seasonal hospital treating gastrointestinal diseases. In the 1930s, it became one of the leading and best equipped hospitals in Shanghai, especially for the treatment of cholera. On this subject, see Chieko Nakajima, *Body, Society, and Nation: The Creation of Public Health and Urban Culture in Shanghai* (Cambridge: Harvard university Asia centre: Harvard University Press, 2018), 51–58.

279 *SB*, April 21, 1934, April 16 and November 15, 1941, July 28, 1942, June 22, 1947, January 31, 1948. Among infectious diseases, tuberculosis was the leading cause of death in the Chinese population of Shanghai (nearly 45,000 victims in the first half of the twentieth century). Cholera came third (more than 8,500 victims). Christian Henriot, Lu Shi and Charlotte Aubrun, *The Population of Shanghai (1865–1953): A Sourcebook*, Brill (Leiden; Boston, 2019), 36–38.

280 *SB*, November 7, December 25, 1947.

In the post-war period, the focus of the Lianhe partners' philanthropic efforts shifted towards national reconstruction and cultural patronage. Between 1942 and 1947, they sponsored various scholarships to support education and academic pursuits, such as the *Shenbao* and Nantong University scholarships, as well as a natural science research prize also sponsored by *Shenbao*. Leveraging his connections in the tobacco industry, Lu Shoulun played a key role in setting up scholarships funded by tobacco companies, particularly the Fuxin Tobacco Company. The Lianhe associates also established literary prizes to encourage and recognise achievements in the field of literature. In 1947, LSL extended his support to the establishment of a learned society called Kongsheng Xuehui, which aimed to foster intellectual and cultural advancement in society. Additionally, the six partners contributed to the creation of a national fund dedicated to education and culture.[281]

In the aftermath of the war, Zheng and Yao supported Lu Meiseng's candidacy in the national legislative elections held in 1948. Defeated by the Nationalists, Lu unsuccessfully took legal action against what he considered electoral fraud.[282] Lu's political awareness can be traced back to formative experiences earlier in his life. During the May Fourth Movement in 1919, while he was a student in Beijing, he participated as a delegate of Qinghua University students in the vast conference organised by the National Students' Federation in Shanghai. The conference resulted in the drafting of a student manifesto that voiced opposition to what they perceived as the "humiliation" inflicted upon China through the Versailles Treaty.[283] Remarkably, Lu's early dedication to anti-imperialism did not hinder his pursuit of education abroad, nor did it impede his embrace of a cosmopolitan way of life.

Ordinary Employees and Women

Little is known about the ordinary employees who worked in the shadows of the managerial and artistic elite. While sources may be scarce on their specific stories, their presence and significance can be glimpsed between the lines and in occasional mentions in local press coverage. For example, Carl Crow acknowledged the remarkable skills of Chinese typographers who were proficient in handling Latin characters, even though they did not understand their meaning.[284]

---

281 *SB*, October 2, 1946, October 1, 1947, January 10, 1948; *SB*, June 2, 1942, May 3, 1944, September 19, 1947; *SB*, June 21, 1942, July 24, 1942, April 8, 1944, March 12, 1945, September 30, 1947; *SB*, September 26, 1947; *SB*, May 1, 1947, May 14, 1948.
282 *SB*, January 6 and 27, February 4, 6, 15 and 29 1948.
283 *SB*, May 15, June 27, July 29, August 27, 1919.
284 Crow, *Four Hundred Million Customers*, 87–88, 100, 110, 178.

Incidentally, the voices of these "undocumented" individuals would emerge in the local press, particularly in cases involving crimes or wage disputes. They may be called upon as witnesses or even be implicated as culprits in trials between employers and employees. In one instance in 1935, two salesmen accused of fraud by Millington narrowly escaped imprisonment, possibly due to their young age. A month later, two coolies were called to testify in a case involving the theft of a typewriter from the same agency.[285]

Advertising remained a predominantly male profession. The women who stood out had remarkable skills and were entrusted with important responsibilities, but their professional activity lasted only as long as their celibacy. The career of Miss Crystal Hut, for example, business manager at Carl Crow Inc., ended after her marriage to entrepreneur George V. Monk.[286]

Elma Kelly, a pivotal figure in the recovery of the Millington agency following the crisis of 1934, played a crucial role in the agency's success, particularly during her tenure as the director of the Hong Kong branch. Born in Melbourne in 1895, Kelly's journey was marked by resilience and determination. Armed with a science degree from Melbourne University, she initially joined Millington in Shanghai, where her talent and dedication quickly became evident. In 1935, she made a significant career move by transferring to the Hong Kong office, setting the stage for the most prosperous period in its history. Kelly's commitment to her profession led her to make personal sacrifices. She made the difficult decision to renounce her marriage, choosing to prioritise her career even amidst the challenging backdrop of the Sino-Japanese War. Her resilience was further tested during her internment in Japanese camps, from which she was liberated in August 1945. Following her release, she embarked on a journey to London, in search of a lover who eluded her. Despite this personal setback, Kelly's determination remained unwavering. Returning to Hong Kong, Kelly ventured into entrepreneurship and established her own publishing and advertising company, Cathay Advertising, Limited. Under her leadership, the company thrived and made significant contributions to the advertising landscape in Hong Kong. Kelly's remarkable career spanned several decades, and she continued to actively manage her company until her retirement in 1973.[287]

---

285 "Two advertising salesmen are fined by court. Millington's employees escape jail because of their youth", *CP*, September 5, 1935; "Shanghai Law Reports: H.M. Police Court. Theft of a typewriter", *NCH*, November 20, 1935.

286 *CWR*, August 10, 1929; *CWR*, September 13, 1930.

287 *NCH*, May 15, 1938, April 22, 1939. Historian J. Dickenson has captured the essence of Elma Kelly's remarkable journey in her fascinating study of Australian advertising women: Jacqueline Dickenson, *Australian Women in Advertising in the Twentieth Century* (2015), 39–53.

Dora Carney's career provides an insightful glimpse into women's achievements in the advertising industry and the evolving nature of advertising as a distinct profession during that time. Her curriculum vitae, submitted to the Shanghai Municipal Council in 1941, highlights her expertise and emphasises that she was not merely a commercial artist but an advertising specialist. Originally from Canada, Dora Carney had accumulated ten years of experience working in the press and radio industry before joining Millington, Ltd. Her responsibilities included overseeing advertising campaigns for notable clients such as the Shanghai Power Company, the Shanghai Telephone Company and the Cathay Laundry. Her diverse skill set encompassed poster design, typography, typesetting, magazine copywriting and radio programming. One notable aspect of Dora's profile was her proficiency in multiple languages, including English, Chinese, Russian and Japanese. Like many women of her time, Dora Carney ultimately had to resign from her professional career to fulfil her roles as a mother and wife. It was the critical situation during the Sino-Japanese War that prompted her to return to work.[288]

Although impressionistic, this evocative portrayal of women in advertising challenges the assumption that they held merely auxiliary roles within the profession. The complexity of their involvement begs further inquiry into critical aspects, such as their entry into the advertising field, the organisation of their work and daily lives, and their interactions with male colleagues under their authority. Additionally, the significance of Chinese women who pursued careers in advertising remains obscured by a dearth of sources, leaving these questions unanswered in the current scholarship. Further research can shed light on these critical aspects, enriching our understanding of gender dynamics within the industry.

Conclusion

This series of portraits demonstrates that there was no predetermined path to becoming an advertising professional. While the pioneers gained their initial experience in the press and journalism, the younger generation born after 1895 had the opportunity to pursue specialised training in universities and new business schools. Before establishing their own businesses, Lin Zhenbin and Lu Meiseng gained practical experience by working for New York-based agencies. These young Chinese individuals, educated in the United States (liumei), played a crucial role in introducing American methods to China. Through their writings and

---

[288] "Advertising Services Offered by Mrs. Carney, PHD Publicity – Propositions from Advertising Agents", SMA (SMC), U1-4-246 (1939).

teachings, they leveraged the first-hand knowledge acquired during their studies abroad to contribute to the professionalisation of their field.

Collective enterprises (Millington, Lianhe) drew strength from the large industrial and financial capitalism that thrived in the treaty ports between the First Opium War (1839–1842) and the Communist revolution (1949). Having a foothold in capitalist circles facilitated market conquest. As entrepreneurs themselves, they were in a privileged position to convince their peers of the necessity of using advertising. Similar to the "political merchants" (zhengshang) studied by historian Feng Xiaocai, advertising professionals frequently intertwined politics with business, without necessarily aligning with the nationalist stance defined by the Guomindang.[289] For most of them, nationalist engagement was as much an entrepreneurial strategy as a political conviction that could be accommodated with working for multinational companies and interacting with foreign professionals. While the veterans such as Zhen Yaonan and Yao Junwei actively participated in the anti-Japanese resistance during the war, the young generation educated in the United States pursued more peaceful and conventional forms of engagement, including holding elective positions within national or international institutions. Vernacular professionals also distinguished themselves through their philanthropic activism in support of children, war refugees and victims of recurring humanitarian crises during the Republican period. While their engagement built upon the traditions of local elites since the late Qing dynasty of the empire, it also drew inspiration from the American-inspired ethic of public service that solidified the new culture of professionalism.

Mobile and versatile, advertising professionals embodied the new class of cultural entrepreneurs that emerged during the Republican era, navigating between the press, industry, philanthropy, arts and academia. They were not only mobile professionally but also geographically. While Carl Crow and Francis Millington were adventurous spirits drawn to the Orient, the remission of the Boxer indemnity from 1908 allowed Lin Zhenbin and Lu Meiseng to study in the United States. Once established, they continued to travel throughout their lives to establish new contacts and stay informed about the latest developments in the field. Their careers were shaped by the tumultuous circumstances that characterised the young Republic. Wars had a particular impact on their lives. While the First World War brought Crow and Millington to Shanghai, the Second World War drove them away. While the war from 1937 to 1945 marked the end of the expatriates' careers in China, it was the Communist takeover in 1949 that interrupted or shifted the

---

289 Feng, Xiaocai, *Zhengshang Zhongguo: Yu Qiaqing yu ta de shidai* (Political Merchands in China: Yu Qiaqing and his time) (Beijing: Shehui kexue wenxian chubanshe, 2013).

trajectories of vernacular publicists. Those like Lin Zhenbin who had established solid foundations overseas were able to continue their businesses in Hong Kong and the United States. While the Communist revolution reshaped Lin Zhenbin's career, the nationalisations carried out in the People's Republic in the 1950s eventually led to the demise of the Lianhe agency. Between the two wars, the "golden age" of the Chinese industry opened up unexpected opportunities for these professionals, giving advertising the chance to scale up and become a full-fledged industry.

Part Two: **Conquering Markets**

Chapter 4
The Rise of Consumer Goods

What did advertisements sell? Previous works, as mentioned in the introduction, have tended to focus on specific products, primarily cigarettes and medicines.[290] Although some attempts have been made to provide a more detailed inventory of advertising offerings, they have failed to capture the relative importance of different products, their evolution over time and how they were articulated within the advertising spaces of the period.[291] This chapter addresses the gap in previous studies by conducting a systematic and longitudinal analysis of the products advertised in the Chinese press, with a specific focus on the influential Chinese newspaper *Shenbao*. Founded in 1872 by British entrepreneur Ernest Major and later directed by Chinese entrepreneur Shi Liangcai, *Shenbao* became a prominent national daily with a wide distribution across China.[292] Its readership com-

---

290 Regarding medicines, see Huang Kewu's pioneering study "Cong Shenbao yiyao guanggao kan minchu Shanghai de yiliao wenhua yu shehui shenghuo (1912~1926) (Medical culture and social life seen through *Shenbao* advertisements, 1912–1926)", *Zhongyang yanjiu yuan Jindai shi yanjiu suo jikan* 17 (1988): 141–94. More recent studies include: Eugenia Lean, "The Modern Elixir: Medicine as a Consumer Item in the Early Twentieth-Century Chinese Press", *UCLA Historical Journal* 15 (1995): 65–92. Regarding cigarettes, see for example: Tani Barlow, "Advertising Ephemera and the Angel of History", *Positions: East Asia Cultures Critique* 20, n° 1 (2012): 111–58; Ulrike Büchsel, "Lifestyles, Gender Roles and Nationalism in the Representation of Women in Cigarette Advertisements from the Republican Period" (Doctoral Dissertation, University of Heidelberg, 2009); David Embrey Fraser, "Smoking out the Enemy: The National Goods Movement and the Advertising of Nationalism in China, 1880–1937" (unpublished Ph.D Thesis, Berkeley, University of California, 1999); Sherman Cochran, *Big Business in China: Sino-Foreign Rivalry in the Cigarette Industry, 1890–1930* (Cambridge, Mass.; London: Harvard University Press, 1980).
291 Barbara Mittler, "Imagined Communities Divided: Reading Visual Regimes in Shanghai's Newspaper Advertising (1860s–1910s)", in *Visualising China, 1845–1965: Moving and Still Images in Historical Narratives*, ed. Christian Henriot and Wen-hsin Yeh (Leiden: Brill, 2013), 267–378; Weipin Tsai, *Reading Shenbao: Nationalism, Consumerism and Individuality in China, 1919–37* (Houndmills, Basingstoke: Palgrave Macmillan, 2008); Wang Runian, *Yuwang de xiangxiang: 1920–1930 niandai "Shenbao" guanggao de wenhua shi yanjiu* (The imaginary of desire: a cultural study of *Shenbao* advertisements in the 1920–1930s) (Shanghai: Shanghai renmin chubanshe, 2007).
292 *Shenbao* reached a national record of 150,000 copies distributed daily in the 1930s and continued its publication until it was confiscated by communist forces in May 1949. The last issue appeared on May 27, 1949. *Shenbao* has been the subject of an abundant literature. See in particular: Terry Narramore, "Making the News in Shanghai: Shen Bao and the Politics of Newspaper Journalism, 1912–1937" (Doctoral Dissertation, Australian National University, 1989); Rudolf G. Wagner, "The Role of the Foreign Community in the Chinese Public Sphere", *The China Quar-*

https://doi.org/10.1515/9783111390000-005

prised intellectual, economic and political elites, with the rising middle-class petty urbanites also becoming an important demographic during the Republican era.[293]

The study examines five pivotal periods in the history of Chinese advertising: 1914, 1924, 1934, 1941 and 1949. The first week of January was selected for each period, except when January issues were unavailable, such as in 1941 where February issues were analysed instead. This sampling strategy proved effective as advertisements tended to exhibit repetitive patterns on a daily basis. In addition to *Shenbao*, advertisements from the *North China Daily News* (NCDN), a leading British newspaper serving the English-speaking community in China, are included for comparative analysis. Additionally, advertisements found in the streets of Shanghai, documented through municipal archives and preserved photographs, are examined to gain insights into outdoor advertising practices.[294]

The chapter is divided into three sections. The first section focuses on the initial dominance of medications in the press and cigarettes in outdoor advertising. The second section explores the gradual shift in dominance as new consumer goods emerge in the 1920s. The final section analyses the transformations that various products underwent within each sector, considering their materiality and usage.

The Initial Dominance of Medicines and Cigarettes

Prior to the outbreak of the First World War, the landscape of Chinese advertising was primarily shaped by two prominent products, each holding its distinct domain: medicines found their place within the pages of newspapers, while cigarettes claimed their presence in outdoor spaces. Historically, the prevalence of medical advertisements can be traced back to the advent of "charlatans" who, in the early nineteenth century, pioneered the utilisation of newspapers as a platform for advertising. Although these patent medicines were often criticised for tarnishing the reputation of advertising, they undeniably played a crucial role in

---

terly, n° 142 (June 1995): 423–43; Barbara Mittler, *A newspaper for China? Power, identity, and change in Shanghai's news media, 1872–1912* (Cambridge: Harvard University Press, 2004); Liu Li, *Zhongguo jindai baoye caifang shilun: yi shenbao wei zhongxin de kaocha* (A history of newspapers interviews in modern China: a study centered on *Shenbao*) (Hefei: Anhui daxue chubanshe, 2014); Song Shuqiang, Yin Zhaolu and Zhao Feifei, eds., *"Shenbao" baodao yu pinglun* (Surveys and commentaries in *Shenbao*) (Nanjing: Nanjing daxue chubanshe, 2019).

293 The expression *petty urbanites* was coined by the historian Yeh Wen-Hsin to refer to the emerging class of office workers and white-collars in Shanghai: Yeh, *Shanghai Splendor*, 129–51.

294 The dataset on which this study is based is available on MADSpace: https://madspace.org/cooked/Tables?ID=111.

fostering the growth of modern journalism by serving as a significant source of revenue for newspapers.[295]

Within the *Shenbao* newspaper, the prominence of medicines is vividly reflected through the abundance of advertisements dedicated to this category. In the year 1914, a remarkable 87 medical advertisements were featured, comprising a substantial 40% of the total number of advertisements. These medicinal advertisements encompassed an expansive 22% of the total surface area of the newspaper, essentially occupying nearly half of the available advertising space, amounting to an impressive 7251 cm^2. One could scarcely turn a page without encountering these medicinal promotions, as they permeated the newspaper from the very first page to the last. The final page, in particular, held a coveted status, as it was believed to leave a lasting imprint on the reader's memory.[296] Moving into the 1920s, medicines continued to hold a prominent position within the pages of *Shenbao*, albeit amidst emerging competition from other product categories. While the number of medical advertisements experienced a slight increase, reaching a total of 89, their proportion in relation to the overall advertising landscape exhibited a significant decline, now accounting for only 30% of all advertisements. Simultaneously, the territorial reach of these medicinal advertisements expanded, covering an area of 8417 cm^2. Nevertheless, their share of the advertising space diminished to 20%, while occupying a mere 13% of the total surface area.

Simultaneously, while medicines were gaining prominence within the realm of newspapers, the tobacco industry held sway over outdoor spaces. This distribution of advertising influence was attributed by experts to the sociological profile of Chinese smokers. Particularly, the coolie population emerged as a significant market for cigarette manufacturers, and outdoor advertising was considered the most effective means of reaching this demographic, given their relatively low level of education. In the pre-World War I era, the Shanghai Municipal Council meticulously recorded approximately 50 billboards dedicated to cigarette advertisements, constituting an impressive 28% of all advertising displayed in the International Settlement.[297] The wide distribution of these billboards across the city served to reinforce their impact and create an omnipresent perception among the public. These billboards were strategically placed along the bustling thoroughfares that intersected the central district of the International Concession, such as Kiangse and Foochow Roads, extending westward to the racecourse at Bubbling Well and north of Soochow Creek. As a result, the influence of cigarette advertis-

---

295 Bacon, 765; Hollington Tong, 30.
296 Wu Tiesheng and Zhu Shengyu, *Guanggaoxue* (Advertising Studies) (Shanghai: Zhonghua shuju, 1946), 59–64.
297 SMA (SMC), U1-14-3267.

ing permeated the urban landscape. As the 1920s drew to a close, the total advertising expenditure dedicated to promoting cigarettes in China surpassed the notable sum of one million dollars. Remarkably, this accounted for nearly 40% of the overall budget allocated to outdoor advertising during that period.[298]

Following the conclusion of the war, the once-dominant presence of cigarettes and medicines in advertising gradually began to wane as they faced competition from emerging consumer goods. Consequently, both industries sought to diversify their advertising strategies by exploring other media avenues. In the case of cigarettes, their representation in *Shenbao* was relatively meagre in 1914, with only a single instance of advertisement. However, they gained traction during the 1920s. The 1924 edition of *Shenbao* featured seven cigarette advertisements, comprising a modest 2% of the total advertisements scattered throughout the newspaper and covering 5% of the overall advertising space. By the end of the 1920s, the tobacco industry had become the second-largest advertiser after pharmaceuticals. However, its momentum was disrupted by the Sino-Japanese War, as evidenced by the presence of merely two cigarette advertisements, accounting for 5% of the newspaper's advertising space in 1941. Nevertheless, the sector experienced a revival post-war, with the January 1949 edition showcasing seven cigarette advertisements, occupying 15% of the advertising space.

Evaluating the growth of medical advertising in outdoor spaces proves more challenging. Before the First World War, photographic evidence and accounts from travellers documented the widespread presence of pharmacy signs adorning the streets of Shanghai.[299] By the end of the war, the Shanghai Municipal Council (SMC) recorded a dozen medical signs that violated municipal regulations, indicating a minor proportion of the operational pharmacies. During the Sino-Japanese War, stricter controls resulted in approximately 50 recorded medical advertisements within the archives of the International Settlement. Besides the signs of pharmacy and bathing establishments, which primarily concentrated on commercial streets in the French Concession (such as avenue Joffre and rue du Consulat) and the International Settlement (such as Nanking Road and Foochow Road), approximately 30 large billboards were erected at crucial intersections, reflecting the growth of the Chinese pharmaceutical industry.

---

298 Bacon, 756, 765.
299 D. Clark, *Sketches in and around Shanghai* (Shanghai: Shanghai Mercury and Celestial Empire Offices, 1894), 80–88.

New Consumer Goods in the 1920s

In the Press

In the 1920s, the landscape of consumer goods in newspaper advertising experienced a notable shift, gradually displacing the dominance of medicines. A range of new products emerged, reflecting the changing interests and preferences of the era [Figure 9]. Following medicines, other sectors began to gain prominence, including financial services (banks, insurance), cigarettes, entertainment (theatre, cinema) and cultural objects (books, magazines). Additionally, energy-related offerings (such as gas and electricity), transport, heavy industry and the culture of appearances emerged as notable contenders.

This distribution pattern continued into the 1920s. The financial sector maintained its lead, accounting for 70 advertisements, which constituted 20% of the advertising population and occupied 10% of the advertising space. Cigarettes and entertainment solidified their presence, representing 20% of the advertisements and capturing one-third of the advertising space. Notably, the culture of appearances experienced a significant breakthrough, with approximately 30 advertisements (10%) covering 10% of the advertising space. Cultural objects made slower progress, comprising around 50 advertisements (10% of the total), but occupying a larger portion of the advertising space at 18%. Conversely, heavy industry and urban services, such as energy and transport, experienced a decline, representing only 2% of the advertisements and 3% of the advertising space. In contrast, new products from the food industry, such as cocoa, biscuits and soft drinks, made their debut in the newspaper with approximately ten advertisements in 1924.

A study conducted in 1923 by scholars from Qinghua University in Beijing corroborated the aforementioned observations. Although the classification system used in their study differed, the findings reaffirmed the preeminent position of medicines, accounting for 27% of the advertisements. Additionally, the study highlighted the growing presence of entertainment (14%), luxury goods such as tobacco and cosmetics (13%), economic and cultural goods (11% each), daily use products (6%) and miscellaneous items (18%).[300] This study not only provided valuable insights into the advertising landscape but also facilitated a comparison of the Shanghai newspaper *Shenbao* with four other Chinese newspapers: *Chenbao* and *Shuntian Shibao* in Beijing, and *Yishibao* and *Dongfang Shibao* in Tianjin [Figure 10]. Three distinct groups emerged from the analysis. The first group included *Yishibao*

---

300 "An Analytical Study of Advertisements in Chinese Newspapers", *Chinese Economic Monthly* 3, n° 4 (April 1926): 139–43.

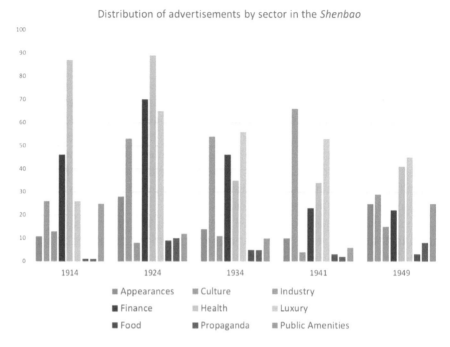

Figure 9: Distribution of advertisements by sector in the *Shenbao*, based on the number of advertisements per day, from the following samples: January 7, 1914, January 3, 1924, January 5, 1934, February 1, 1941, January 1, 1949. Legend: Appearances: cosmetics, clothing, accessories, interior decoration. Culture: books, periodicals, music, photography, office equipment. Industry: construction, chemicals, petroleum, automotive, electrical appliances. Finance: banking, insurance, real estate, commerce, lawyers. Health: medicines, hygiene products. Luxury: cigarettes, spirits, entertainment. Food: food and non-alcoholic beverages. Propaganda: municipal announcements, charities. *Public amenities*: gas and electricity, transport, communications.

and *Shuntian Shibao*, where medical advertising continued to dominate. In these newspapers, medicines occupied half of the advertising space, followed by economic goods (22%), entertainment (9.4%), daily necessities (5.8%), luxury goods (2.8%) and educational items (2.2%). *Dongfang Shibao* displayed similarities to foreign press, with medical advertising comprising a smaller proportion (4%) and economic goods being overrepresented (40%). Other categories included daily necessities (15%), luxury goods (12%), entertainment (5%) and educational ads (5%). The third group, represented by *Shenbao* and *Chenbao*, exhibited an intermediary position. While pharmaceutical advertisements had a stronger presence compared to *Dongfang Shibao*, it was still weaker than *Yishibao*, accounting for a maximum of a quarter of the advertisements. The educational sector followed (17%), followed by economic goods (14%), entertainment (13%) and luxury goods (10%).

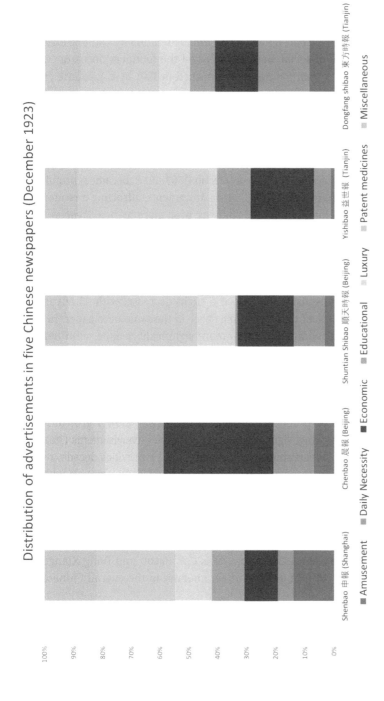

Figure 10: Distribution of advertisements in five Chinese newspapers (December 1923), expressed in terms of surface area (square inch). From: "Analytical Study of Advertisements in Chinese Newspapers". *Chinese Economic Monthly* 3, n° 4 (April 1926): 139–43.

These differences in advertising distribution partly reflected the historical background of the newspapers and their readership profiles. The persistence of medical advertising in *Yishibao*, a newspaper founded in 1915 by Catholic missionaries under the theme of social welfare, reflected the founders' focus on social and health concerns.[301] *Shuntian Ribao*, established in 1901 by a Japanese entrepreneur with philanthropic intentions, continued to attract major sponsors from the Japanese pharmaceutical industry, such as Morishita, the manufacturer of the renowned drug "Jintan".[302] *Dongfang Shibao*, the Chinese edition of an English-language publication, represented a distinct profile with reduced emphasis on medical advertising (4%) and a greater presence of economic goods (40%). *Chenbao*, founded in 1916 by Chinese intellectual Li Dazhao (1889–1927), became a prominent platform for the May Fourth and New Culture Movements, attracting a readership primarily comprised of intellectuals and students, even more so than *Shenbao*.

The trends that emerged in the 1920s persisted throughout the following decade, with notable shifts in various product categories. Medical advertising continued its decline, with less than 30 advertisements recorded in 1934, accounting for 10% of the total advertisements and occupying only 15% of the advertising space in *Shenbao*. Financial goods also experienced a slight decrease, with 45 advertisements (15%) covering 10% of the advertising space in the same newspaper. In contrast, the culture of appearances faced a more significant decline, with only 14 advertisements (5%) occupying a mere 2% of the advertising space. On the other hand, cigarettes, entertainment and cultural goods continued their growth trajectory. Each of these sectors featured approximately 50 advertisements, representing between 20% and 40% of the newspaper's advertising space. Industrial products, tertiary services and food products experienced stagnant or slower growth rates. Heavy industry demonstrated signs of recovery, with ten advertisements (3%) and a doubled share of the advertising space compared to the previous decade, reaching 5% of the newspaper. Tertiary services maintained a steady presence with approximately 10 advertisements, accounting for 1% of the advertising space. Food products occupied the same amount of space but with half the number of advertisements (5).

The advertisements in *Shenbao* mirrored broader trends observed in the Chinese press during the early 1930s. Journalists C.A. Bacon and Dong Xianguang noted the progress of cultural goods and automobiles in the overall Chinese ad-

---

301 Laurent Galy, "Yishibao (Social Welfare)", in *Encyclopédie des historiographies: Afriques, Amériques, Asies: Volume 1: sources et genres historiques (Tome 1 et Tome 2)*, ed. Nathalie Kouamé, Éric P. Meyer and Anne Viguier, (Paris: Presses de l'Inalco, 2020), 1975–87.

302 Janet Y. Chen, *Guilty of Indigence: The Urban Poor in China, 1900–1953* (Princeton University Press, 2013), 22.

vertising landscape. While acknowledging that automobiles remained out of reach for the majority of the population, they anticipated that the improving standard of living and the expansion of road networks would contribute to the development of the automobile market.[303] However, Dong also critically pointed out certain shortcomings in advertising practices. He believed that Chinese entrepreneurs did not fully harness the power of the press and expressed disappointment that department stores primarily relied on temporary, small-scale campaigns to announce seasonal sales.[304]

During the war, the advertising landscape underwent minimal changes. Medicines and entertainment maintained their prominence, accounting for 34 advertisements (15%) and 53 advertisements (28%), respectively, in *Shenbao*. These two sectors continued to occupy roughly one-third of the advertising space. Cultural goods experienced further growth, reaching 66 advertisements, although they occupied only 10% of the advertising space. The other sectors exhibited contrasting developments. The culture of appearances and urban amenities witnessed a quadrupling of their advertising space, increasing from 2% to 8% and from 1% to 4%, respectively. However, the number of advertisements in these sectors slightly decreased to ten and six ads, accounting for 5% and 2% of the total advertisements, respectively. In contrast, the financial sector experienced a more significant decline. Both the population and territory of financial advertisements were halved, decreasing from 46 to 23 advertisements, which constituted 10% of the total advertisements and occupied 5% of the advertising space.

On the eve of the Communist revolution, the distribution of newspaper space among different product categories became more equitable. Medicines maintained a presence with around 40 advertisements, although they experienced a decline, accounting for 15% of the total advertisements. The finance and entertainment sectors remained relatively stable in terms of advertisement numbers, with 22 and 45 advertisements, respectively, representing 10% and 20% of the total advertisements. These sectors also maintained a consistent share of the advertising space, with finance occupying 22% and entertainment occupying 5%. Cultural goods encompassed less than 30 advertisements, accounting for 10% of both the advertisement population and the advertising space. While heavy industry experienced growth, increasing from four to 15 advertisements and occupying 2% to 4% of the advertising space, it remained a marginal sector in terms of overall advertisement presence. In contrast, the culture of appearances and transport

---

303 In the late 1920s, there were less than 12,000 cars in circulation in China (half of them in Shanghai), compared to 400 million inhabitants. Bacon, 758; Tong, 1936, 30.
304 Tong, 31.

advertisements demonstrated notable advancements. Both sectors witnessed a doubling in the number of advertisements, with 25 ads each. Moreover, their territorial presence quadrupled, with the culture of appearances accounting for 20% of the advertising space and transport occupying 10% of the advertising space.

In contrast to *Shenbao*, medical advertisements in the *North China Daily News* (NCDN), a leading British daily, held less prominence. As early as 1914, the *NCDN* seemed to distance itself from patent medicines and announcements associated with "quackery". This shift created space for a wider range of goods, particularly financial services, entertainment and urban amenities, which gained prominence over time, particularly towards the end of the period under consideration. A closer examination reveals which products were common to both newspapers and which were exclusive to either *Shenbao* or *NCDN*. While medicines and cigarettes were commonly advertised in both publications, the culture of appearances and cultural goods, such as books and musical instruments, exhibited significant differentiation. Entertainment served as an intermediate case, experiencing substantial changes during the Republican period. Prior to the First World War, the two communities (referring to readerships) were entertained separately. However, with the emergence of cabarets and the rise of cinema following the war, both newspapers began featuring numerous advertisements for the same shows.[305] Starting from the Sino-Japanese War onwards, however, the advertising spaces in *Shenbao* and *NCDN* became more compartmentalised, indicating a greater separation in the types of advertisements published in each newspaper. The advertising content and emphasis shifted, aligning more distinctly with the target audiences and market preferences of each publication.

In Outdoor Spaces

Like medicines in the press, cigarettes faced competition for outdoor advertising space from other product categories. Until the late 1920s, their main competitors included the energy sector (gas, electricity), alcoholic beverages (such as P&O Scotch whisky, Asahi beer, Castillon wine and Monopole champagne), other non-alcoholic drinks (such as Watson mineral water), food products (such as Nestlé, Quaker Oats and Bournville Cocoa) and the automobile industry (including garages and service stations). Entertainment advertisements remained relatively discreet until the 1930s when the night culture began to flourish, particularly

---

305 Andrew Field, *Shanghai's dancing world: cabaret culture and urban politics, 1919–1954* (Hong Kong: Chinese University Press, 2010).

with the introduction of neon lighting. This shift brought increased visibility and promotion to entertainment venues and events, transforming the advertising landscape associated with entertainment. It is worth noting that the municipal archives poorly represented banks and insurance companies, which tended to favour advertising in the press.[306]

During the 1930s, two sectors notably expanded their presence in outdoor advertising spaces: automobiles and services. Restaurants accounted for 17% of the advertisements, followed by hotels at 8%. Entertainment venues, including cinemas, theatres and nightclubs, held a 5% share, while bars and cafes occupied 4%. These activities were concentrated in lively districts that thrived during the night, such as the Great World (Dashijie) neighbourhood and Avenue Joffre in the French Concession. On the other hand, garages and service stations, which supported the growing automobile industry, comprised a significant portion (20%) of the advertisements. They were predominantly located on the outskirts of the city, accompanying urban expansion and the extension of the road network to the western areas of the concessions. Propaganda activities, including hygiene education campaigns, charitable initiatives and exhibitions, ranked third with an 11% share of the advertisements. These activities were supported by banners and other temporary forms of media. The medical sector and cultural activities, such as schools, newspapers, bookshops and music shops, followed suit. Avenue Joffre, which was establishing itself as the fashion centre of the French Concession, witnessed the flourishing of beauty salons, tailors and jewellers. These establishments catered to the growing demand for fashion and luxury on the bustling avenue. Despite Shanghai's reputation as one of the best-equipped cities under the Republic, advertisements for urban amenities related to water, energy, public transport and communications still lagged behind.[307]

---

306 Bacon, 766; "The Advertiser's Dilemma: Another Chinese Puzzle", *North China Herald*, June 15, 1929.

307 Shanghai was at the forefront of infrastructure development in China. The city had a system for distributing running water as early as 1862, followed by the provision of gas and electricity shortly after. Electricity became available in the International Settlement around 1885, while the first tramway line began operations in 1907. Buses were in circulation prior to the outbreak of WWI. See: Zheng Zu'an, "Jindai Shanghai dushi de xingcheng – yibasisannian zhi yijiuyisinian Shanghai chengshi fazhan shulue" (The formation of the modem city of Shanghai – the story of the development of Shanghai as a city, 1843–1914), in *Shanghai shiyanjiu* (Studies in Shanghai history), ed. Wang Pengcheng et al. (Shanghai, 1984), 181. Wu Shenyuan 吴申元, Shanghai zui zao de zhongchong 上海最早的种种 (The earliest species of Shanghai) (Shanghai: Huadong shifan daxue chubanshe, 1989), 49–50; Sherman Cochran, ed., *Inventing Nanjing Road: Commercial Culture in Shanghai, 1900–1945* (Ithaca, NY: Cornell University Press, 1999), 5; Leo Ou-fan Lee, *Shang-*

During the war, the tobacco industry maintained its dominance in the streets of Shanghai, with over 56% of the 1,250 billboards recorded by the Shanghai Municipal Council (SMC) in May 1943 dedicated to tobacco advertising. Hotels, restaurants, bars, cafes and theatres followed, accounting for 17% of the signboards. Pharmacies and hygiene products claimed 11% of outdoor advertising. Fashion, food and motor vehicles held marginal positions, with 3%, 2% and less than 2% respectively.

As documentation becomes scarcer after the rendition of foreign concessions, historians have had to rely on scattered photographs, often lacking precise dates and locations. The photographs taken by Jack Birns for *Life magazine* in January 1948 have proven invaluable. Although Birns concentrated on capturing the busiest places, such as the Racecourse or the Great World, at a specific time of day, his photos reaffirmed the tobacco industry's dominance through its colossal and omnipresent billboards. These images also depicted the rise of cosmetics and hygienic products, characterised by extravagant displays that rivalled the impact of cigarette advertisements. Other photographs illustrated the revival of nightlife culture following the war, showcasing the gradual reopening of restaurants, bars and theatres. The proliferation of garages and service stations on the outskirts of the city further indicated the significant developments of the automobile and petroleum industries.[308]

New Products, New Uses

The Rise of the Pharmaceutical Industry

Despite the relative decline of medical advertising, medical products were undergoing a significant transformation rather than disappearing altogether. A longitudinal analysis of advertisements in *Shenbao* reveals two main generations of medicines, which partly overlapped in their presence.

The first generation, inherited from the Chinese pharmacopoeia, dominated until the 1920s and encompassed a wide range of ailments and remedies. In the study conducted by Qinghua scholars in 1923, medicines were classified into 11 categories. The most prominent category, accounting for 26% of the advertisements, fo-

hai Modern: The Flowering of a New Urban Culture in China, 1930–1945 (Cambridge, Mass.: Harvard University Press, 1999), 7.

308 Jack Birns, "China, Last Days Of Shanghai" (Shanghai, 1949), Google LIFE Photo Archive (https://www.virtualshanghai.net/Photos/Images?ID=25618); Billboard advertising a Chinese brand of toothpaste (Guchiling yagao) near a Caltex service station, Shanghai, 1948, Jack Birns, Google LIFE Photo Archive (https://madspace.org/Photos/?ID=34376).

cused on the "social diseases" prevalent in the nineteenth century, particularly venereal diseases (20%) and opium addiction. Another significant category included ginseng and longevity elixirs (13%), reflecting the interest in traditional Chinese remedies for health and vitality. Some advertisements addressed diseases associating the liver and brain or heart and kidney, showcasing residual expressions of vernacular medicine.[309] Foreign-origin cod liver oil products also gained popularity during this period, with their advertisements increasing from 2% to 4% between 1914 and 1924. Advertisements for remedies targeting infectious and respiratory diseases were well-represented, reflecting the concerns and anxieties surrounding recurring epidemics since the nineteenth century.[310] Additional advertisements focused on treatments specific to women and children, nervous disorders and sight and hearing issues.

Advertisements for hospitals and doctors were relatively scarce, accounting for less than 5% of the total. Despite approximately 1,000 registered practitioners with the Shanghai Municipal Council during the 1920s, few independent physicians actively advertised in *Shenbao*. According to Carl Crow, the best doctors did not rely heavily on advertising because their reputations were built on mutual trust and recommendations. Crow attributed the limited representation of hospitals in advertisements to the persistence of self-medication practices among the Chinese population. Additionally, it could be argued that overburdened hospitals had little need for advertising given the high demand for their services.[311]

During the mid-1920s, new ailments of nervous or cerebral origin began to emerge in *Shenbao*. In addition to the already dreaded insomnia that was prevalent in 1914, headaches were becoming a significant hindrance in an increasingly urbanised, productivity-driven and noisy society. Advertisements for psychiatric clinics and specialist practitioners indicated a growing recognition of mental disorders as distinct pathologies in their own right. Advertisements addressing hair problems, such as baldness or grey hair, highlighted concerns about aging and issues related to masculinity. These advertisements tapped into societal anxieties surrounding appearance and societal expectations tied to youthfulness and vitality. The decline of specific maternity treatments (accounting for 3% of advertisements) may seem paradoxical in an era marked by natalist culture. However, it is important to note that childhood and femininity were being addressed in other

309 Wen Chunying and Zhu Chen, "Zhong-Xi ronghe: jindai yiyao guanggao de 'shen' yu 'nao' – yi Shanghai *Xinbao, Shenbao* weili (1862–1915) (Liver and brain in the medical ads of *Xinbao* and *Shenbao*)", *Guanggao daguan*, 2012, 84–88.
310 Christian Henriot, Lu Shi and Charlotte Aubrun, *The Population of Shanghai (1865–1953): A Sourcebook* (Leiden; Boston: Brill, 2019), 51–58.
311 Carl Crow, *Four Hundred Million Customers*, 202.

sectors, including education, hygiene and infant nutrition. This shift reflected changing societal perspectives and a broader recognition of the multifaceted needs and care required during the stages of childhood and maternity.

During the 1930s, a new generation of medical advertisements emerged, introducing novel products from the pharmaceutical industry. Influenced by the cosmetics industry, there was an increased emphasis on skin problems, with 13% of advertisements dedicated to this category. Skin issues became associated with appearance rather than solely with health concerns. Hearing problems began to fade in prominence, while eye disorders took centre stage, accounting for 6% of medical advertisements. The demand for glasses shifted from being a fashion accessory to a reflection of the growing emphasis on physical comfort and academic performance. The development of ophthalmology further contributed to the medicalisation of sight problems.[312] Nervous disorders gained ground as another symptom of urbanisation, representing 9% of medical advertisements. The increasing prevalence of these disorders reflected the stresses and challenges of urban life. Additionally, there was a growing demand for vitamins (3%), reflecting the societal expectation of productivity in both physical and mental realms. This "vitamania" phenomenon, although a global trend, took over from ginseng as a popular product in China while not fully replacing it.[313]

The renewal of medical advertising was evident not only in the nature of the products but also in their materiality and methods of administration. For example, Doan Backache & Kidney Pills adapted to the increased mobility of city dwellers by offering their pills in a tablet form that could be easily carried and consumed during journeys, with the advertisement claiming that it would not affect their effectiveness. The discourses surrounding medical products were also changing. Kepler Cod Liver Oil, for instance, shifted its image from being a panacea to adopting the characteristics of a modern *weitaming* (vitamin) product.[314]

During the Sino-Japanese War, the trends observed in the 1930s continued to shape medical advertising. In 1941, the decline of social diseases, Chinese tonics and organ combinations persisted, each accounting for only 3% of the advertisements. Vitamins, on the other hand, remained resilient, maintaining a significant presence along with the resurgence of panaceas and cod liver oil, which represented 6% of the advertisements. Sight problems and nervous disorders contin-

---

312 "Weekly Report for the Week ended June 29, 1918", Julean Herbert Arnold Papers, 1905–1946, Box 4, f.2 (Stanford, Calif: Hoover Institution Archives, 1918).

313 Rima Apple, *Vitamania: Vitamins in American Culture* (New Brunswick, N.J.: Rutgers University Press, 1996).

314 "Doan Backache & Kidney Pills", *SB*, January 1, 1934, 20; "Kepler Cod Liver Oil", *Shenbao*, January 1, 1934, 24.

ued to be major concerns, each accounting for 9% of the advertisements. With the professionalisation of medicine, there was a notable increase in advertisements for medical practitioners (3%) and hospitals (13%). X-rays also gained popularity as a fashionable treatment, occupying 9% of the advertisements.

By 1949, the landscape of medical advertising became more varied. While newer pharmaceutical products such as vitamins and X-rays maintained their presence, older remedies experienced a comeback. Ginseng and longevity elixirs accounted for 16% of the advertisements, and disorders related to the heart and kidney or liver and stomach represented 13%. Ailments specific to urban modernity, such as nervous disorders and sight problems, began to fade from the newspaper's advertisements. With the development of gynaecology and paediatrics, women and children regained prominence in medical advertising. However, it was primarily the food industry that provided them with new visibility, as their health and nutrition became important considerations in advertising campaigns.

The Tentative Breakthrough of the Food Industry

Before the outbreak of the First World War, the food industry had little presence in *Shenbao*. Food packaging constraints hindered import and distribution possibilities. In addition, differences in dietary preferences and habits made it challenging for foreign food products, particularly dairy products, to gain widespread adoption. Food, whether it was a matter of survival or gastronomy, received minimal advertising attention in the Chinese press. In 1914, *Shenbao* featured only one advertisement for meat produced in Yunnan province. Luxury spirits such as French cognac and German beer were among the first edible products to be advertised. The presence of these high-end alcoholic beverages in advertisements reflected the influence of elite clubs like the French Cercle Sportif and the German Concordia Club in treaty ports like Shanghai, where they played a role in promoting new drinking habits among the Chinese elite.[315] Some food brands were making strides in Shanghai, thanks to the efforts of the Oriental Advertising Agency. Nestlé brand products and Watson and Aquarius mineral waters were beginning to feature in press advertisements, marking their establishment on the streets of Shanghai.

After the war, food advertising in *Shenbao* experienced a significant increase both in quantity and diversity. Cocoa and powdered milk emerged as prominent

---

315 Norwood Allman, "Transliteration of 'Coca-Cola' Trade-Mark to Chinese Characters", *The New Yorker*, February 1959, 61–62.

food products, capturing attention in the newspaper. Condiments and health foods, such as Vitamin Milk, dominated outdoor advertising spaces. Advertisements for biscuits and sweets shifted the focus of food from necessity to pleasure and indulgence. Dairy products occupied a somewhat ambivalent position in the advertising landscape. On one hand, they were associated with health, as seen in the promotion of powdered milk for consumption by children and invalids. On the other hand, they were also presented as sources of pleasure, as exemplified by the use of dairy in the preparation of Bournville hot chocolate.[316] In the 1930s, the market for dairy products underwent a radical transformation with the development of industrial dairies like Shanghai Dairy Farm and Liberty Dairy. These local dairies brought a significant shift by reducing dependence on imports from countries like New Zealand and Australia. Supported by nationalist elites, producers and advertisers collaborated to promote the consumption of fresh milk among the entire Chinese population.[317] Previously limited to powdered milk primarily for infants (such as Glaxo and Klim), pasteurised milk began to target adults and schoolchildren. The introduction of flavoured milk drinks, such as strawberry or chocolate varieties by Newmilks, aimed to make milk more appealing and adaptable to a wider range of tastes.[318]

With the emergence of American sodas and soft drinks, European spirits faced a decline in advertising prominence in *Shenbao*. Brands such as German beer and British whisky did not vanish completely but encountered stiff competition from new American (Johnny Walker), Chinese (UB Beer) and Japanese (Asahi) brands. The introduction of these new players in the beverage market altered the landscape and posed challenges for traditional European spirits. During the Second World War, the food industry aimed to simplify daily life by introducing new additives, such as Henningsen and Royal Baking Powder, which helped housewives in meal preparation. After the war, however, these American brands gradually disappeared from the advertising scene as vernacular products like Maling canned foods gained preference among consumers. It is worth noting, however, that the Chinese food industry had a relatively minor presence in *Shenbao* throughout the republi-

---

316 Klim, *SB*, January 3, 1924, 5; Glaxo, *SB*, January 3, 1924, 20; Bournville Cocoa, *SB*, January 3, 1924, 16.

317 Crow, *Four Hundred Million Customers*, 211–12. Regarding milk consumption in China, see: Susan Glosser, *Chinese Visions of Family and State, 1915–1953* (Berkeley: University of California Press, 2003); Jia-Chen Fu, *The Other Milk: Reinventing Soy in Republican China* (Seattle: University of Washington Press, 2018); Wang Zhenzhu, "Popular Magazines and the Making of a Nation: The Healthy Baby Contest Organized by The Young Companion in 1926–27", *Frontiers of History in China*, n° 4 (2011): 525–37.

318 Label for Sun Chocomilk and Sun Milk Shake Strawberry (Newmilks, Ltd), SMA (SMC), U1-4-1793 (1936).

can period. The newspaper predominantly featured imported food products and international brands, while Chinese food products had limited visibility in its advertising pages.[319]

Democratising the Culture of Appearances

Before the outbreak of the First World War, the culture of appearances in Shanghai was primarily manifested through luxury accessories such as jewellery, furs, hats and umbrellas. This was evident both in the advertisements of *Shenbao* and the physical presence of these items on the streets of Shanghai. Along Broadway, located to the north of the International Settlement, tailors, jewellers and watchmakers vied for the attention of passers-by, showcasing their exquisite offerings.[320] Following the war, there was a notable refinement and diversification in textiles. *Shenbao* began featuring silk and satin alongside furs, reflecting the changing landscape of fashion and luxury goods. In the streets of Shanghai, the signs of luxury jewellers and tailors began to illuminate the night, further enhancing the city's vibrant and glamorous atmosphere.

In the subsequent decades, the textile and clothing industry experienced significant innovations and transformations. The introduction of new materials, such as cotton and Manchester calico, brought more accessible options to the market and found their way into the advertisements of *Shenbao*, while manufacturers of silk and satin continued to promote their higher-end and more luxurious products. The changes in clothing trends had indirect effects on various players in the industry. Pawnshops, as noted by Carl Crow, became fashion experts who could anticipate seasonal effects and identify clothes that could be resold in the following year.[321] In the streets of Shanghai, silk and fur retailers like the Fortune Silk Store and Hsin Feng Factory persisted despite increasing competition from the wool industry, represented by shops like Teh Tsang Woollen Piece Goods Shop.[322] Simultaneously, new brands emerged in the market, offering fine lingerie (such as the Great Eastern Hosiery Company and The World Hosiery

---

319 Maling (Meilin guantou shipin), *SB*, February 1, 1941, 7.
320 Clark, 80–88. See also: Cécile Armand, "Monstres publicitaires (1) – Les lieux d'enseignes", Blog post, *Advertising History*, https://advertisinghistory.hypotheses.org/3088 (last accessed on April 26, 2020).
321 Crow, *Four Hundred Million Customers*, 37.
322 On the development of the wool industry, see: Carles Brasó Broggi, *Trade and Technology Networks in the Chinese Textile Industry: Opening Up Before the Reform* (New York: Palgrave Macmillan: Palgrave Macmillan, 2015).

Company), hats (like the Shanghai Hat & Cap Manufacturing) and shoes (including Bata, Parisian/European Shoe Store and Tajima Brothers).

During and after the Sino-Japanese War, there was a shift in the popularity of different materials in the clothing industry. Cotton began to overshadow furs and satin, becoming a more prevalent choice for garments. Simultaneously, sewing equipment aimed to empower housewives and make them more independent in clothing production. Carl Crow's estimates revealed that approximately two billion needles were sold annually throughout the country. On average, each woman over the age of five consumed one needle per month, indicating the significant role of sewing in households.[323]

Despite these changes, the luxury industry remained resilient. In the shopping streets of the foreign concessions, jewellers and tailors continued to flourish despite the competition posed by large billboards advertising major industrial brands. The clothing market on the eve of the Communist revolution remained diverse, encompassing a range of materials such as silk, cotton, leather and calico. The rubber industry experienced notable success in outdoor advertising, capitalising on the newspaper readers' sensitivity to weather conditions. *Shenbao*'s advertisements for Red Star Rubber Factory highlighted the benefits of rubber as a new material, specifically in the production of raincoats and shoe soles.[324]

In the early stages, cosmetics were primarily marketed as remedies for skin problems, available in the form of powders and lotions. In the 1920s, however, beauty products began to gain autonomy and diversified in their offerings. They expanded beyond their curative function and took the form of scented soaps, ointments, eau de Cologne, beautifying pills, powders, vanishing creams and lipsticks. The emergence of the term *huazhuangpin* (cosmetics) in a 1934 advertisement for the Oriental Chemical Society marked the recognition of cosmetics as a distinct category.[325] It reflected the growing awareness that cosmetics had evolved into a specialised field, separate from medicinal products. Hygiene products also underwent a similar transition, moving away from being primarily associated with medicine and adopting cosmetic forms such as creams, perfumes and scented soaps. Toothpastes (yachi, yagao), initially marketed as powders (yafen), made their debut, of-

---

323 Crow, 20–21.
324 "Red Star Rubber Factory (Kedapai)", *SB*, January 1, 1949, 3. Regarding the history of the sensitivity to the weather see: Alain Corbin, *La pluie, le soleil, le vent: une histoire de la sensibilité au temps qu'il fait* (Paris: Aubier, 2013).
325 *SB*, January 5, 1934, 6. On terminology and the emergence of the cosmetics industry, see: Tzu-Hsuan Sung, "Cosmétiques, beauté et genre en Chine. Une analyse de la presse et des publicités (Fin des Qing – 1930)", (Doctoral dissertation, École Normale Supérieure de Lyon, 2015).

fering alternative options for dental care.[326] Despite the relatively low prevalence of hair growth among the Chinese population, Ever-Ready razor blades from Laboratoires Midy attempted to establish a market presence in *Shenbao*. Barbershops and beauty salons set up in foreign concessions, such as the Shanghai Toilet Club and Simon's Beauty Parlour, aimed to attract newspaper readers to their establishments.[327]

Conclusion

During the pre-World War I era, the advertising landscape in China was primarily shaped by the prominence of medications and cigarettes. Medicinal products were predominantly advertised in print media, while cigarettes enjoyed prominent displays in outdoor advertising. However, following the war, these two sectors encountered escalating competition from emerging consumer goods, leading to a transformation in the advertising landscape. The advent of food products, hygiene items and cosmetics posed a formidable challenge to the long-standing dominance of medications and cigarettes. This shift in the advertising landscape brought about significant changes in the nature and utilisation of these new consumer goods. Traditional remedies offered by dubious purveyors gradually yielded ground to pharmaceutical products, marking a notable transformation. While the panaceas inherited from Chinese pharmacopoeia endured, their essence underwent considerable modification with the introduction of pharmaceutical innovations. Concurrently, the realm of cosmetics, hygiene products and food items embarked on a trajectory towards independence from their conventional curative functions. These products began to be marketed not solely as remedies for health concerns but also as agents of beauty, hygiene and pleasure. This pivotal shift in their positioning allowed them to resonate with a broader consumer demographic beyond their therapeutic attributes, heralding a new era of appeal and consumer engagement.

Luxury goods, including spirits, confectionery, fur and jewellery, retained their position as niche products despite ongoing efforts to diversify the market. Throughout the Republican era, advertisers in the financial sector, such as banks, insurance companies and real estate agencies, recognised the significance of targeting the business community, which constituted a substantial segment of *Shenbao*'s reader-

---

326 Sodozont (Kangjian zhi jichu), *SB*, January 3, 1924, 16.
327 See for instance: Ever-Ready Blades (Changbei daopian), *SB*, January 5, 1934, 19. The comment on hairiness came from trade commissioner Sanger, who felt that razors had no chance of finding a market locally, because the Chinese were beardless and generally despised the barber profession. Sanger, 70.

ship. They strategically utilised advertising space in the newspaper to reach this influential audience. The intellectual fervour surrounding the May Fourth Movement and the New Culture Movement created a demand for educational and cultural products. Advertisements for schools and educational institutions proliferated catering to the readership of students and intellectuals actively involved in the intellectual and cultural discourse of the time. Additionally, the advertising landscape encompassed a focus on entertainment and social distinction. Abundant advertisements for gramophones, musical instruments, photo studios and projection devices catered to the desires of readers seeking entertainment and cultural enrichment. As the 1930s approached, advertisements for shows and films gained increasing prominence, mirroring the growing popularity of these emerging forms of entertainment.

This chapter provides a valuable initial exploration of the available goods during the pre-communist era, yet it is crucial to acknowledge its limitations in capturing the entirety of the material culture of the time. The selection of advertisements analysed in this chapter represents only a portion of the broader consumer landscape, influenced by factors such as the nature of the newspaper, its target readership and the strategies employed by advertisers. As a generalist daily focused on consumer goods and catering to the urban upper classes, *Shenbao* provides insights primarily into personal consumption rather than industrial or professional realms. Therefore, it may not fully encompass the diverse range of material culture and consumer behaviour during that period. It is important to recognise that other publications likely served different audiences and offered a wider array of products and services. Specialised journals, brochures and catalogues may have been more suitable platforms for promoting industrial or professional goods. These alternative sources could shed further light on the broader spectrum of material culture and consumption patterns. Furthermore, the advertisers featured in *Shenbao* were part of an elite group of rational entrepreneurs who recognised the value of advertising as a strategic promotional tool. Their financial capacity to afford advertising space in one of the most prestigious newspapers of the Republican era highlights their understanding of the impact and reach of this medium. Their presence in *Shenbao* signifies the significance of targeting the affluent readership and underscores the importance placed on advertising as a means of enhancing visibility and reputation.

Chapter 5
The Gradual Conversion of Advertisers

Who advertised in the *Shenbao*? Who were the advertisers and where did they come from? Was there stronger competition in certain sectors than in others? Did the advertisements reflect the emergence of national or regional specialisations? How did the political and economic context reshape the distribution of advertisers? Drawing on the same samples as in the previous chapter, this chapter analyses the profile of *Shenbao*'s advertisers between 1914 and 1949, with a particular focus on the industry structure and geographical origins of the advertisers. The two first sections compare the level of competition in each sector based on the number of advertisers within them. The next sections highlight the continuous growth of Chinese advertisers despite the rising American competition at the end of the First World War. The final section examines finer regional reconfigurations shaped by the political and economic context.

General but Uneven Growth

Towards the end of the 1920s, advertising professionals experienced satisfaction as a growing number of entrepreneurs embraced advertising as a means of promotion. The advertising population, which had been limited to a few advertisements before the First World War, had now expanded to several hundred by 1929. Furthermore, advertising expenditures showed a consistent increase year after year.[328] Nevertheless, this overall growth masked significant disparities. On the eve of the Sino-Japanese War, Dong Xianguang expressed his disappointment over the limited number of Chinese industrialists who still relied on advertising as a promotional tool.[329] Furthermore, the allocation of advertising budgets significantly varied depending on the media platforms and specific sectors of activity.

Uneven Appropriation Across Media

Between 1914 and 1949, the number of advertisers in *Shenbao* increased only slightly, from 240 to 270 per day on average. However, this relative stability con-

---

328 Carl Crow, *Four Hundred Million Customers*, 7–11, 202, 205; Bacon, 757, 765–766.
329 Tong, 30.

https://doi.org/10.1515/9783111390000-006

ceals important variations over time, and must be seen in relation to the size and total number of advertisements, as well as the volume of pages in the newspaper, indicating the editorial space available. The number of advertisers doubled between 1914 and 1924, rising from 242 to 450, but fell back to 298 in 1934 despite the increase in the number of pages (from 22 to 32). Until the Sino-Japanese War, the number of advertisers continued to decrease, though less sharply. It fell to 234 in 1941, but the drop was less dramatic than it might seem because the newspaper's volume had been divided by three during the war, reduced to 14 pages in 1941. The population of advertisers stabilised at around 272 in 1949, for the same amount of editorial space. In retrospect, the spectacular growth of the 1920s was mainly due to the general increase in the advertising population. The drastic fall in the 1930s should be seen in the context of the unequal occupation of space. Even as the newspaper doubled in size, certain advertisers such as Huamei Tobacco Company restricted the space available to their competitors by monopolising entire pages [Figure 16].[330] In the 1940s, the reduction in the number of pages and advertisements implied that the number of advertisers stabilised at around 250 per day. Towards the end of the period, there was a shift towards a more balanced allocation of advertising space, indicating a return to moderation and a more equitable sharing of space among advertisers.

The same advertisement also displayed several advertisers. This was the case with collaborative advertising and foreign exporters listing their local distributors. In the mid-1920s, the American watch manufacturer Heacock & Cheek Company held the exceptional record of 17 distributors in a single advertisement.[331] As seen in chapter 2, collaborative advertising (lianhe guanggao) brought together a number of entrepreneurs from the same industry or participating in a collective campaign. These ads were favoured by professional organisations, such as the Shanghai Electrical Industries Association [Figure 11], and by promoters of national products, such as the cigarette manufacturer Huamei Tobacco Company (Huamei yangongsi), which had joined forces with the nationalist China National Products Company (Zhongguo guohuo gongsi).[332]

In the streets of Shanghai, the appropriation of advertising space is more difficult to assess due to the incomplete nature of municipal records. As highlighted in the previous chapter, shop signs largely eluded municipal surveys. Permits issued for billboards rarely indicated the names of advertisers, who changed regularly. The Public Works Department was interested in the material structure of

---

330 Maskee (Huamei Tobacco Company), *SB*, January 5, 1934, 1.
331 *SB*, January 3, 1924, 20.
332 *SB*, January 5, 1934, 1, 7.

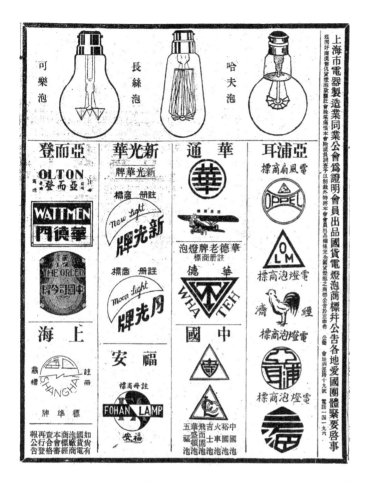

Figure 11: Advertisement for Shanghai Electrical Manufacturers' Association (Shanghaishi dianqi zhizaoye tongye gonghui), *Shenbao*, 5 January 1934, 7.

billboards rather than the nature of the product they displayed. Despite these gaps in the documentation, the number of advertisers in the International Settlement rose significantly, from around ten for three hundred billboards in 1914 to over a hundred for 1,250 billboards in 1943.[333]

---

333 General Buildings Advertisements – Taxation of Street Advertising. Measuring Advertising Space, Shanghai, May 20–July 14, 1914, SMA (SMC), U1-14-3267; Hoardings – Advertising Space. List of Hoardings, Shanghai, May 21–June 10, 1943, SMA (SMC), U1-14-3256.

Uneven Appropriation Across Sectors

The population of advertisers varied significantly across different sectors. In 1914, the medical sector had the highest number of advertisers in *Shenbao*, with 90 advertisers. By 1924, this number had increased to 120. However, it subsequently declined and stabilised at around 50 advertisers in the 1930s. The financial sector initially had fewer advertisers but followed a similar trend, increasing from 50 advertisers in 1914 to 80 in the 1920s, and then declining to around 30 by the end of the period. On the other hand, the leisure sector showed an opposite trajectory, with the number of advertisers initially decreasing but stabilising at around 60 in the 1920s. In the cultural industry, the population of advertisers remained relatively stable over the long term, averaging around 60. However, there were significant fluctuations, with a minimum of 25 advertisers in 1914 and a maximum of 85 in 1924. The remaining sectors, such as the food industry, had a relatively small number of advertisers throughout the period, typically fewer than ten. On the other hand, sectors like the culture of appearances, heavy industry, services and transport gradually opened up towards the end of the period, attracting more advertisers.

On the streets of Shanghai, all the sectors experienced a general increase in competition, albeit unevenly. In the entertainment sector, the number of advertisers tripled between 1914 and 1937, from five to around 15, and exceeded 100 in 1943. The pharmaceutical sector also recorded robust growth, reaching around a hundred advertisers in 1943. Next came industrial products (between ten and 15), the culture of appearances (around ten), food and cultural goods (around 20 each in 1943), finance (between eight and 15) and finally transport (between eight and ten). These different sectors were characterised by a modest but steady increase in the number of advertisers. The tobacco industry presents a more unusual profile. Highly selective during the two first decades (fewer than five advertisers), the tobacco sector opened up in the 1930s and its population doubled during the war (from five to ten).

Several factors explain these differences, starting with the relative age of the companies and the industry they represented. According to Carl Crow, the pioneers had the advantage of precedence, and it was difficult for newcomers to break into sectors where competition was fierce, particularly medicines, cigarettes and soaps. The degree of competition also depended on the political situation. Before the First World War, there were still few advertisers and competition was quite limited. European and Japanese companies dominated the press and the streets of Shanghai. From the war onwards, these pioneers faced increasing competition from American multinationals and Chinese industrialists, which grew stronger under the Nationalist regime. Although many vernacular companies were short-lived, the sinicisation movement gained momentum with the Sino-Japanese War, which wiped out most foreign advertisers.

Two Divergent Trajectories: Medicines and Cigarettes

A comparative study of cigarette and drug advertisers provides a more detailed picture of changes in supply during the Republican period. While these two sectors are well-studied in the scholarship, they are rarely examined from this angle. They were chosen here because, as shown in the previous chapter, they were the first to invest in advertising, and in different areas, making it possible to carry out both a global and longitudinal study. From the point of view of competition, these two sectors present contrasting situations. While the tobacco industry remained very closed until the 1930s, the medical sector was initially made up of a multitude of small advertisers. The situation was reversed after the First World War. As the tobacco empire gradually fragmented, the rise of the pharmaceutical industry made advertising less accessible to smaller drug manufacturers.

The Gradual Closure of the Medical Sector

If there was one sector in which market professionals dissuaded their clients from venturing, it was that of medicines. Apart from the comparative advantage of newcomers, vernacular medicine was reputedly impervious to foreign pharmacopoeia.[334] Furthermore, the medical sector was highly vulnerable to counterfeiting. Historian Sherman Cochran, for example, has devoted an in-depth study to the Rendan brand (人丹), a local counterfeit of the Japanese brand Jintan (仁丹), which became very popular with the rise of anti-Japanese sentiment during the Republic.[335] By 1914, competition was already stiff in *Shenbao*. Nearly 100 advertisers vied for the newspaper's pages, with great inequalities in terms of surface area occupied (from a tenth to half a page), positioning (beginning or middle of the newspaper, centre or margin of the page) and frequency of appearance (from one to five occurrences per day). Competition diminished over the following decades.

---

334 Crow, *Four Hundred Million Customers*, 202, 205.
335 Cochran Sherman, "Marketing Medicine and Advertising Dreams in China, 1900–1950", in *Becoming Chinese: Passages to Modernity and Beyond*, ed. Wen-Hsin Yeh (Berkeley: University of California Press, 2000), 62–97. For examples of Jintan advertisements, see for instance: *SB*, January 4, 1914, 9 (https://madspace.org/Press/?ID=110). For Rendan, see: *SB*, January 20, 1919, 1 (https://madspace.org/Press/?ID=443).

The number of advertisers halved in the 1930s and stabilised at around 40 by 1949. On the streets of Shanghai, developments are again more difficult to measure. The advertisers fell into four categories: a declining majority of local pharmacies (16 in 1930–1937, four in 1938–1943), a growing minority of national or multinational pharmaceutical firms (two in 1930–1937, 12 in 1938–1943), a handful of health establishments (Hung-Jao Sanatorium in 1938–1939) and independent practitioners (Dr. Kurt Noll and Dr. T. Murata in 1936).

The longevity of advertisers is another important factor in assessing their significance. Prior to the First World War, there was a diverse mix of local pharmacies alongside major European and Japanese pharmaceutical companies. In the 1920s, however, there was a complete turnover of small advertisers, and multinational corporations such as Chamberlain, Chesebrough and Himrod entered the market. Concurrently, Cantonese department stores like Sincere (Xianshi) and Wing On (Yong'an) emerged as preferred distributors for the flourishing Chinese pharmaceutical industry, with Sine Laboratory being a prominent representative of this sector. The sinicisation of the sector accelerated over the next two decades. While some pioneers remained (Bayer, Burroughs Wellcome, Foster-Mcclellan), many disappeared (Allen & Hansbury, Kofa, Himrod, Scott & Bowne), supplanted by American (Health Products Corporation) and Japanese manufacturers (Kimura Chemical Company, Takeda Chemical Company) and the new national champions of the chemical industry (New Asiatic Chemical Works, Min-Yee Chemical).

As a result of the disappearance of foreign advertisers, the pharmaceutical sector became entirely sinicised after the Second World War. *Shenbao*'s pages remained a dual space where small local advertisers (pharmacies and dispensaries, doctors, hospitals and clinics, Shanghai doctors' associations) coexisted with a new generation of vernacular companies, which sometimes concealed their origin by adopting foreign-sounding names, such as Strand (Xinguang yaochang) or Gianter Chemical Works (Zhengde yaochang).

Growing Competition in the Tobacco Industry

As shown in the previous chapter, cigarettes were a relatively recent product in the history of consumerism. Introduced into China at the turn of the twentieth century, cigarettes played a key role in the development of outdoor advertising.[336] In con-

---

[336] Sherman Cochran, *Big Business in China: Sino-Foreign Rivalry in the Cigarette Industry, 1890–1930* (Cambridge, Mass.; London: Harvard University Press, 1980); Carol Benedict, *Golden-Silk Smoke: A History of Tobacco in China, 1550–2010* (Berkeley: University of California Press, 2011).

trast to the pharmaceuticals industry, the number of cigarettes advertisers was initially very small. On average, *Shenbao* carried four advertisers a day for the whole of the period 1914–1949. This average ranged from a single advertiser in 1914 – British-American Tobacco Company (BAT) – to a maximum of seven in 1924 and 1949. From the outset, BAT reigned supreme over the newspapers and streets of Shanghai. Before the First World War, only one local company, Tsong Hsing Tobacco (Shanghai zhenshen yangongsi), competed for the pages of *Shenbao*.

After the war, the tobacco sector underwent a series of phases marked by increased competition and changing dynamics. The first phase occurred in the 1920s when Chinese advertisers capitalized on boycott campaigns sparked by the Treaty of Versailles (1919) and the May Thirtieth Incident (1925). During this period, Chinese advertisers made significant progress, overshadowing their foreign competitors. In 1924, the *Shenbao* featured only one American manufacturer (Williams Company) compared to six Chinese advertisers, including Nanyang Brothers, Wing Tai Vo (Yongtaihe) and Lixing. Encouraged by the Nationalist government and the National Products Movement, Chinese companies experienced continued growth throughout the Nanjing decade. However, they still faced competition from foreign companies such as Major Drapkin (British), indicating that the tobacco industry remained a battleground between domestic and international players.

The impact of the Sino-Japanese War was significant for both Chinese and foreign companies. By 1941, the *Shenbao* displayed only two Chinese names, Nanyang and Huacheng, indicating the decline of foreign companies in the cigarette industry, similar to the medical sector. Most foreign companies had disappeared before the restitution of the foreign concessions. By May 1943, only BAT and its British partner W.D. & H.O. Wills remained as foreign advertisers, competing against a dozen Chinese competitors, including the prominent Huacheng, Wing Tai Vo and Yee Tsoong (Yizhong yunxiao). After the war, a final renewal took place in the advertising landscape. With the withdrawal of foreigners, the vernacular tobacco industry experienced a new boom. Four new advertisers joined the previous generation: Dadongnan, Yuhua, Yili and the Shanghai Tobacco Manufacturers Association (Shanghaishi juanyan zaozhu huochai shangye tongye gonghui). By 1949, only the British company Major Drapkin persisted in both the newspaper and outdoor advertising spaces.

The cigarette sector in the advertising landscape exhibited significant inequalities, particularly until the Sino-Japanese War. Companies such as BAT and its Chinese competitors, including Huacheng and Huamei, dominated the front page of *Shenbao*, while smaller companies were relegated to less prominent positions in the newspaper. These inequalities were also evident in the physical spaces of Shanghai, with small local shops like Longyanhao and The Smoke Shop overshadowed by the oversized billboards of BAT, Wing Tai Vo and Yee Tsoong.

Furthermore, the lifespan of advertisers varied greatly, highlighting further disparities in the sector. Established companies such as BAT and Nanyang Brothers had a longer presence in advertising spaces, having been present in newspapers and on the streets of Shanghai before the First World War and continuing their advertising activities until 1941. On the other hand, many vernacular companies established during the Nanjing decade had a relatively short lifespan. National champions like Huacheng and Wing Tai Vo managed to survive the Sino-Japanese War, with some, like Yee Tsoong, persisting until the Communist revolution. Assessing the longevity of companies that emerged after the war became more challenging with the demise of *Shenbao* in May 1949.

Sitting on the U.S.-China Fence

If we take a broader perspective on the origin of advertisers, two significant trends become apparent. Chinese advertisers, who were already the majority in *Shenbao* in 1914, experienced significant growth and dominance in all sectors under the Nationalist regime, particularly after the Sino-Japanese War. On the other hand, American multinationals made remarkable progress at the end of the First World War, surpassing European and Japanese advertisers who had been present in the advertising landscape since the Opium Wars in the mid-nineteenth century. This shift in dominance reflects the changing dynamics of the global economic and political landscape during that period.

Until the end of the 1920s, the clientele of advertising agencies mainly consisted of foreign multinationals (see chapter 2). Nevertheless, Chinese advertisers accounted for more than half of advertising expenditures in China in 1929. Their aggregate expenditure amounted to six million Mexican dollars, of which nearly four million were spent on the press and just over one million on outdoor advertising.[337] This distribution may seem surprising in a political context that was *a priori* unfavourable to Chinese companies. Under the "unequal" treaties regime, foreign imports benefited from low import taxes in treaty ports such as Shanghai, Tianjin and Guangzhou.[338] Conversely, Chinese companies faced internal customs barriers, particularly the *lijin* system that hindered the circulation of goods between provinces, thereby maintaining the national market's fragmentation.[339]

---

337 Bacon, 754.
338 Sanger, 49.
339 Sanger, 49–50.

Although until the 1930s the agencies' clientele was predominantly of foreign origin, vernacular advertisers largely dominated in *Shenbao*. By 1914, more than three quarters were Chinese (177), compared with 20% Europeans (53) and less than 5% Japanese (nine). These figures, however, hide important variations across sectors and among advertisers. In the medical sector, local pharmacies dominated in terms of numbers but were outweighed by British (Burroughs, Wellcome, Foster-Mcclellan), American (Kofa, Scott & Bowne), Japanese (Morishita) and French (Laboratoires Gallia) multinationals. Before the war, only two vernacular companies, Anglo-Chinese Dispensary (Zhongying dayaofang) and International Dispensary (Wuzhou dayaofang), were able to compete with the foreign giants.[340] Chinese advertisers, on the opposite, reigned supreme over the written word. With the founding of a new educational system and the intellectual ferment that characterised the early days of the Republic, schools, newspapers, and publishers were stepping up their advertising.[341] Addressing a local, Chinese-speaking audience, cultural advertisers waged a fierce war, but did not face competition from foreign advertisers, who favoured the English-speaking readership of the *North China Daily News* and other foreign publications.

Foreign advertisers, on the other hand, dominated visual and audio culture, as well as office equipment, targeting the westernised elite and the emerging class of white-collar workers. Until Hollywood cinema was introduced at the end of the war, the entertainment sector was animated by local theatre groups (Xinmin xinjushe, Hankou dalüguan) and dancing halls (Dawutai, Danguidiyitai, Xingwutai). In the world of finance, most of the vernacular advertisers were small establishments that had nothing in common with the major representatives of British (London Insurance), Japanese (Yokohama Specie Bank) and Sino-American capitalism (China Mutual Life Insurance). While the British duo Moore & Company (Lüyishimo yanghang) and Noel Murray & Company (Ruihe yanghang) ruled over the auctions market, local lawyers were abundant in *Shenbao*. Chinese advertisers were lagging behind in all other sectors. Foreign competition was particularly fierce in the cosmetics and fashion industries. European (Rose, Downs & Thompson, Bucheister & Bidwell, Peninsular & Oriental) and Japanese companies (Onoda Cement, Nippon Yusen Kaisha) dominated heavy industry, transport and energy. Chinese advertising was notably weak in the three sectors that had been controlled by foreign

---

340 *SB*, January 7, 1914, 8 (Wuzhou dayaofang), 11 (Zhongying dayaofang).

341 Regarding educational reforms in Republican China, see: Marianne Bastid and Chien Chang, *Educational Reform in Early Twentieth Century China* (Ann Arbor: Center for Chinese Studies, University of Michigan, 1985); C.H. Becker, *Reorganisation of Education In China* (Paris: League of Nations' Institute of Intellectual Cooperation, 1932); Thomas D Curran, *Educational Reform in Republican China: The Failure of Educators to Create a Modern Nation* (Lewiston, NY: Mellen, 2005).

powers since the Opium Wars – mining, transport, and finance – which, during the Republic, became symbols of imperialism to be fought or emulated.[342]

During the 1920s, there were notable developments in the chemical and cosmetics industry, with companies like Yashua, Great China Dispensary and Guangsheng making significant strides with successful brands such as Three Stars, Tiger brand Snow Cream and Two Sisters. In the 1930s, Chinese advertisers further expanded their presence in various industries, capitalising on the development policies pursued by the Nationalist regime. They made significant advancements in sectors like cement, rubber, mechanical engineering and electrical engineering. The chemical industry also experienced growth with companies like Oriental Chemical Works, Sine Laboratory and Great Eastern Dispensary. In the entertainment sector, vernacular advertisers gained a strong foothold with the opening of new theatres and amusement parks. In the fashion industry, local boutiques like Dafeng rubbed shoulders with textile industry leaders such as Sanyou and Huaxin, supported by nationalist organizations like China National Products Company. In the finance and services sector, the number of banks, lawyers and real estate promoters increased, although they faced competition from American multinationals such as China Realty and Realty Investment Company.[343]

The Sino-Japanese War marked a period of uncertainty and transition between sinicisation and Americanisation. In 1941, Chinese advertisers experienced a decline in the pharmaceutical sector (15%), finance (14%) and the culture of appearances (5%). However, they maintained their presence in the entertainment sector (26%) and made progress in the cultural industry (32%). Conversely, they were noticeably absent in the transport sector (4%) and the food industry (1%). With the withdrawal of foreigners during the war, Chinese advertisers seized the opportunity to establish themselves across various sectors. By the eve of the Communist revolution, foreign presence had become exceptional. A few surviving American advertisers left their mark in tertiary services and long-distance transport.

---

342 Elisabeth Köll, *Railroads and the Transformation of China*, Hardcover (Harvard University Press, 2019); Anne Reinhardt, *Navigating Semi-Colonialism: Shipping, Sovereignty, and Nation-Building in China, 1860–1937* (Harvard University Press, 2018). See also: David Faure, éd., *China and Capitalism: Business Enterprise in Modern China* (Hong Kong: Division of Humanities, Hong Kong University of Science and Technology, 1994), 42–43; Gerth, *China Made*, 46–48.
343 Cheng, Linsun. *Banking in Modern China: Entrepreneurs, Enterprises, and the Development of Chinese Banks, 1897–1937* (Cambridge, Cambridge University Press, 2002).

Multinational Advertising Space

Despite imports from all countries being subject to the same tax rate under the "unequal treaty" regime, the advertising spaces in *Shenbao* reveal significant inequalities between foreign advertisers and a notable decline in their diversity during the Republican period [Figure 12].[344]

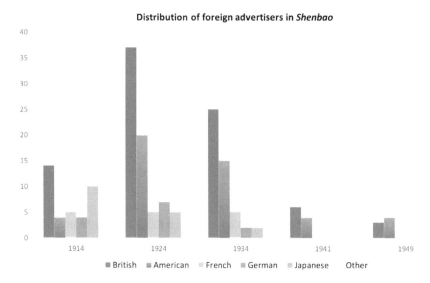

Figure 12: Distribution of advertisers by geographical origin (excluding Chinese advertisers) in *Shenbao*, based on the following samples: January 7, 1914, January 3, 1924, January 5, 1934, February 1, 1941, January 1, 1949.

The Decline of Japanese and German Advertisers

In the pre-World War I era, the advertising landscape in *Shenbao* encompassed a diverse range of nationalities, including German, British, French, Japanese, Dutch and North American. At that time, Japanese advertisers held a significant presence, accounting for 20% of the total advertisers in 1914. However, their numbers gradually declined in the following decades, with a halving of Japanese advertisers during the 1920s and their complete disappearance by the 1930s. In contrast, the withdrawal of German advertisers was relatively slower and occurred at a later stage. Throughout the 1910s and into the 1920s, German advertisers maintained a

---

344 All importers paid a 5% tax *ad valorem*, regardless of their origin. Sanger, 49.

consistent presence, with their numbers ranging between four and seven. However, the 1930s witnessed a sharp decline in German advertisers, ultimately leading to their complete disappearance from *Shenbao*'s advertising spaces.

The withdrawal of both Japanese and German advertisers can be attributed to the impact of successive wars and the rise of nationalism. In 1917, the Chinese government imposed a ban on German advertisements in newspapers, in response to the hostilities of World War I. Similarly, following the disappointment of the Treaty of Versailles in 1919, Chinese newspapers, including *Shenbao*, decided to ban Japanese advertisers.[345] However, these measures were temporary and implemented unevenly across different newspapers. Navigating the delicate balance between nationalism and economic rationality, *Shenbao* continued to publish advertisements by German and Japanese companies until the outbreak of the Second World War.

The retreat of German and Japanese advertisers in *Shenbao* created opportunities for other nationalities, particularly the British and Americans, to establish a stronger presence in the advertising landscape. By 1914, the British already held a dominant position in *Shenbao*, with 14 different advertisers accounting for nearly 35% of foreign advertising. This dominance can be attributed to the long-standing British presence in China since the early nineteenth century and the influence of its expansive colonial empire. Between 1914 and 1924, the British presence in *Shenbao* doubled, with the number of British advertisers rising from 14 to 37, representing 50% of foreign advertisers. This trend continued in the 1930s, with British advertising expanding to encompass 60% of the foreign advertising space. However, the number of different British advertisers decreased to six during this period, as they now had to share the advertising landscape with American competitors who represented a slightly smaller minority with four advertisers, or 40% of the foreign advertising presence.

From 1941 onwards, the composition of foreign advertisers in *Shenbao* further shifted. Three British companies (30%) remained, competing with four American advertisers (40%), as well as advertisers representing European minorities such as Bata shoes from Czechoslovakia, Lazaro pianos from Portugal, Norwegian shipping (Norway Steamship) and Dutch shipping (Java-China-Japan Lijn). French advertising remained relatively discreet, with an average presence of five advertisers per day until the Sino-Japanese War, accounting for around 10% of foreign advertising. Collectively, other European nationalities such as Dutch, Italian, Norwegian, Russian and Swedish never exceeded 5% of advertisements.

---

345 Sanger, 58. See also: Gerth, *China Made*, 167.

Contested Americanisation

In 1914, American advertisers were a minority, but they made a remarkable breakthrough after the war, increasing from four (10%) to twenty advertisers (30%) by the 1930s. With the disappearance of European minorities in the 1940s, they found themselves in a head-to-head competition with British advertisers. Although they remained slightly outnumbered in 1941 (four versus six), the Second World War shifted the balance of power in their favour and allowed them to assert dominance until the Communist revolution. However, their influence varied across different sectors. While they held sway in the food and automotive industries, British advertisers continued to dominate the pharmaceutical and financial sectors.

The pharmaceutical industry provides a noteworthy illustration of the process of Americanisation at play in the Chinese press. In 1914, the sector was characterized by a diverse representation of more than six nationalities. Leading the way were British multinationals (Yinshang anchang yanghang, Yingguo luoyishengzong yaoju), American companies (Kofa, Scott & Bowne), and Dutch enterprises (Holland China Handels, Llewellyn), each accounting for three advertisers (10%). Following closely were Japanese (Jingdu tianbaozhai, Rixin dayaofang), Germans (Carlowitz, Schmidt), and French (Chapoteaut/Gallia, Orimault), each with two advertisers. The reduction in the number of nationalities occurred gradually through successive withdrawals. The Dutch companies faded away in the 1920s, followed by the Germans and Japanese in the 1930s. By the mid-1920s, the sector was dominated by Americans (12 advertisers, comprising 35%) (Himrod, Muller, Phipps, Chesebrough), closely pursued by the British (nine advertisers, representing 25%) (Brunner Mond, De Witt), Japanese (five advertisers, constituting 15%), and then Germans (Berlin Medical Imports) and French (Etablissements Byla) (three advertisers each, accounting for 8% each). According to Carl Crow's estimations, this distribution roughly corresponded to pharmaceutical sales figures.[346] By the mid-1930s, only three nationalities remained in contention: the British (17 advertisements, making up 70% of medical advertisements), Americans (Allen & Hanbury's, Lambert Pharmacal) (five advertisers, totalling 20%), and the French (Laboratoires Midy, Louis Rondon) (three advertisers, contributing 10%). During the war, the British continued to lead the race with six advertisers (65%) (including Burroughs Wellcome and De Witt) against three Americans (35%) (including Health Products Corporation and Foster-Mcclellan). On the eve of the

---

346 Crow, *Four Hundred Million Customers*, 204–205.

Communist revolution, foreigners had completely withdrawn from the sector, allowing the Chinese industry to take over.

The British continued to maintain their dominance in the financial sector, despite the evolving landscape of competition. Up until the 1920s, the sector was unevenly divided between the British (China Mutual Life, London Insurance) (85%) and the Japanese (Yokohama Specie Bank) (15%). Russian (Russo-Asiatic Bank) and French banks (Banque de l'Indo-Chine) entered the scene in the 1920s, but the British retained their advantage in the banking sector (Hong Kong Shanghai Banking Corporation, Chartered Bank of India, Australia, and China), insurance (Yorkshire Fire & Life Insurance), and auctions (Moore, Noël Murray). During the 1930s, the emergence of new services such as savings and real estate favoured Americanisation at the expense of national diversity. The British remained the majority in the banking sector (65%), but the Americans (35%) established themselves in the real estate sector (China Realty, Realty Investment). Financial advertising faced challenges during the Sino-Japanese War. In 1949, only one American insurance company, Asia American Insurance, remained in *Shenbao*.

The sector of long-distance transport in *Shenbao* provided a platform for greater diversity among advertisers, particularly in the realm of steamship lines. Depending on their origin and destination, different nationalities had the opportunity to showcase their services and products. Prior to the First World War, the dominance of the British (Peninsular & Oriental) and Japanese (Nippon Yusen Kaisha) steamship lines in the sector was notable. The long-standing British presence on the seas and China's geographical proximity to Japan contributed to their dominance. After the war, however, the Japanese steamship lines disappeared from the advertising landscape, making way for British (China Mutual Steam Navigation), American (Pacific Mail Steamship) and Swedish (Moller) shipowners who took control of the lines to Northern Europe.

During the Sino-Japanese War, the advertising activities of shipping companies came to a halt. Following the withdrawal of British shipowners during the war, the sector experienced a resurgence with the emergence of American lines (American President Lines, Everett Steamship, Columbia Pacific) that largely surpassed their Dutch (Java-China-Japan Lijn), Norwegian (Norway Steamship) and Taiwanese (Taiwan Navigation) counterparts in terms of competition and presence in advertising. While foreign airlines were well represented in English-language newspapers, they notably lacked a presence in *Shenbao*. Instead, the China National Aviation Corporation (Zhongguo hangkong gongsi) held a dominant position in the advertising spaces of *Shenbao*, establishing its supremacy in the field of aviation services in China.

Circulations and Comparison with the Foreign Press

In contrast to *Shenbao*, the *North China Daily News* (NCDN) maintained a greater level of national diversity in its advertising composition throughout the period. Interestingly, the British presence was in the minority, accounting for an average of 10% of advertisers and reaching a maximum of one-third of the total. Chinese advertisers also held a marginal position, with an average representation of 10% and a maximum of three advertisers in 1949. On the other hand, the dominance of American advertisers prevailed in the *NCDN* until the Sino-Japanese War, with an average representation of 40%. However, they disappeared from the advertising landscape before the Communist revolution. As the boycotts imposed during the war did not extend to the foreign press, German and Japanese advertisers continued to appear in *NCDN* until the end of the period. These two nationalities experienced a remarkable peak in the 1920s and 1930s, each accounting for 10–15% of advertisers. French advertising held a relatively strong position in the British newspaper, representing an average of 20% of advertisers compared to 10% in *Shenbao*. French companies, with less focus on Chinese-speaking consumers, targeted a niche market consisting of expatriates and Chinese elites educated abroad.

The preference of foreign advertisers for the British newspaper and Chinese advertisers for *Shenbao* was evident, with only a few exceptions of advertisers appearing in both publications. This division reflected both the language barriers faced by advertisers and the differences in consumption practices among readers. Between 1934 and 1941, the two newspapers became more similar in content and advertisers, but they drifted apart again after the Sino-Japanese War. As Barbara Mittler's research has highlighted, circulations between the two newspapers were generally asymmetrical.[347] Foreign advertisers showed a greater interest in reaching readers of the Chinese press compared to the level of interest shown by Chinese advertisers in the English-language press. Among the advertisers that appeared in both newspapers, they were mainly multinational companies that had established a presence in China in the latter half of the nineteenth century, such as British-American Tobacco, Bayer and the Standard Oil Company. The fate of Japanese advertisers in the two newspapers depended on their seniority. Pioneering Japanese companies like the manufacturer of Jintan, Morishita, disappeared entirely from *Shenbao* after the First World War. However, the new generation of companies

---

347 Barbara Mittler, "Imagined Communities Divided: Reading Visual Regimes in Shanghai's Newspaper Advertising (1860s–1910s)", in *Visualising China, 1845–1965: Moving and Still Images in Historical Narratives*, ed. Christian Henriot and Wen-hsin Yeh (Leiden: Brill, 2013), 267–378.

founded in the 1930s, such as Wakamoto, managed to secure advertising space in the British daily during the Sino-Japanese War.[348]

Reshaping Local Identities

As noted by historian Karl Gerth, the notion of the "nationality" of products is a complex discursive construct that became institutionalised during the nationalist regime but remained challenging to define throughout the Republican period.[349] In *Shenbao*, there was no systematic emphasis on the national origin of products in advertising. Chinese advertisers only highlighted their national identity during specific historical moments, such as the officially proclaimed National Products Year in 1934 and as part of the broader National Products Movement (guohuo yundong). Moreover, the affirmation of nationalism did not result in the disappearance of local and regional specialties in advertising. Local and regional products continued to be promoted alongside national products, reflecting the diverse cultural and economic landscape of China.

Prior to the First World War, *Shenbao*'s advertising primarily focused on Shanghai and the Yangtze Valley region. Outside of Shanghai, Cantonese advertisers played a significant role in sectors such as services (banks, pharmacies) and distribution (department stores, grocery stores). After the war, there was an expansion of the geographical scope of advertisers, with an increase in the number of advertisers from outside Shanghai. *Shenbao* began featuring advertisements for businesses such as a wool merchant in Nanjing, several banks in Tianjin and pharmacies based in Hankou and Hangzhou. During the 1930s, publishing companies from outside Shanghai also emerged as strong competitors to the dominant Shanghai publishers. Companies like Modern Publishing House in Guangzhou, Zhengzhong Publishing House in Nanjing, Baicheng Publishing House in Tianjin and Zhuzhe Bookstore in Beijing posed serious competition to publishers in Shanghai such as Commercial Press, Oriental Press and China Publishing House. This expansion of advertisers to the north and south of the country indicated a process of economic integration and the growing readership of the newspaper in various directions.

This expansion, however, was primarily limited to major treaty ports such as Guangzhou, Tianjin and Hankou, as well as provincial capitals like Beijing and Hangzhou. Inland rural provinces, except for isolated cases such as a mining com-

---

348 Wakamoto Yeast Tablets, *North China Daily News*, February 2, 1941, 7.
349 Gerth, *China Made*, 185–202.

pany in Luanzhou (Hebei) and a textile factory in Changsha (Hunan), remained largely out of reach. The limited presence in these outlying regions can be attributed to factors such as distance, communication difficulties and the predominant focus on rural or heavy industrial activities that were not inclined towards advertising. The period of geographical expansion and increased presence of non-Shanghai advertisers in *Shenbao* was relatively short-lived. The outbreak of the Sino-Japanese War (1937–1945) followed by the civil war (1945–1949) disrupted territorial unity and had a significant impact on advertising patterns. As a result, geographical proximity to Shanghai once again became the prevailing norm. With the exception of larger national and multinational companies, the number of advertisers from outside Shanghai in *Shenbao* decreased as one moved further away from the metropolis. The turbulent events and territorial conflicts of the time limited the reach of advertisers, and the focus returned to the immediate vicinity of Shanghai.

Conclusion

The Republican era witnessed a notable growth in the significance of advertising, as an increasing number of advertisers recognised its importance and embraced its potential. This led to heightened competition across various sectors, both in the print media and in the bustling streets of Shanghai. Industries such as tobacco, pharmaceuticals, finance and entertainment experienced particularly intense competition.

The origin of advertisers underwent two significant shifts during this period. Initially, local Chinese advertisers held a dominant position, consistently contributing to the advertising landscape of the newspaper. After the conclusion of the First World War, notable figures from the national industry began to emerge and join the ranks of these local advertisers. Additionally, American multinational corporations emerged as influential players, overshadowing the earlier European and Japanese pioneers who had held sway since the era of the "unequal treaties". Notably, British companies continued to maintain a strong presence in the finance and services sectors. Chinese advertisers, spurred on by the nationalist regime, made continuous progress and eventually established their presence across all sectors during the Sino-Japanese War. Despite the rise of nationalism and anti-American sentiment during the subsequent civil war (1945–1949), American influence continued to prevail until the Communist revolution, as Chinese advertisers embraced the style and visual codes of American brands.

Chapter 6
The Invention of Branding

> Not only do Chinese have very decided ideas as to what they like and dislike, but once they have become accustomed to a certain brand, no matter whether it be cigarettes, soap or tooth paste, they are the world's most loyal consumers, and will support a brand with a degree of unanimity and faithfulness which should bring tears of joy to the eyes of the manufacturer.[350]

In the opening lines of his autobiographical account, Carl Crow commends the unwavering loyalty displayed by the Chinese people towards the brands that had earned their trust – an aspiration coveted by advertisers worldwide. The historical roots of this profound attachment, however, warrant a closer examination. As previous scholarship has demonstrated, commercial brands are a relatively recent social construct in the history of marketing and consumption.[351] Against this backdrop, the primary objective of this chapter is to meticulously trace the formation and evolution of commercial brands within the context of Republican China, drawing insights from the advertisements published in the *Shenbao*. By delving into the varied conceptions expounded in professional literature, the first part analyses the ways in which these brands were interwoven within the pages of the Chinese newspaper from 1914 to 1949. The second section highlights their uneven progression across different sectors and the fluctuations in their availability over time. The final part seeks to understand how brands gave rise to new categories of consumers, particularly women and children.

From Chops to Trademarks

During the Republican era, some observers drew a direct connection between modern trademarks and the traditional use of chops in China. Chops were seals that had been employed since ancient times to identify goods and their manufacturers. In the nineteenth century, the term "chop" specifically referred to the copper roll

---

350 Carl Crow, *Four Hundred Million Customers*, 3.

351 Franck Cochoy, *Une histoire du marketing: discipliner l'économie de marché* (Paris: La Découverte, 1999); Michel Callon, Yuval Millo and Fabian Muniesa, *Market Devices* (Malden, Mass.: Blackwell, 2008); Frank Trentmann, *The Empire of Things: How We Became a World of Consumers, from the Fifteenth Century to the Twenty-First* (2016); Hartmut Berghoff, Philip Scranton and Uwe Spiekermann, *The Rise of Marketing and Market Research* (New York: Palgrave Macmillan, 2011).

https://doi.org/10.1515/9783111390000-007

used to authenticate cotton bales. At the turn of the twentieth century, its usage extended beyond commercial contexts, encompassing any element, signature, or seal employed to validate an object or document.[352] In the 1920s, the notion of chops acquired a more antiquated connotation. Legal professionals regarded it as a local idiosyncrasy, linking it to the ancestral Chinese reverence for products with a well-established reputation. Market professionals, however, criticised this genealogy and sought to dispel its picturesque associations. For trade commissioner J. Sanger, for example, chops were simply the Chinese equivalent of Western trademarks, which had two main functions: to protect the manufacturer from fraudulent imitations and to guarantee the consumer the consistent quality of the product.[353]

Following the Opium Wars, the concept of trademark was generally applied to foreign imports. It was translated as *shangbiao* in the vernacular language and came into widespread use during the Republic. In the 1920s, it was mainly associated with industrial property issues and the risk of counterfeiting. While the culture of imitation had not always been viewed negatively, under the "unequal" treaties regime it became a thorny issue in trade policy. After the First World War, many voices were raised to decry the impunity enjoyed by counterfeiters. In 1919, only Chinese-language literary works were officially protected against intellectual property infringement.[354] Passed in 1923, the first trademark law attracted more than 25,000 applications in its first year. However, political instability, the relative weakness of the central state and the multiplicity of legal systems in the treaty ports complicated its application and made the law largely ineffective.[355]

With these loopholes in the legal system, advertising became an indispensable resource for manufacturers constantly on the lookout for fraud. British-American Tobacco was among the first to use the press to alert consumers and appeal to their vigilance. One of its advertisements entitled "Unfair trading" declared:

---

352 Frank Dikötter, *Exotic Commodities: Modern Objects and Everyday Life in China* (New York: Columbia University Press, 2006), 45.
353 Sanger, 66.
354 William P Alford, *To Steal a Book Is an Elegant Offense: Intellectual Property Law in Chinese Civilization* (Stanford: Stanford University Press, 1995), 53. On intellectual property issues, see: Fei-Hsien Wang, *Pirates and Publishers: A Social History of Copyright in Modern China*, Histories of Economic Life (Princeton, New Jersey: Princeton University Press, 2019).
355 Dikötter, *Exotic Commodities*, 36–45. Kennett, "Trademarks in China", *North China Herald*, August 2, 1919. Norwood Allman, *Handbook on the Protection of Trade-Marks, Patents, Copyrights, and Trade-Names in China* (Shanghai: Kelly & Walsh, Ltd., 1924). Regarding the Trademark law of 1923, see: Zuo Xuchu, *Zhongguo jindai shangbiao jianshi* (A brief history of modern trademarks in China) (Shanghai: Xuelin chubanshe, 2003), 51–56. Zuo considers this law as a manifestation of Western imperialism in China.

We find that there have been put upon the market in China various soaps and other toilet articles packed in packets which are close imitations of the packets in which some of our well-known brands of cigarettes are sold. The manufacturers of these toilet articles undoubtedly seek by this to obtain the benefit of our advertising and to mislead the public to suppose that we have some connection with their productions. We therefore publish here full-color reproductions of certain of our packages which have been imitated, together with representations of the packings of the toilet articles above referred to, and we warn the public that such toilet articles are not manufactured by us and that we have nothing to do with them. (Signed) British-American Tobacco Co. (China), Ltd.[356]

The advertisement prominently showcased a vivid colour illustration that strikingly juxtaposed the original product with its counterfeit counterpart, purposefully highlighting their differences. Considering that colour printing was a rare and costly technique at the time, the deliberate use of colour in the illustration was a notable choice, which underscored the company's serious concern and its commitment to tackling the issue of counterfeiting.

Imitations not only affected the materiality of products, but also the semantics of brands. In a predominantly Chinese-speaking environment, the most famous foreign brands were prime targets. A simple letter was sometimes enough to distinguish the original from the copy. For example, the American cosmetics brand "Pond" became "Rond" by the discreet addition of a pencil stroke. The fraud was invisible to the uneducated, hurried or simply distracted eye.[357] The lack of legal protection therefore prompted professionals to rethink the nature and function of trademarks. From the 1920s onwards, advertising began to supplement traditional trademarks with a new type of cultural branding. Designated by the Chinese character *pai* or its derivatives (laopai, paizi, paihao), these new kinds of brands detached the product from its manufacturer and involved consumers more directly in the fight against fraud.

Semantics of Brands in *Shenbao*

In the early years of the Republic, the notion of trademark was little used in *Shenbao*. In 1914, the term *shangbiao* essentially appeared on medical advertisements warning of cases of counterfeiting. Until the mid-1920s, it was used mainly for pharmaceutical and food products, such as Stearns Headache Wafers, Bournville Cocoa and Klim Milk. In the case of food products, the addition of a name served to blur their medical connotations and enhance their taste content. Prior to the

---

356 Sanger, 66–67.
357 Sanger, 66–67.

First World War, the Chinese character *pai* was primarily employed to caution against fraudulent imitations, as exemplified in the expression *maopai* (counterfeit goods). It also appeared in auction advertisements and in the term *zhaopai*, referring to the signs of warehouses and trading houses. In these advertisements, a tone of politeness and gentleness was typically employed, inviting customers to personally inspect the goods and verify their authenticity (renming paihao, renming zhaopai).[358] By the end of the war, however, a significant shift occurred. The character *pai* began to be associated with consumer goods, accompanied by a distinctive visual representation and a proper name.

Under the Nationalist regime, there was a notable shift in the advertising landscape of the *Shenbao*, with foreign brands gradually receding and making way for new vernacular brands. In the realm of pharmaceutical advertisements, the terms *pai* and *shangbiao* were used interchangeably, at times even appearing side by side within the same advertisement. In a broader context, the character *pai* was predominantly associated with luxury products such as cosmetics, cigarettes and automobiles. On the other hand, the term *shangbiao* frequently appeared in the expression *zhuce shangbiao* (registered trademark), especially in relation to the introduction of new national certifications. An illustrative example can be seen in a 1934 advertisement for the Shanghai Electrical Manufacturers' Association (Shanghaishi dianqi zhizaoye tongyegonghui), which proudly displayed the term to emphasise that its products adhered to national standards [Figure 11].[359]

During the Sino-Japanese War, the usage of the phrase *zhuce shangbiao* extended beyond its previous applications and encompassed cigarettes (such as Hanyantong) and cultural objects (like Yada Radio). Concurrently, the terms *pai* and *shangbiao* became closely associated with legal standards and fraud trials, highlighting their relevance in matters of legal compliance and authenticity verification. In the post-war era, there were contrasting developments in terminology. The expression *shangbiao* gradually fell out of use, while the traditional term *pai* experienced a revival. Notably, the application of the character *pai* became more diverse, extending to encompass medicines, cigarettes, cosmetics and fashion accessories. In contrast, the term *shangbiao* was primarily limited to cultural goods and heavy industry, indicating a more restricted scope of usage within those specific sectors.

---

358 *SB*, January 7, 1914, 3, 4, 5. Regarding the use of forms of politeness in *Shanghai Xinbao* advertising in the last decades of the nineteenth century, see: Barbara Mittler, "Imagined Communities Divided: Reading Visual Regimes in Shanghai's Newspaper Advertising (1860s–1910s)", in *Visualising China, 1845–1965: Moving and Still Images in Historical Narratives*, ed. Christian Henriot and Wen-hsin Yeh (Leiden: Brill, 2013), 267–378.
359 Shanghaishi dianqi zhizaoye tongye gonghui, *SB*, January 5, 1934, 7.

Uneven Progress Across Sectors

During the 1920s, the emergence of cultural brands had a varying impact on different products and advertisers. The influence of this process was not uniform across all sectors. In highly competitive industries like pharmaceuticals, manufacturers employed branding techniques to differentiate their products from competitors and protect against counterfeiting. In sectors that were still developing, such as cigarettes and the food industry, brands played a pivotal role in introducing new products to the market. Brands were used as a means to reshape consumer habits, introduce innovative offerings and attract new customers. This was particularly evident in the dairy products and soft drinks segments, where brands were utilised to win over consumers who were unfamiliar with these products or hesitant to try them. Branding in these sectors served as a catalyst for consumer acceptance and adoption of new products.

Prior to the First World War, the use of distinctive names and logos in advertisements was primarily seen in the domains of medicines (56%), alcohol, cigarettes, industry (such as Portland Dragon cement and Liga Tiger tyres), hygiene products (like Sanmeipa shampoo and Three Beauties) and the culture of appearances exemplified by Pegasus hats (Feima laopai) and Feiying weaving machines. These sectors were at the forefront of adopting branding strategies to establish their unique identities. In the 1920s, branding efforts persisted in luxury spirits (like Peter Dawson Whisky), cigarettes (such as Aiguo and Victory), hygiene products (like Tiger toothpaste) and the culture of appearances. Additionally, brands expanded into new sectors like the food industry (with brands like Bovril and thermos Isola [Figure 15]) and electrical appliances (such as Philips light bulbs and sewing machines). Notably, financial services, transport and entertainment industries remained relatively immune to extensive branding practices during this period. Moving into the following decade, brands continued to dominate the pharmaceutical, electrical appliances, cigarette and alcohol industries. Weekly supplements served as platforms to showcase new brands emerging in the automobile sector (including Fiat, Ford and Breda) and the petroleum industry (with brands like Socony, Shell and Texaco). These sectors embraced branding as a means to differentiate themselves and attract consumer attention.[360] Logotypes also began to appear on cultural objects such as Parker pens, Radio Corporation of America (RCA Victor) records and Pathe-Orient projection equipment.

---

360 In the 1920s–1930s, *Shenbao* published an automobile supplement every Saturday and then every Monday. This study is based on the automobile supplements of January 5, 1924 and January 3, 1934.

The Sino-Japanese War was characterised by contrasting developments. Key sectors like the pharmaceutical industry, culture of appearances, cigarette manufacturers and the food industry maintained their prominence in the world of brands. These sectors continued to prioritise branding strategies to effectively market their products. In contrast, branded alcoholic beverages were less prevalent during this period. Meanwhile, the sector of cultural goods, along with services and entertainment, remained relatively untouched by extensive branding practices. On the eve of the Communist revolution, shoe brands like Keds and Three Bells, as well as hygiene products such as 999 bathroom linen and Heiren toothpaste, dominated the branding landscape. Meanwhile, emerging sectors including school equipment, musical instruments and airlines began to embrace branding practice to establish their presence in the market and attract consumers. On the other hand, food and pharmaceutical products took on a more subdued approach to branding during this time.

Variations in Brand Offering

The brand offerings in various sectors exhibited significant variations over time, with pioneers in advertising, pharmaceuticals and cigarettes providing notable examples of these changes. The 1930s emerged as a particularly productive decade for both sectors, although their situations diverged after the Sino-Japanese War. In the pharmaceutical sector, the number of medical brands experienced a significant increase between 1914 and 1934, more than tripling from around 30 to over 80 brands. Towards the end of the period, however, the number of medical brands began to decline, with fewer than 60 brands in 1941 and barely 20 in 1949. Cigarettes, on the other hand, witnessed a proliferation of brands during the Republican period. Historian Carol Benedict estimates that several thousand cigarette brands were in circulation during this time.[361] In the pages of the *Shenbao*, an average of seven different cigarette brands were displayed daily, with a minimum of three in 1914 and 1941, and a maximum of 11 in 1934 and 1949. While the brand offering experienced a period of intense creativity until the 1930s, it collapsed during the war, but rebounded to pre-war levels prior to the Communist revolution.

The range of brands also varied from company to company. In the pharmaceutical industry, only a minority of multinational companies were able to offer more than two brands a day. Prior to the First World War, the British firm Burroughs, Wellcome & Company held the record with five concurrent brands, in-

---

361 Benedict, 158.

cluding Kepler, Hazeline Frost, Tabloid and Bivo. Under the Nationalist regime, the Chinese company New Asiatic Chemical Works offered up to six different brands. Generally, the vernacular industry giants proved to be more productive in terms of brand offerings compared to foreign multinationals. Companies such as International Dispensary (Wuzhou dayaofang) and Great China Dispensary (Zhongxi dayaofang) each offered over ten brands throughout the entire period. While the proliferation of medical brands helped break away from the era of panaceas, featuring too many brands under a single company could potentially weaken the consistency of its image. Some manufacturers, such as Bovril or Scott & Bowne, adopted the opposite strategy by promoting a single brand consistently throughout the period. In the tobacco industry, only a few manufacturers had the capacity to offer more than two brands simultaneously. British-American Tobacco (BAT) stood out as an exceptional case, with more than eight different brands identified in the *Shenbao* samples analysed. Notably, Three Castles, Hatamen, and Ruby Queen were among the most frequently featured brands.

The longevity of brands exhibited significant variation within different sectors. In the pharmaceutical industry, Scott's Emulsion was the only brand in the samples analysed that persisted throughout the entire period. Introduced prior to the First World War, brands like Doan's Backache & Kidney Pills, Kepler and Waterbury Cod Liver Oil managed to survive until the Sino-Japanese War. The majority of brands had relatively short lifespans. Many brands failed to gain traction in the market, while others barely survived for a single advertising campaign. Similarly, in the tobacco industry, only a few names displayed longevity. Three brands – Pirate, Ruby Queen and The Rat – remained in circulation for over 20 years (1924–1949), while My Dear and Pyramid endured for more than 15 years (1934–1949).

Comparison with the Foreign Press

Due to the niche readership and declining popularity of the foreign press during the Sino-Japanese War, the range of brands featured in the *North China Daily News* (NCDN) was not as extensive as that of *Shenbao*, and it experienced a significant reduction towards the end of the period. The pharmaceutical offerings in the *NCDN* decreased from around 50 brands before the First World War to only 15 in 1941, eventually completely drying up by 1949. In contrast, *Shenbao* showcased almost a hundred brands in 1934 and still featured around 20 brands in 1949. Similarly, in the tobacco industry, the brands spectrum in the British newspaper declined from seven to just one brand between 1914 and 1949, while the range in *Shenbao* increased from three to 12 brands during the same period.

Moreover, the brands offered in each newspaper could differ for the same product category or advertiser. In the pharmaceutical sector, products from Foster McClellan (American) and International Dispensary (Wuzhou dayaofang) were exclusively featured in *Shenbao*, while brands like Cuticura and Germol (British) only appeared in the British newspaper. In the cigarette sector, British-American Tobacco (BAT) had a marked presence in both newspapers but did not consistently feature the same brands. While Three Castles in 1914 and Capstan in 1924 were common to both newspapers, Hatamen and Ruby Queen were exclusively offered to *Shenbao* readers, whereas Clipper and Gold Flake were reserved for the British newspaper. While these differences reflected advertisers' efforts to adapt to the cultural preferences of readers, they also reinforced market compartmentalisation.

Brand Differentiation and Market Segmentation

Advertisers employed various criteria to differentiate brands, and the nature of the product itself played a crucial role in this process. In the pharmaceutical sector, brand names often explicitly stated the nature of the ailments and affected organs they targeted. Examples such as De Witt Backache & Kidney Pills, Doan Ointment and Kepler Cod Liver Oil clearly indicated their intended uses. Some advertisers specialised in specific illnesses, while others aimed to address a broader range of ailments and target a wider patient base. A notable example of diversification is seen in the American company Foster-McClellan, which, over its 30-year presence in China, offered over seven different brands, each focusing on a different organ or condition. For instance, Doan's Backache & Kidney Pills targeted back pain, Doan's Anti-Constipation Pills addressed intestinal disorders, Doan Ointment treated skin issues, an analgesic catered to athletes, and two other brands targeted lung diseases (Dou'an shibufei shengyao) and cough (Dou'an shikesou yaopian). The recurring motif of the fictional doctor's name "Doan" helped maintain brand identity and visibility across its multiple variations. In the realm of cigarettes, the origin of the tobacco played a significant role in brand differentiation, leveraging both the objective qualities of the tobacco and the subjective perceptions associated with it by smokers. Carl Crow noted that the Chinese favoured Virginia raw tobacco while being less fond of aromatic cigarettes like Camels, Chesterfield and Lucky Strike, which were more preferred by American smokers.[362] Indeed, blended tobacco cigarettes were infrequent in *Shenbao*, although the Victory brand, sold in the mid-1920s, represented an exception with its short-lived existence.

---

362 Crow, *Four Hundred Million Customers*, 6–7.

The variety of cigarette brands was also influenced by both the price range and the social status of smokers. Lu Xun, a renowned Chinese writer, noted that luxury brands like Craven A and Black Cat were preferred by urban elites, while brands such as Ruby Queen, Pirate and Pin Head were more popular among the general population. However, it is essential to recognise that the imagery associated with brand names alone is not sufficient to determine the social category of consumers. While certain brands may convey associations of luxury or popularity, the selling price of the cigarettes served as a more reliable indicator of social status, although explicit pricing information was rarely provided in advertisements.[363] Furthermore, the act of being advertised and associated with a branded product itself became a criterion of distinction. As Carol Benedict has demonstrated, smokers from lower socioeconomic backgrounds often could not afford luxury branded cigarettes and instead turned to locally manufactured generic cigarettes produced through cheap labour.[364]

Determining the gender of brands is more challenging and requires careful consideration of various factors. The case of My Dear cigarettes illustrates how feminine representations can be misleading, as the brand used feminine elements in its name, logo and scenarios to attract male smokers. Towards the end of the period, the brand also associated itself with male figures, blurring the gender categorisation further.[365] In the case of Santal Midy, a medication for venereal diseases, the presence of a nude woman in the advertisement served as a deterrent rather than an indicator of the brand's gender appeal. On the other hand, the figure of a moustachioed man representing the Japanese brand "Jintan" and the tiger emblem of Sincere cosmetics does not necessarily make these brands masculine. Gender associations can be complex and not solely reliant on visual cues. Some brands, however, did exhibit clearer gender differentiation. For example, the pharmaceutical company Burroughs Wellcome produced cosmetics like Hazeline Snow and Hazeline Rose Frost, which were positioned towards a feminine market, while also offering more neutral brands like Kepler Cod Liver Oil. Furthermore, there were advertisers, such as the Cantonese manufacturer of "Two Sisters" cosmetics (Guangsheng), who specifically targeted the female market, indicating a deliberate gender segmentation in their branding approach.

---

363 Crow, *Four Hundred Million Customers*, 5–6.
364 Benedict, *Golden-Silk Smoke*, 160–62.
365 "My Dear", *SB*, January 6, 1934, 1; February 1, 1941, 3.

Gender Differentiation

During the Republican era, the changing social roles assigned to women, the increase in their level of education and the emergence of women's magazines fostered the creation of a market specifically oriented towards women.[366] Cosmetics, during this Republican period, were among the few products that could unequivocally be labelled as feminine. According to Carl Crow, the practice of make-up has long held a central place in Chinese body culture. The advertising expert explains that Chinese women consumed significant quantities of makeup, varying in quality depending on their social status. Paradoxically, he observed that unmarried women seeking suitors tended to use makeup less intensively than married women who were concerned with maintaining their husbands' desire. In the 1920s, the growth of the cosmetic industry brought about a renewal of mentalities and practices. According to Carl Crow, advertising played a role in legitimising the practice of make-up, which had long been kept secretive and associated with prostitution. Advertisements also served an educational function. Crow asserted that young Chinese women learned to use vanishing creams as a base for applying powder and blush through these advertisements. However, women consumers were also able to liberate themselves from the normative power of advertising by repurposing products beyond their intended uses as defined by the manufacturers. For instance, Crow observed that young Chinese women came up with the idea of using medical hot water bags to create a flushed effect on their cheeks.[367]

Beyond the cosmetics sector, it is crucial to approach the feminisation of commercial images during the Republican era with caution. While scholars such as Tani Barlow and Ellen Laing have shed light on the rise of the modern woman as a prominent figure in global advertising, it is important to recognise that the presence of women in advertisements does not automatically imply that they were the intended target audience or the primary consumers of the advertised products.[368] Despite the considerable amount of research dedicated to women in ad-

---

366 Regarding women's education during the Republic, see: Bailey, *Gender and Education in China*. On gender roles, see: Schneider, *Keeping the Nation's House Domestic Management and the Making of Modern China*. The most popular women's magazines included: *Funü zazhi* (1915–1931), *Xin funü* (1920–1921), *Xin nüxing* (1927–1929), *Linglong* (1932–1937), *The Young Companion/Liangyou* (1926–1941). Several of these magazines have been digitized by the University of Heidelberg: https://kjc-sv034.kjc.uni-heidelberg.de/frauenzeitschriften/ (last consulted July 2, 2022).
367 Crow, *Four Hundred Million Customers*, 23–35; Crow, "Advertising and Merchandising", 195.
368 Alys Eve Weinbaum and Tani Barlow, *The Modern Girl around the World Consumption, Modernity, and Globalization* (Durham, N.C.: Duke University Press, 2008); Ellen Johnston Laing, *Selling Happiness: Calendar Posters and Visual Culture in Early Twentieth-Century Shanghai* (Honolulu: University of Hawai'i Press, 2004).

vertising, their representation in *Shenbao* was relatively limited and inconsistent over time. Before World War I, women appeared in only 20% of advertisements, while men were represented in 50% of advertisements during the same period. Moreover, women were often depicted in couples or mixed groups. The ratio reversed after the war. In the 1920s, women occupied 60% of advertisements, compared to 25% for men and 20% for mixed groups. It is worth noting that until the 1920s, certain sectors, such as heavy industry, were considered inappropriate for the portrayal of feminine images. Manufacturers of cosmetics and cigarettes often objectified women as objects of seduction, while the food industry restricted their depiction to traditional roles as mothers and homemakers.[369] Although the number of women images multiplied in the 1930s, their popularity faded towards the end of the period, accounting for only 20% of advertisements in 1949. Market professionals, noting consumer weariness, began exploring alternative means of persuasion.[370]

Throughout the Republican era, it is clear that male figures dominated the advertising landscape, reaching their peak representation during the Sino-Japanese War (accounting for 60% of advertisements). Moreover, men were portrayed differently from women, both in terms of the products they were associated with and the postures they adopted. In medical advertisements, they often assumed roles such as the family patriarch, employee, or scholar. With cigarettes in their mouths, they took on the image of the dandy and transformed into businessmen in educational and financial advertisements. While hygiene products were initially associated with femininity due to their proximity to cosmetics, they gradually expanded their appeal to the male market through the introduction of razors and shaving creams.

In summary, despite the apparent feminisation of images in the Chinese press, the majority of advertisements in *Shenbao* focused on products that were either gender-neutral or had an uncertain gender association. Apart from the cosmetics sector, assessing the "gender" of products based solely on advertisements can be challenging. The intended end user was not always explicitly stated, and the boundaries between masculinity and femininity were influenced by evolving societal norms and perceptions. It is therefore crucial to consider the broader context and factors beyond advertising images when analysing the gender associations of products.

---

369 C.P. Yeh, "The Ideal Chinese Advertisement: Suggestions, Hints and Warnings", *North China Herald*, October 18, 1919.
370 "Publicity for Shanghai Said Mostly Bad. Book of Information on this city planned to popularize us abroad. Millington tells Rotary all about Advertising", *China Press*, May 11, 1934.

Age Differentiation

Different age groups were represented to varying degrees in Chinese advertising, with children being the most prominently featured in commercial images. Other generations were also present, although in a subtler manner. During the Republican period, advertisers increasingly focused on children as their target audience. This new emphasis on children was influenced by factors such as the relatively young population in China, the pro-natalist climate of the interwar period that encouraged child-rearing and family growth, and various initiatives aimed at national "regeneration" and the cultivation of future citizens under the Nationalist regime.[371]

Starting from the 1920s, children were offered a wider range of products in advertisements. Three sectors, in particular, showed significant interest in young consumers: the pharmaceutical industry, food products and educational goods. Even before the First World War, numerous medical advertisements specifically targeted children, featuring products such as Kepler Cod Liver Oil, Virol, or Scott's Emulsion. In the 1920s, there was further specialisation in infant medicines. As highlighted in chapter 4, children's medicines were identified as a distinct category in the study conducted by Qinghua researchers in 1923.[372]

In the mid-1930s, new medical brands which specifically targeted children were introduced to the market, such as Baby's Own Tablet, manufactured by Foster McClellan. This specialisation in favour of the youngest age group went hand in hand with the development of paediatrics, as emphasised in chapter 4. In the realm of taste and health, infant foods flourished after the First World War, representing approximately half of the newspaper advertisements. Glaxo powdered milk appeared in the mid-1920s, while Betavit cereals was introduced during WWII.[373] With the profound restructuring of the educational system in Republican China, educational offerings quickly expanded. Primary schools, textbooks and children's magazines accounted for half of *Shenbao* advertisements in 1924 and nearly 80% in 1941. A careful examination of educational advertisements highlights a specialisation towards young children and childcare. Manufactured

---

371 A good illustration of this can be found in the cover of the magazine *Arts and Life* (Meishu shenghuo) published in September 1934. In the centre of the page, the child representing China proudly waved the national flag while proclaiming that it was not the "sick man of Asia" (Wo fei ya bingfu!). Regarding nationalist programs focused on children, see: Margaret Tillman, *Raising China's Revolutionaries: Modernizing Childhood for Cosmopolitan Nationalists and Liberated Comrades, 1920s-1950s* (Columbia University Press, 2018).

372 "An Analytical Study of Advertisements in Chinese Newspapers ", 139–43.

373 Glaxo Powdered Milk, *SB*, January 3, 1924, 20; Betavit, *SB*, February 5, 1941, 4.

toys, which were more commonly associated with children's magazines and other specialised publications, remained marginal in daily newspapers like *Shenbao*.[374] It is worth noting that certain products deemed harmful or inappropriate, such as cigarettes, alcoholic beverages and entertainment, were not targeted towards children in advertising campaigns.

In the advertising imagination, the concept of childhood gradually took shape and differentiate itself over time. Prior to World War I, childhood was portrayed as a relatively vague and undifferentiated category. The various stages of childhood were primarily indicated by the nature of the products being advertised, such as infant milk for babies and educational literature for school-age children and young adults. In the 1920s, however, the division between different ages of childhood became more refined. Through the use of language and imagery, the concept of the newborn (ying'er, yinghai) started to stand out from preschool or already-schooled children. In 1934, an advertisement for Quaker Oats even quantified the appropriate age for consumption, stating that the product could be consumed from the age of three months.[375] During the 1930s, advertisements began featuring older children (ertong) or children in the growth phase (shengzhang qizhong). Kepler, for example, showcased products targeting older children, while China Publishing House (Zhonghua shuju) offered textbooks which aligned with the official curriculum of the Ministry of Education for primary and middle school students.[376] On the other hand, the notion of adolescence struggled to emerge in Chinese advertising during this period, even though it had been well represented in American advertising since the 1910s.[377]

Children featured in *Shenbao* advertisements primarily served as a commercial appeal, regardless of their age. They were often prominently displayed in the main illustrations and sometimes incorporated discreetly into the brand's logo, as seen in examples like Virol, Glaxo, or Baby's Own Tablet.[378] In the 1930s, children were frequently placed at the centre of scenes depicting happy families, looking directly at the viewer to evoke sympathy.[379] During this period, baby contests also emerged, and advertisers took advantage of these events to promote various infant

---

374 Susan Fernsebner, "A People's Playthings: Toys, Childhood, and Chinese Identity, 1909–1933", *Postcolonial Studies* 6, n° 3 (2003): 269–93.

375 Quaker Oats, *SB*, January 1, 1934, 16.

376 Kepler, *SB*, January 1, 1934, 24; Zhonghua shuju, *SB*, January 5, 1934, 1.

377 Jeffrey Jensen Arnett, *Emerging Adulthood the Winding Road from the Late Teens through the Twenties* (New York; Oxford: Oxford University Press, 2004); Paula S Fass, *The Routledge History of Childhood in the Western World* (London: Routledge, 2012), 229–48.

378 Virol, *SB*, January 6, 1914, 14; Scott's Emulsion, *SB*, January 3, 1924, 20; Glaxo, *SB*, January 3, 1924, 20.

379 Kepler, *SB*, January 1, 1934, 24; *SB*, February 1, 1941, 7.

or household products in popular magazines like *Liangyou* (Young Companion) and commercial exhibitions such as the Better Homes Exhibition (chapter 2).[380] Under the nationalist regime, advertisers began making more politically motivated use of childhood, capitalising on nationalist programs for their commercial purposes. For instance, in 1934, the Beixin Bookstore (Beixin shuju) aligned its textbooks with the officially proclaimed Year of Childhood by the government, appealing to readers' patriotic sentiments.[381]

Despite their visual presence, children were seldom the intended audience of advertisements due to their limited purchasing power, which diminished their direct appeal to advertisers. The popular tale of a young Chinese boy diligently saving his meagre resources to indulge in the luxury of a handful of raisins was a fabricated fable crafted by the Californian company Sun-Maid to cater to the Orientalist desires of its Western customer base. While the practice of providing pocket money to children began to gain traction among the American middle class, it was not a widespread phenomenon in China during the period under consideration.[382] However, an examination of advertisements featured in *Shenbao* from the 1930s reveals an emerging trend of advertisers seeking to establish more direct connections with children. Illustrations assumed the role of intermediaries, particularly when targeting non-schooled children who had not yet attained reading proficiency. Notably, in 1934, the American brand Listerine employed the endearing character of Mickey Mouse to cultivate a sense of rapport with young consumers, enticing them with the promise of a complimentary toy upon the purchase of a toothbrush.[383]

Nevertheless, these instances of direct engagement with children through advertisements remained exceptional. In the context of a general newspaper like *Shenbao*, such approaches imply that children either perused the daily press independently or with the guidance of an adult who would serve as an interpreter of the content. To reach a less-educated young audience, some advertisers preferred to turn to outdoor advertising strategies. In the bustling streets of Shanghai, they employed attention-grabbing techniques such as light projections, parades, hot

---

380 Wang Zhenzhu, "Popular Magazines and the Making of a Nation"; "Chinese Baby Contest Due at Homes Exhibit – Details will be told soon by the China Press", *China Press*, February 11, 1937.

381 *SB*, January 1, 1934, 6.

382 "Only raisins supremely fine could win such world-wide favor", *Saturday Evening Post*, August 6, 1927. On this subject, see: Cécile Armand, "The Grapes of Happiness: Selling Sun-Maid Raisins to the Chinese in the 1920s-1930s", *Asia Pacific Perspectives* XIII, n° 2 (Fall/Winter 2015). On the history of pocket money, see: Cécile Armand, "WWII (3-2-2) – Les âges en guerre: les jeunes et les vieux (l'interdépendance des générations)", Blog post, *Advertising History*, consulted April 19, 2020, https://advertisinghistory.hypotheses.org/2547.

383 Listerine, *SB*, January 6, 1934, 13.

air balloons, radio trucks and animal processions specifically designed to captivate children's children. Some promoters even made appearances in schools and other venues dedicated to youth. An intriguing example of such engagement occurred in 1935 when producer W.H. Jansen proposed screening semi-commercial films in Shanghai schools. These educational films served the dual purpose of imparting elementary public hygiene rules while simultaneously promoting Lactogen milk. Building upon this concept, the China Soap Company adopted a similar approach the following year, expanding the reach of their outdoor screenings.[384] It is plausible that both advertisers drew inspiration from similar campaigns conducted by the Colgate Company in the United States prior to World War I.[385]

Despite the central importance of filial piety in Chinese society, older individuals remained in the background of *Shenbao* advertisements (15%). The presumed weakening of needs and desires over the years, the life expectancy shortened by wars, famines and epidemics, the loss of autonomy and the insufficient personal resources in a society where intergenerational solidarity continued to play an essential role are all factors that diverted advertisers from the senior market. Old age, being close to death, was generally depicted in a negative light, as the inevitable extension of middle age that one must strive to delay. In 1924, an advertisement for the International Correspondence School (ICS) portrayed a man's life from the perspective of his professional career divided into decades. The active years were depicted as occurring between 30 and 50 years old, with no consideration given to the later years.[386] The fear of old age was evident in numerous medical advertisements as well, such as De Witt and Doan Backache & Kidney Pills, which promised to increase longevity and alleviate rheumatism, digestive, or urinary disorders.[387] However, old age had multiple facets in the advertising imagination. The negative aspect, associating it with illness and death, faded in the 1930s, and old age became synonymous with wisdom and longevity. During the war, it was embodied through the figure of Santa Claus and scenes of multi-generational families. By 1949, the portrayal of a smiling old age began to prevail over anxiety, reflecting the more general trend in post-war advertising towards optimism.[388]

---

384 Advertising by Means of Cinematograph Displays. W.H. Jansen Cinema exhibitions in Markets, Schools, etc., The China Soap Company, Limited. Advertising by Means of Cinematograph Displays, SMA (SMC), U1-4-3820 (1935).

385 J. Walter Thompson Company, Newsletter Collection. Box MN2 (1916–1922).

386 International Correspondence School (ICS), *SB*, January 1,1924, 1.

387 De Witt Longlife Pills (Qinchuan meirong zhi mijue), *SB*, January 3, 1924, 8; Longlife Vita-Spermin, *SB*, January 4, 1934, 11; De Witt Kidney Pills (Diweide bushenwan), *SB*, February 1, 1941, 7.

388 Sanatogen (Sannatujin), *SB*, January 3, 1924, 16; Kepler Cod Liver Oil, *SB*, February 1, 1941, 7; 99 Vitamin (Jiujiu weita), *SB*, January 8, 1949, 1.

Adults, as the primary consumers of interest to advertisers, played a central role in advertising campaigns. They were the ones who possessed purchasing power, entertained various needs and desires, and held the ability to make decisions and take action. Implicitly present in advertisements, adults were associated with all categories of products. They were not only regular readers of the press, but they also encountered numerous posters and billboards as they navigated through the bustling streets. The active age of adulthood, on the other hand, was characterised by its main limitation: a lack of time and availability to thoroughly read advertisements. While rarely named or quantified, the concept of the average age emerged as a default interval in some advertisements for products like Kepler Cod Liver Oil, International Dispensary and Fourvita.[389] Adulthood occupied a unique position between childhood and degeneration. It oscillated between a positive pole that assimilated it to strength, youth, health and pleasure, as exemplified in advertisements for companies like Huamei Tobacco or Taogu Shuntian guan,[390] and a negative pole that portrayed it as susceptible to illness, professional failure and social decline, as seen in advertisements for products like De Witt or Fuji Kidney Pills.[391] Despite a brief phase of pessimism in the 1930s, the positive aspect of adulthood generally prevailed and eventually triumphed toward the end of the period.

Conclusion

During the early years of the Republic, commercial brands emerged as successors to traditional seals used for marking goods. These new cultural brands, characterised by distinctive names and logos, filled gaps in industrial property protection laws and granted products a sense of autonomy from their manufacturers. By endowing products with their own identities, these brands also aimed to establish a closer connection with consumers. The rise of identity brands, however, did not lead to the disappearance of older forms of marketing. Under the Nationalist regime, trademarks experienced a resurgence with the establishment of certified standards by the Ministry of Industry. While the initial wave of renowned brands came from a select group of multinational corporations like BAT and vernacular

---

389 Kepler Cod Liver Oil, *SB*, January 3, 1924, 8; International Correspondence School, *SB*, January 1, 1924, 1; International Dispensary Cod Liver Oil (Wuzhou rubai yuganyou), *SB*, January 6, 1934, 8; Fourvita (Fuweita), *SB*, February 2, 1941, 7.
390 Taogu Shuntian guan, *SB*, January 3, 1914, 8; Huamei Tobacco Company (Maskee), *SB*, January 5, 1934, 1.
391 De Witt Kidney Pills, *SB*, February 1, 1941, 7; Fuci Kidney Pills, *SB*, February 3, 1941, 7.

industrialists like Huang Chujiu and Chen Diexian, the advent of professional advertising agencies in the 1920s brought about a step change, as they facilitated the widespread use of brands across various sectors and enabled smaller advertisers to develop their own brand image, fostering competition in the marketplace.

The adoption of brands, however, was not uniform across sectors and underwent significant changes over time. In the pre-World War I era, cultural brands were primarily associated with luxury products, such as cigarettes, alcohol, patent medicines and items related to personal appearance. After the war, there was a significant increase in the number of brands, driven by the growth of consumer industries, particularly in the food and cosmetics sectors. The 1930s marked the peak of creativity in branding efforts, followed by a decline during the Sino-Japanese War, although branding experienced a final resurgence before the Communist revolution. The proliferation of brands also contributed to a more nuanced differentiation of consumers, although it is challenging to determine their age, gender and social status solely based on advertisements. Professional literature provides a more reliable source of information to gain a deeper understanding of the intentions of advertisers and their clients.

Part Three: **Advertising Theories and Practices**

Chapter 7
Insights from Textbooks

What constitutes effective advertising? What rules should it adhere to, and what mistakes should it avoid? The 1920s witnessed the proliferation of a body of professional literature in two distinct categories. On one side, there were surveys that provided an overview of the state of advertising in China, and on the other side, there were instructional manuals designed to offer practical guidance to young professionals in crafting their advertisements. This chapter marks the initial study dedicated to the advertising literature produced in China between the conclusion of World War I and the Communist revolution. It demonstrates how these texts contributed to a more comprehensive codification of advertising practices and the development of a specific doctrinal framework for the profession. Within this chapter, the manuals are systematically analysed to comprehend how the socio-political context and the contributions of emerging cognitive sciences informed the construction of advertising theories and practices during the republican period. The first section provides a broad survey of the professional literature and highlights the emergence of a Chinese-language literature in the late 1920s. The subsequent two sections scrutinize, in detail, how printed advertising and outdoor advertising were addressed within these manuals.

The Emergence of Professional Literature

The first professional texts on advertising in China were primarily written in English by expatriates or special correspondents of North American origin. These texts were directed towards an audience of entrepreneurs or foreign investors who were interested in exploring the Chinese market. Typically, these early texts took the form of reports, newspaper articles, or book chapters and were relatively concise in nature. They were authored by individuals like journalist Carl Crow or specialised institutions such as the Bureau of Foreign and Domestic Commerce, affiliated with the U.S. Department of Commerce. While some surveys were also published by Chinese institutions, such as the Bureau of Economic Information (Jingji taolun chu), these early ethnographic texts often reflected the prevailing prejudices of their authors and their contemporaries towards Chinese society.

The U.S. Department of Commerce played a significant role in producing important texts related to advertising in China. Notable among these works was the survey conducted by trade commissioner J. Sanger in 1921, mentioned in the first chapter, which covered the history of advertising, media, products and Chinese

https://doi.org/10.1515/9783111390000-008

consumer habits. This survey encompassed not only China but also included Japan and the Philippines. Another influential publication was the comprehensive commercial handbook edited by commercial attaché Julean Arnold in 1926. While it contained a special chapter on advertising authored by Carl Crow, advertising was not the central focus of the book. Apart from the published texts, American archives have also preserved several well-documented reports on Chinese advertising. Among these, one of the most substantial reports was compiled in 1932 by the U.S. consul in Shanghai, J. Black. This comprehensive report consisted of three parts covering various aspects of advertising activity, different advertising mediums, composition techniques, market studies, municipal regulations, newspaper surveys and a list of professional agencies operating in China.

In the 1920s, the *Chinese Economic Monthly* (Zhongguo jingji yuekan), the official journal of the Bureau of Economic Information, published two significant articles on advertising that were previously mentioned in earlier chapters.[392] The first article, published in 1926, presented the findings of a study conducted by two researchers from Qinghua University, analysing the nature of advertisements in five Chinese newspapers.[393] The second article, published in 1929, resulted from an investigation conducted by American journalist C.A. Bacon, focusing on the development of advertising in China. Bacon's analysis covered various aspects, including the media, methods, nature of products and active agencies in Shanghai.[394] Aside from these official texts, the local press also frequently reported on the activities of professional organisations and covered conferences organized by associations and universities related to advertising in China.

Unlike some other professions like engineering and medicine, the advertising field lacked dedicated journals from professional associations. Instead, discussions on advertising and its societal significance were found in publications related to

---

392 Published between 1921 and 1937, the *Chinese Economic Bulletin/Monthly/Journal* (Zhongguo jingji yuekan) was the official journal affiliated with the Bureau of Economic Information (Jingji taolun chu), operating under the authority of the Ministry of Industry. In 1928, it underwent reorganisation and became known as the Bureau of Industrial and Commercial Information (Gongshang fanwen ju), only to be further renamed as the Bureau of Foreign Trade (Guoji maoyi ju) in 1931. In parallel with these changes, the publication itself underwent a series of rebrandings, evolving from the *Chinese Economic Monthly* to the *Chinese Economic Journal* in 1931 and ultimately adopting the name *Chinese Economic Journal and Bulletin* in 1935. On this journal, see: Cécile Armand, 'X-perts (1): Digging up the Chinese Economic Journal', Blogpost, *Advertising History* (blog), October 26, 2018, https://advertisinghistory.hypotheses.org/3372.

393 "An Analytical Study of Advertisements in Chinese Newspapers", *Chinese Economic Monthly* 3, n° 4 (April 1926): 139–43.

394 C.A. Bacon, "Advertising in China", *Chinese Economic Journal and Bulletin* 5, n° 3 (September 1929): 754–67.

national exhibitions and other relevant subjects. National exhibition catalogues, for example, highlighted advertising as an indispensable weapon in the commercial competition against foreign powers.[395] On the other hand, in his comprehensive history of journalism published in 1927, Chinese journalist Ge Gongzhen criticised advertising for its potential negative impact on newspaper reputation and the ethics of professional journalists.[396] Apart from such general works, the only known specialised publication was the quarterly journal *Guanggao yu tuixiao jikan* (Advertising and Promotion), edited by Xu Baiyi, the director of the Lianhua agency (Lianhua guanggao gongsi). However, this journal emerged only a few months before the outbreak of the Sino-Japanese War. Despite its limited run, the journal provided a valuable resource as it featured rich illustrations, colourful printing and various thematic sections that explored all aspects of the advertising profession. Moreover, it included comparative studies with other countries, offering a comprehensive view of the field at that time.[397]

The earliest Chinese-language textbooks on advertising, published in the early 1920s, were translations of American textbooks, sometimes with the involvement of Japanese translators as intermediaries.[398] For instance, the manual titled *Guanggao xinglixue* (Psychology of Advertising), published in 1925, was a translation by Japanese author Iseki Jiro from the work of American psychologist Walter Dill Scott's *The Psychology of Advertising*, originally published in 1908.[399] As the late 1920s approached, Chinese authors began to distance themselves from foreign literature and started incorporating new first-hand knowledge gained during their studies in the United States. These manuals were intended for a different audience – the new generation of advertising professionals who were educated in Chinese universities. The increasing number of publications in the subsequent

---

395 Ma Yinchu, "Zhongguo guohuo shiye fazhan zhi zhang'ai jiqi jiuji zhi fangfa (The obstacles to the development of the Chinese industry and the means to overcome them)", in *Zhonghua guohuo zhanlanhui jinian tekan* (Special issue on the national products exhibition) (Shanghai: Guomin zhengfu gongshangbu, 1928); Pan Junxiang, *Zhongguo jindai guohuo yundong* (The National Products Movement in China) (Beijing: Zhongguo wenshi, 1995).

396 Ge Gongzhen, *Zhonguo baoxue shi* (History of journalism in China) (Shanghai: Commercial Press, 1927).

397 *Shenbao*, May 12, 1936.

398 On the mediating role of Japanese translators in other fields of knowledge, see: Hsiao-yen Peng and Isabelle Rabut, *Modern China and the West: Translation and Cultural Mediation* (Leiden; Boston: Brill, 2014); Natascha Vittinghoff et Michael Lackner, ed., *Mapping Meanings the Field of New Learning in Late Qing China* (Leiden; Boston: Brill, 2004).

399 Iseki Jiro, *Guanggao xinglixue* (Psychology of Advertising) (Commercial Press, 1925); Walter Dill Scott, *The Psychology of Advertising: A Simple Exposition of the Principles of Psychology in Their Relation to Successful Advertising* (Boston: Small, Maynard & Co., 1908).

decades reflected a strong demand for these manuals. Between 1918 and 1948, over 15 different titles were published, with a notable peak in 1930 [Table 2]. In this market, two major commercial publishers dominated – the Commercial Press (12 titles, 48%) and China Bookstore (Zhonghua shuju) (eight titles, 32%). The frequent reprints of some works underscored the rapidly evolving nature of the discipline and the need for regular updates. For example, Gan Yonglong's bestseller underwent four successive reprints between 1927 and 1939.[400] While a few authors were practitioners like Lu Meiseng, most were academics, such as Sun Xiaojun, who taught journalism at Nanyang University, or Ding Xingbo, an economics professor at the Huaxi School of Commerce.

The manuals on advertising in China displayed strikingly similar titles, and their contents often followed a stereotypical pattern. They typically began with an introductory section covering the general history of advertising, followed by chapters on copywriting, production techniques, campaign planning and market research. However, over time, the content of these manuals evolved to accommodate new media, such as mobile and illuminated advertising, and embraced fresh approaches inspired by cognitive sciences. Chinese authors were committed to translating concepts from English-language literature into the vernacular language. To facilitate memorisation and showcase their cultural capital, neologisms were thoughtfully placed in parentheses within the Chinese text.[401]

The Foundations of Copywriting

The term "copy," originally coined by American professionals in the early twentieth century, referred to the elements that constituted an advertisement. In China, it was introduced in the 1920s and translated as *guanggao gao*. According to Lu Meiseng, a well-crafted copy needed to demonstrate originality, honesty and empathy with the reader, which necessitated literary skills and knowledge in psychology and commercial sciences.[402] In the post-World War II era, the term took on a more technical meaning. Wu and Zhu, in their 1946 manual, outlined a structured approach to copy preparation, involving product research, market analysis and an understanding of available media. Influenced by emerging marketing sciences, they emphasised that the copy should emanate from the product itself, considering its materials, manufacturing process and the manufacturer's history.

---

400 Gan Yonglong, *Guanggao xuzhi* (Advertising Principles) (Shanghai: Commercial Press, 1927).
401 On the function of neologisms in scientific texts, see: Vittinghoff, *Mapping Meanings the Field of New Learning in Late Qing China*; Mullaney, 2017, 206–50.
402 Lu Meiseng, *Guanggao* (Advertising) (Shanghai: Commercial Press, 1940), 40, 65.

Additionally, the copywriter must adapt to the economic situation and the characteristics of the target consumers, including age, gender and purchasing habits.[403]

Despite varying definitions, all authors agreed that a copy always comprised at least two key elements: text and image.

The Ideal of Simplicity

The early foreign pioneers of advertising stressed the importance of using clear and straightforward language in the text, avoiding any ambiguity. Although advertising was not considered a form of literature, they believed that the copywriter should refrain from using vulgarity or excessive informality. Maintaining a respectful tone was essential, achieved through the use of conventional polite expressions. Carl Crow particularly emphasised that Chinese language advertisements should be more literal and educational compared to those tailored for the American market. This approach was necessary to introduce products that were still unfamiliar to the Chinese audience.[404]

Chinese authors embraced the principle of simplicity in their advertising texts as part of the broader linguistic reform during the early Republic, which aimed at creating a vernacular language (baihua) that would be accessible and understandable to all citizens.[405] In his 1928 textbook, Kuai Shixun devoted a chapter to advertising text, where he discouraged the use of classical Chinese and literary proverbs, especially when targeting the general population. He stressed that the language used should match the average educational level of ordinary people, and the text should be both simple and clear, with a compelling conclusion to prompt purchasing decisions. Kuai also emphasised the importance of infusing the text with an emotional element to give it life and appeal.[406] Other subsequent manuals built upon these principles, adding psychological elements to the mix. Authors like Wu and Zhu further emphasised the need for concise and immediately comprehensible language, considering that readers had limited attention spans.[407]

---

403 Wu Tiesheng and Zhu Shengyu, *Guanggaoxue* (Advertising Studies) (Shanghai: Zhonghua shuju, 1946), 110.

404 Carl Crow, "When You Advertise to Orientals", 116, 119. A.C. Row, "The Art of the Poster", *North China Herald*, February 1920.

405 On the linguistic reform, see Elisabeth Kaske, *The Politics of Language in Chinese Education, 1895–1919*, vol. 82, Sinica Leidensia (Leiden: Brill, 2007).

406 Kuai Shixun, *Guanggao ABC* (The ABC of Advertising) (Shanghai: Shijie shudian, 1928), 38–51.

407 Wu and Zhu, 81.

Titles and Slogans

The concept of a title (biaoti) emerged in Chinese advertising manuals in the late 1920s, a feature not commonly found in foreign literature on the subject. Regarded as the "soul" (guihun) of advertising, the title was considered a critical element for the success of an advertisement. It was believed that the title's brevity and prominent position played a significant role in the reader's ability to remember it, with shorter titles being more easily recalled. Experiments conducted in the 1920s aimed to determine the ideal length of a title, and the consensus settled on an average of five to seven characters. Just like the main text, the writer was advised to use simple words, avoiding exaggeration and literary subtleties. Lu Meiseng, for example, praised the Far East Saving Company for its effective and catchy title: "Decide (Juexin)!"[408]

Some advertising manuals took on the task of classifying and analysing existing titles. Notably, titles that used the name of the brand or company were preferred by advertisers with well-established reputations, such as the Commercial Press (Shangwu yinshuguan). On the other hand, factual titles (fufan biaoti), commonly used for cosmetics, became less common in the late 1920s. Authors of these manuals advised caution in using injunction titles (mingling biaoti) because they could potentially offend clients sensitive to courtesy rules. Surveys published in the *China Yearbook* and the Japanese newspaper *Mainichi* in the late 1920s provided insights into title preferences among advertisers. The surveys revealed that approximately 75% of advertisements had nominative titles, simply using the brand or company name. About 20% of advertisements featured factual titles, focusing on presenting factual information about the product. A smaller proportion, less than 5%, relied on injunction or seduction (quanxiu biaoti) titles, which took a more assertive approach to urging readers to take action.[409]

The concept of a slogan, known as *biaoyu* in Chinese, emerged relatively late in professional advertising literature, notably after World War II, and was not present in foreign texts. According to Wu and Zhu, slogans served two main purposes: familiarising consumers with brands and providing retailers with a compelling selling point. The authors recommended using slogans for "superfluous" products like cigarettes and cosmetics. Chinese advertising witnessed limited adoption of slogans, with some notable exceptions, particularly in the tobacco industry, exemplified by the Chinese giant Huacheng. Two of its flagship brands, My Dear (Meili) and The

---

408 Kuai, 23. Lu, 78–83.
409 Su Shangda, *Guanggaoxue gailun* (The Fundamentals of Advertising) (Shanghai: Commercial Press, 1929), 33–40.

Rat (Jinshu), featured their own slogan, which ingeniously played on the sound and meaning of Chinese characters. My Dear promised, "When you have beauty, you have everything" (You mei ji bei, wu li bu zhen), while The Rat highlighted its aromatic qualities and reasonable price (Yanwei hao, jiaqian qiao). The use of internal rhyme not only appealed to the visual sense but also engaged the consumer's musical and olfactory sensibilities, imbuing the advertising message with memorability and captivation.[410]

Logo and Typography

As highlighted in the previous chapter, brands were commonly accompanied by a visual element that ensured instant recognition. American trade commissioner Sanger observed that the most popular brands all had a logo, which he deemed a crucial element for effectively reaching less educated populations:

> The best "chop" is nearly always pictorial, supplemented in most cases with a few easily read Chinese characters. One of the very best chops is that used by the Japanese "Jintan," which is advertised and used all over China. This chop consists of nothing but the head and shoulders of a man wearing a distinctive kind of hat, together with two simple Chinese characters that even the most illiterate coolie can read and remember.[411]

Chinese authors further elaborated on the logo's versatility, noting that it could take the form of a symbol, a Chinese character, or a simple image.[412] To overcome technical constraints that affected illustration quality and limited the use of colours in print, they recommended employing typographic resources (ziti). Some advertisements drew inspiration from ancient calligraphic styles, a practice noted by Lu Meiseng and Su Shangda. However, they observed that this tradition was fading away with the emergence of a new generation of professionals. These individuals had undergone training after the abolition of the imperial examination system in 1905 and lacked the classical education that their predecessors had received.[413]

---

410 Lu, 92–94.
411 Sanger, 67.
412 Kuai, 87–88.
413 Su, 48; Lu, 108. Regarding the abolition of the imperial examinations and its impact on the formation of Chinese elites, see: Benjamin A Elman, *Civil Examinations and Meritocracy in Late Imperial China* (Harvard University Press, 2013).

A New Emphasis on Composition

Introduced in Chinese textbooks during the late 1920s, the concept of composition (jiegou) referred to the rational combination of textual and visual elements in advertising. The authors of these textbooks observed that advertising texts often appeared dense and overloaded, prompting them to emphasise the importance of incorporating white space (kongbai). However, this recommendation was not universally embraced, as advertising costs were typically based on the occupied space in newspapers and outdoor advertising. Kuai Shixun's advice in particular highlighted the significance of proper aeration and avoiding overcrowding in advertisements. He explained that effectively using empty space could enhance the legibility of the text and allow the message to stand out more effectively.[414]

Following World War II, Wu and Zhu's manual ventured into a more theoretical realm by introducing the three "laws of composition" – laws of magnitude, separation and movement – derived from the insights of experts in cognitive science. Inspired by the work of American psychologist Daniel Starch (1883–1979), the authors extensively discussed the psychology of forms. They also offered a detailed examination of composition stages using Gemey cosmetics as an illustrative example, starting from sketching (lunkuotu) to transfer onto zinc plates (xinban) and final proofs (guanggaoyang).[415]

The concept of the border (bianyuan) emerged as an essential element of composition in Chinese advertising textbooks, despite its absence from foreign texts. In an increasingly crowded advertising environment, incorporating a border became a valuable tool for attracting attention and distinguishing an advertisement from its neighbouring content.[416] Borders served multiple functions, including providing a decorative element and serving as a substitute for illustrations. In the interest of effective pedagogy, Lu Meiseng illustrated different types of borders using concrete examples from his clientele. From a technical standpoint, Lu emphasised the importance of adjusting the thickness of the frame to the size of the advertisement. For instance, he advised drawing thin and unadorned borders for classified ads and advertisements inserted in newspaper columns.[417]

---

414 Kuai, 23.
415 Wu and Zhu, 96, 103–8; Daniel Starch, *Advertising: Its principles, practice, and technique* (Chicago; New York: Scott, Foresman and Company, 1914).
416 Kuai, 23.
417 Lu, 102–7.

A Visual Turn in Advertising

Foreign pioneers in China recognised the potential of images to communicate with the supposedly illiterate Chinese population. Carl Crow, for instance, believed that the ideal advertisement should solely rely on visual elements. According to him, every ad should feature a reproduction of the product along with an illustrated user manual. He cautioned against using the sketch style popular in Anglo-Saxon advertising at the time, advocating for faithful representations that would enable the Chinese to appreciate the product's quality and quantity. Crow stressed the importance of accuracy in depicting the advertised item, ensuring that the number of elements shown precisely matched what was being offered. To illustrate the consequences of inaccuracy, he recounted the misfortune of a tobacco manufacturer who depicted only nine cigarettes instead of the promised ten on their packaging, likely resulting in customer dissatisfaction and loss of trust.[418]

For Chinese authors, in contrast, illustrations (tuhua) held a dual purpose in advertising. They served not only an educational function but also aimed to entice and influence the consumer's purchasing decision.[419] Lu Meiseng recognised that images could complement the written copy, making the message more engaging and memorable.[420] It was crucial for illustrations to adhere to the same principles of clarity and originality as the written text. Just like words, images should be aligned with the nature of the product being advertised. Luxury and beauty products, for instance, warranted a more sophisticated and refined imagery to appeal to the target audience effectively. Overall, the illustrations needed to be tasteful, avoiding any elements that might offend the readers' sensibilities. Su Shangda, among others, advised using positive and favourable scenes in the illustrations to create a positive emotional impact on the potential buyer. By depicting scenes that evoke positivity and joy, advertisers sought to put consumers in a receptive and optimistic mood, increasing the likelihood of a successful purchasing decision.[421]

In advertising textbooks, images were commonly categorised into seven types: (1) reproductions of packaging, which were prevalent; (2) situational depictions, preferred for services and intangible goods; (3) result illustrations or before/after comparisons, widely used in medical advertisements; (4) partial representations of products, often for food items; (5) emotionally-driven images to elicit empathy, especially for medicines and family-oriented goods; (6) historical scenes, relatively

---

418 Crow, "When You Advertise to Orientals", 119, 123; Crow, *Four Hundred Million Customers*, 10–11, 170–71; Bacon, 764.
419 Kuai, 53–54.
420 Lu, 106–8.
421 Su, 41–42.

rare; and (7) instances where an enlarged logo replaced the illustration. Some authors delved into the technical aspects of image production. For instance, Kuai recommended using photographs as a basis for more realistic illustrations. He advised creating the initial sketch larger than the desired final image to account for the reduction during printing.[422]

During the Republican period, illustrations in the press, apart from major national newspapers like *Shenbao*, were generally of mediocre quality. Pencil drawings (gangbihua) and black and white illustrations (heibaihua) remained the prevalent norms until the 1940s. Techniques such as ink wash painting (moshuihua) and halftone printing (tongban) yielded unsatisfactory results on newsprint, limiting their use. Photography (zhaopian) was captivating for its realism and impact, but only a few printers had access to the required photogravure plates (yingxieban). As a result, photography was not widely utilised. Colour printing also intrigued advertising professionals, but it was sparingly employed due to technical constraints and high production costs. It only appeared occasionally in luxury advertisements for products like cigarettes and spirits. Even in the weekly supplements and illustrated magazines that emerged in the 1930s, the colour range was limited to two or three hues.

The use of colours in advertising elicited different perspectives among experts. While Millington advocated leveraging the particular sensitivity of Chinese people to colours, Carl Crow and A.C. Row advised a more restrained approach. Crow observed that certain colours appreciated in the West, such as blue, might have a less favourable reception in China and could potentially have the opposite effect of what was intended.[423] A.C. Row noted that Chinese posters typically featured more muted colours compared to Western designs, discouraging the use of overly bright hues.[424] On the other hand, trade commissioner Sanger cautioned against overestimating the importance of colour in advertising. He based his assertion on a recent survey, suggesting that racial differences had only limited influence on colour preferences, and opinions on colours were as diverse as individuals themselves.[425]

Under the influence of Chinese professionals, traditional taboos surrounding colours gradually diminished. Challenging the earlier intuitive and ethnocentric theories put forth by foreign pioneers, Chinese authors delved into rigorous studies on the influence of consumers' age and gender on colour preferences. Inspired by an American company's research, Kuai observed that advertisements for cos-

---

422 Kuai, 57.
423 Crow, "When You Advertise to Orientals", 117–19; Bacon, 758. See also: "Advertising in China", *NCH*, March 20, 1926.
424 A.C. Row, "The Art of the Poster", *North China Herald*, February 1920.
425 Sanger, 70–1.

metics were often printed in colour, hypothesising that women might be more sensitive to colours than men.[426] Regarding age, Kuai's analysis revealed that younger individuals tended to prefer yellow and red, while older consumers were more attracted to green. With a well-informed understanding of recent research in cognitive science, Wu and Zhu meticulously analysed the colours that the human eye could perceive based on light waves and the associated emotions they evoked.[427]

Translating and Sinicising the Copy

The translation of advertising texts became a pressing concern for advertising professionals, especially for foreign advertisers aiming to place their advertisements in the Chinese press. They grappled with the question of whether they could directly use advertisements designed for their domestic market or if they needed to redesign them to suit local conditions. In the early 1920s, pioneers like Carl Crow highlighted the challenges of translation. He advised his American clients that the original text could not be simply translated literally but had to be entirely rewritten in the vernacular language by a native of the country. While this principle applied to any target country, A.C. Row pointed out that the difficulties were further compounded in China due to the diversity of local dialects.[428]

Translating brand names was a highly sensitive task, as experts emphasised. Carl Crow cautioned that an ill-conceived translation could irreparably damage the reputation of a product and its manufacturer. The challenge lay in finding a translation that was both straightforward and distinctive enough to avoid confusion with rival brands. While Sanger suggested giving translators full creative freedom to invent a new and unique name, pioneers often encountered resistance from their foreign clients, who were hesitant to alter their established identity to enter the Chinese market. Before the brand was launched, it underwent rigorous testing to ensure that it would not be susceptible to imitation or mocking parodies. The careful consideration of the translated brand name was critical to its success and acceptance in the Chinese market.[429]

Chinese authors made distinctions among different types of brand names. Some brands simply used the company's name, like the sock manufacturer Jinglunshan or the pharmacy Yong'an. Other brands incorporated names of places,

426 Kuai, 37, 61.
427 Wu and Zhu, 114–25.
428 Row, "The Art of the Poster". See: Sanger, 72.
429 Sanger, 68. Crow, *Four Hundred Million Customers*, 192–93.

often China, Shanghai, or one of the five continents. Additionally, some brands were created to evoke positive values, such as luck (fugui) or money (jinqian) in the case of the company Huafeng. Lu Meiseng noted that certain English brand names, like U-needle, were constructed as portmanteau words resulting in unexpected semantic effects (You need). However, he discouraged the use of such wordplay in Chinese brand names, as the language did not lend itself well to this type of linguistic creativity. Instead, the focus was on simplicity and clarity to ensure the brand name resonated effectively with the Chinese audience.[430]

Translating new or locally unknown products into the Chinese language presented significant challenges for market professionals. Carl Crow noted that prior to the introduction of automobiles in China, there were no existing words in the vernacular language to describe them. As a solution, a specific lexicon was created, drawing inspiration from sailor jargon and the language used by horse carriage drivers. Crow compiled a bilingual glossary to cater to the advertising needs in the emerging automotive market. In other instances, advertising professionals encountered genuine linguistic difficulties. Some terms proved to be untranslatable, making it hard to effectively convey the product's features or benefits. For instance, the expression "cosmetic skin" might have posed challenges in finding an accurate Chinese equivalent. Additionally, selecting the right translations for certain products was crucial, as inappropriate choices could render the product unpopular among consumers. This was exemplified with cheese, where a less appealing translation could have hindered its acceptance in the Chinese market.[431]

Similar to texts, commercial illustrations also required a local touch, crafted by artists well-versed in Chinese culture.[432] Cigarette manufacturers drew inspiration from Chinese mythology, incorporating auspicious animals like bats, cleverly playing with acronyms like BAT (British-American Tobacco). Huacheng Tobacco Company embraced the rat, naming its brand "The Rat" (Jinshu pai). Nanyang Brothers Company opted for the symbol of imperial power, the Golden Dragon, which regained prestige in the 1930s. However, certain taboos governed the use of images. Sanger discouraged depicting animals considered contemptible, such as dogs, or Orientalist motifs that might evoke cultural backwardness.[433] American journalist Bacon expressed concern over Hollywood movie posters that featured scenes of love and violence, fearing they might convey a negative image of Western civilisation to Chinese viewers.[434] Yet, over time, these taboos relaxed,

---

430 Lu, 93.
431 Crow, *Four Hundred Million Customers*, 23–24, 185–89, 225.
432 Sanger, 68; Bacon, 757.
433 Sanger, 68, 70.
434 Bacon, 762–63.

and orientalist themes found their way into vernacular brands, like Pyramid cigarettes and Betelnut in the 1930s. Western pets, particularly cats, became popular
in local advertising, seen in brands like Philips light bulbs and Three Cats cigarettes.[435] Even the dog symbol made its way into advertising, featured in educational textbooks published by Beixin in 1936 and the women's lingerie brand
"Doghead" (Goutou laopai) after the war.[436]

The Making of Appeals

The concept of appeal, introduced in foreign literature during the early 1920s, referred to the persuasive techniques used in advertising to influence consumers'
purchasing decisions.[437] Carl Crow, in particular, employed the term *health appeal* to describe advertisements that emphasised the curative properties of products.[438] Later studies examining the influence of gender on appeals were cited in
Kuai Shixun's manual, revealing that women tended to respond more favourably
to appeals that emphasised beauty, morality, product quality and effectiveness,
while men showed greater interest in appeals related to health, science and
safety. Nevertheless, advertising practitioners acknowledged that the boundary
between these appeal categories was not rigidly defined, and experimentation
was often necessary to determine the most suitable approach for targeting specific audiences.[439]

   After the Sino-Japanese War, the concept of appeal, translated into the vernacular language as *suqiu*, took on a more theoretical significance. Influenced by the
ideas of American industrialist Percival White (1857–1912), Wu and Zhu provided a
comprehensive framework for understanding desired consumer reactions. They
identified three levels of desired response: attracting attention, engaging readers
with the advertisement and, ultimately, prompting a purchase decision. These responses were further categorised into four types of appeals. The consciousness-

---

435 Betelnut (Binglangpai xiangyan), *SB*, January 1, 1934, 1; January 5, 1934, 1; Pyramid (Jinzita
xiangyan), *SB*, January 6, 1934, 1.
436 Philips (Feilipu dianpao), *SB*, January 3, 1924, 16. Beixin Bookstore (Beixin shuju), *SB*, January 1, 1934, 6; Advertisement for Goutou laopai, Shanghai, 1949 (photograph), Harrison Forman
(1904–1978) Collection, University of Wisconsin-Milwaukee Libraries, box L10, Forman 1340, Gift
of Sandra Carlyle Forman, 1987.
437 See for instance: International Textbook Company, *Engraving and Printing Methods, Advertisement Illustration, Technical- and Trade-Paper Advertising, Street-Car Advertising, Outdoor Advertising, House Publications* (Scranton, Pa.: Smithsonian Libraries, 1909).
438 Crow, *Four Hundred Million Customers*, 209–10.
439 Kuai, 28–39.

based appeal (zhijue) relied on repetition and association of ideas to evoke sensory experiences such as taste, scent, or sound related to the advertised product. The comparative appeal (chabie) aimed to demonstrate the product's superiority over others in the market. The affective appeal (qingxu) targeted readers' emotions, while the conceptual appeal (guannian) sought to engage their intellect and stimulate thought. Wu and Zhu emphasised that advertising appeals should be tailored to consider factors such as the economic situation, standard of living, consumption habits and the media channels used for advertising.[440]

The different appeals in advertising can be understood through three major discursive registers, corresponding to three significant phases in the history of advertising: the hyperbolic discourse, characterising the era of quacks; the rational discourse, coinciding with the beginnings of professional advertising; and the emotional discourse, which emerged in the 1920s to complement rational advertising.

From Exaggeration to Reason

During the early stages of advertising in China, there was a prevalent use of hyperbolic language, particularly in what came to be known as "quack" advertisements. These ads were characterised by excessive superlatives and extravagant promises, often making miraculous claims about the products being promoted. However, such exaggerations were met with suspicion by the audience and led to reader fatigue, ultimately contributing to the discredit early advertising faced. To counter this negative perception and promote honesty and transparency, advertising professionals began advocating for a shift towards rational advertising. This new approach involved the use of simple language that appealed to the reader's reason and logic.[441] Instead of making extravagant claims, rational advertising focused on describing the product's properties and providing explanations for why it would be beneficial to acquire it. Rational advertising was particularly preferred for products such as medicines, food items, cosmetics, hygiene products and other items that needed clear explanations and justifications for their usage.[442]

Among the rational advertising techniques, consumer testimonials were prominently used in medical advertisements during the early stages of advertising in China. This genre of advertising was introduced by American advertisers in the 1920s and made its way to China through pharmaceutical companies like Fulford &

---

440 Wu and Zhu, 76.
441 "'Truth in Advertising' As Problem For China's Reading Public Discussed By Mason", *China Press*, June 1933; Hollington Tong, "Newspapers as an Advertising Medium in China", 29–32.
442 Crow, "When You Advertise to Orientals", 116; *Four Hundred Million Customers*, 23, 260–80.

Company, the manufacturer of the renowned Dr. William's Pink Pills, and advertising experts such as Carl Crow. Testimonials relied on the principle of proof and sought to appeal to the empathy of readers by presenting narratives that extensively described the suffering endured by patients. According to experts, these stories captivated readers and added credibility to the effectiveness of the advertised products. Occasionally, lucky publicists were able to capitalise on spontaneous testimonials from satisfied customers. For example, in one instance, a Hankou railway employee wrote a letter to Carl Crow, recounting how Bournville cocoa had cured him of insomnia and chronic indigestion, which doctors attributed to excessive tea consumption. Nevertheless, such fortuitous testimonials were rare, and market professionals often resorted to fabricating fake testimonials to promote their products.[443]

Towards the end of the republican era, rational advertising techniques became more sophisticated, with Lu Meiseng making notable distinctions between different approaches.[444] One such distinction was between educational advertisements, also known as "motif-based" advertisements (jiaoyu guanggao or liyoushi), and the genre of notification or warning (tishi). Educational advertisements combined words and images to highlight the qualities of a product. They had a short-term effect and were particularly recommended for advertisers introducing a new product (kaichuangshi) or aiming to emphasise the comparative advantages over competitors (bijiaoshi). On the other hand, the genre of notification was reserved for well-known products and relied on a cumulative logic to create long-term effects. Unlike educational advertisements, there was no need to explain the superiority of the product, which allowed the copywriter to rely solely on images or brief texts. A good example of this approach can be seen in the announcements of sales at Wing On department stores (Yong'an), which were of extreme simplicity and solely indicated the dates of the sales.[445]

After the Sino-Japanese War, the concept of rational advertising was introduced into the vernacular language as *jieyou guanggao*. This term encompassed various forms of testimonials, with Wu and Zhu noting distinctions between ordinary confessions and those that relied on the authority of experts or celebrities, such as movie stars. The use of rational discourse was further reinforced by incorporating statistical data or the results of scientific surveys, although their authenticity could vary. In their writings, Wu and Zhu cited the works of American

---

443 Crow, *Four Hundred Million Customers*, 197–210.

444 Lu, 67–71.

445 Lu, 67–71.

psychologist Walter Dill Scott (1869–1955), highlighting that rational advertisements always contained an implicit element (anshi) that went beyond pure reason.[446]

From Reason to Emotion

Under the influence of commercial psychology, Chinese advertisers began to increasingly tap into consumers' emotions, marking a shift in their advertising strategies. This trend was complemented by the growing use of images, which aimed to create a sense of tangible connection between the readers and the products being promoted. The concept of emotional or suggestive advertising was introduced in Chinese as *anshi guanggao* and manifested in the expression *renxing xingwei suqiu guanggao* (human interest copy). Lu Meiseng briefly touched upon this concept while discussing sensory stimulation techniques and the development of humorous advertising (huajishi).[447] Wu and Zhu further endorsed this approach, particularly for food products, so-called luxury items like cigarettes, cosmetics, fashion accessories and entertainment, as well as services centred on comfort and security, such as insurance. When comparing suggestive advertising to rational advertising, Wu and Zhu noted that the former was often associated with women and aimed for immediate, short-term effects. In contrast, rational advertising was perceived as effective in the long run and was typically targeted at intellectuals, businessmen and men in general.[448]

Outdoor Advertising in Professional Literature

In the realm of professional literature, outdoor advertising received relatively little specific instruction, with pioneers primarily focusing on press advertisements and making comparisons between Chinese and Western posters. Foreign authors simply emphasised the need for outdoor text to be even briefer and simpler than in print ads. Given the limited visibility conditions, characters should be large enough to be legible from a distance. Notably, Bacon observed that the Oriental Advertising Agency used font size as a basis for pricing their services.

In this context, the image took centre stage in outdoor advertising, similar to newspapers, with a faithful depiction of the product, which, however, needed to be

---

446 Wu and Zhu, 82–85.
447 Lu, 75–76.
448 Wu and Zhu, 89–90.

enlarged for visibility from a distance. A photograph reproduced in the U.S. trade commissioner's report showcased billboards placed along the railway line between Beijing and Tianjin by British-American Tobacco. In this photograph, the size of Three Castles cigarettes was deliberately disproportionate to match the speed of the train, ensuring visibility and impact [Figure 13]. On the contrary, another photograph of a billboard in a street in Tianjin presented a counterexample, where the poster was saturated with text, resembling a direct replica of a newspaper page [Figure 14].[449] Sanger's recommendations also included animating advertisements with illustrated scenes of life. The pioneers stressed the importance of having images created by local artists, although this imperative diminished in treaty ports that were more exposed to foreign influences.[450]

FIG. 25.—PAINTED SIGN ALONG RAILWAY, NEAR TIENTSIN.
Note the Chinese characters in addition to the English name.

Figure 13: "Painted sign along Railway, near Tientsin [Tianjin]", from Sanger, 77.

During the late 1920s, while foreign professionals were primarily focused on traditional advertising mediums, Chinese authors were actively exploring the emerging techniques of mobile and illuminated advertising. Among the pioneers in this field was Kuai Shixun, who extensively studied advertising on trams and buses in major Chinese cities. His observations revealed that advertisements were commonly placed at the front of buses and at the back of trams, as well as on the

---

449 Sanger, 77–78.
450 Row, "The Art of the Poster".

FIG. 22.—SIGNBOARDS FOR CHINESE PRODUCTS.
Notice that no pictures are used—only text matter.

Figure 14: "Signboards for Chinese products. Notice that no pictures are used – only text matter".
From Sanger, 74.

sides of both vehicles. The limited available space on these mobile platforms compelled copywriters to condense their messages to the utmost, highlighting one or two carefully chosen product features. Additionally, Kuai stressed that, inside the vehicles, the size of the advertisements needed to be larger than that of newspapers but smaller than standard billboards to ensure optimal visibility. Attention to composition and colour selection was crucial to enhance the effectiveness of mobile ads. To maintain the interest of regular passengers, Kuai recommended changing the advertisement regularly, ideally every week and at a minimum every three weeks. By employing dynamic and engaging content, advertisers could prevent monotony and capture the attention of their audience effectively in the bustling urban environment.[451]

In 1929, neon lighting made its debut in Shanghai; however, it initially went unnoticed by the first generation of advertising professionals. It was only after the war that Wu and Zhu's manual addressed the realm of electric advertising, but with a specific focus on the most striking and visually captivating installations. For instance, the manual highlighted BAT's illuminated clock and the captivating mobile bees that represented the Beehive textile brand.[452] As the 1930s unfolded, illuminated advertising began to emerge as a specialised and technical field, surpassing the scope of general advertising manuals. The unique and dynamic nature of illumi-

---

451 Kuai, *Guanggao ABC* (The ABC of Advertising), 77–78.
452 Wu Tiesheng and Zhu Shengyu, *Guanggaoxue* (Advertising Studies), 288.

nated advertisements presented new challenges and opportunities for advertising professionals, which will be analysed in the second volume of this research.

Conclusion

The three decades between the First World War and the Communist revolution witnessed a significant development in professional literature, which contributed to shaping the advertising profession by providing it with a coherent body of doctrines and specific practices. Early English-language texts, primarily directed at foreign entrepreneurs, often carried ethnocentric biases. However, as the 1920s progressed, vernacular manuals emerged, targeting the new generation of Chinese publicists educated in local universities. Initially, these manuals were translations from American or Japanese sources, but Chinese authors eventually carved their own path, drawing on their first-hand knowledge gained during studies in the United States.

Despite facing technical constraints, advertising professionals were united in their pursuit of a more visually oriented approach that placed a strong emphasis on illustrations and evoking emotions. Amidst linguistic reforms impacting language usage and typography, Chinese authors emphasised the importance of simplicity and clarity in language, carefully selecting headlines and slogans, and crafting persuasive copy adapted to the product and intended consumer. By embracing imagery and the vernacular language, the post-WWI generation of market professionals connected with the aspirations of vernacular industrialists, such as Chen Diexian, who aimed at promoting popular knowledge (changshi). Nevertheless, they also asserted their professionalism and the academic foundations of their scientific approach, setting themselves apart in their commitment to a more refined and sophisticated practice of advertising.[453]

---

453 Lean, *Vernacular industrialism in China* (chapter 3).

Chapter 8
Implementation by Practitioners

This chapter investigates how practitioners applied the instructions from advertising manuals. Did their ads transition towards a more visually oriented approach? Did they abandon exaggerations, appealing instead to consumers' reason and emotions? To explore these questions, we adopt an empirical methodology, comparing textbook theories with "real" advertisements found in newspapers and on the streets of Shanghai. This approach offers an alternative perspective to cultural studies that view advertising as a "distorting mirror" of social reality.[454] Rather than focusing on the relationships between representations and reality, this chapter analyses the connections between normative literature and practical implementations. The first section examines the implementation of manual instructions in press advertisements from 1914 to 1949, using the samples from *Shenbao* featured in the preceding chapters (Chapters 4 to 6). In the second section, we apply the same approach to outdoor advertising, utilising the municipal archives of Shanghai and street photographs collected during our research.

Imperfect Application in the Press

As per the manuals examined in the previous chapter, an exemplary advertisement should ideally include a headline, concise text and an illustration, while optional elements like a slogan, border and elaborate typography could enhance its impact. However, the practical implementation of these elements in *Shenbao* advertising did not always align with the ideal standards. The adoption of the ideal copy emerged gradually and exhibited uneven application across different products. Model advertisements, representing the highest standard of compliance, accounted for an average of 15% of the advertising population between 1914 and 1949. However, until the 1920s, only 10% of advertisements fully adhered to the ideal criteria, and this number only modestly increased a decade later. Interestingly, the progression was not linear, and model advertisements experienced a decline towards the end of the period.

---

454 Laikwan Pang, *The Distorting Mirror: Visual Modernity in China* (Honolulu: University of Hawai'i Press, 2007).

https://doi.org/10.1515/9783111390000-009

The Resilience of Text

Before the First World War, text held a dominant position over images in *Shenbao* advertisements, with textual elements occupying between half and three-quarters of the advertising space. The main text, particularly dense in medical advertisements, gradually decreased over time. By the mid-1920s, the prominence of text gave way to visual elements and white spaces, which now occupied more than half of the advertising surface. Advertisements began to appear more spacious, with some, like those for Philips electric bulbs and Isola thermos flasks, almost entirely reliant on visual elements, aligning closely with the ideal envisioned by Carl Crow [Figure 15].[455] In contrast, advertisements in the genre of notifications, such as national lotteries and fundraising campaigns, maintained lengthy texts throughout the period, retaining their emphasis on informative content until 1949.[456]

Throughout the period, aside from the main text, other textual elements remained prevalent in advertisements. The brand or product name, crucial in advertising, often served as the headline of the advertisement. In the case of foreign brands, the name appeared in both its original language, typically English, and transliterated into Chinese. As recommended in the manuals, the headline held a prominent position, often placed centrally in the advertisement, as evident in examples like Bovril in 1924 or Federal cigarettes in 1934.[457] Sometimes, the headline was embellished with elaborate typography, although this occasionally risked compromising legibility, as observed in advertisements for Nanyang Socks Factory in 1924, Foci Pharmacy in 1934 or Yuwentai dancing in 1941.[458]

From the 1920s onwards, the manufacturer's name becomes more discreet, sometimes merging with the brand name. In the case of lesser-known foreign companies in China, the manufacturer's name was occasionally entirely omitted. An illustrative example is Dr. Williams' Pink Pills, which enjoyed global fame, overshadowing the identity of its manufacturer, Fulford & Company, a multinational corporation of Canadian origin.[459] The manufacturer may also hide behind its local representative. For instance, the British confectionery manufacturer Cadbury took a backseat, repre-

---

455 Philips (Feilipu), *SB*, January 3, 1924, 16; Isola Thermos, *SB*, January 3, 1924, 18.

456 Kangyuan Canned Factory (Kangyuan zhiguanchang), *SB*, February 1, 1941, 1; Smart Shirt (xin guangbiao zhuo neiyi ranzhi zhengli chang), *SB*, January 1, 1949, 3; Chicago (Zhijiage), *SB*, January 1, 1949, 9.

457 Bovril, *SB*, January 1924, 20; Federal Cigarette, *SB*, January 5, 1934, 2.

458 Nanyang Socks Factory (Nanyang wachang), *SB*, January 3, 1924, 18; Foci Pharmacy (Foci yaochang), *SB*, January 5, 1934, 16; Tiger Balm (Hubiao wanjingyou), *SB*, January 5, 1934, 11; Yiwentai dancing (Yiwentai wutai), *SB*, February 1, 1941, 8.

459 Dr. Williams' Pink Pills for Pale People, *SB*, January 29, 1914, 11.

Figure 15: Advertisement for Isola thermos (Zhonde shangdian), Shenbao, January 3, 1924, 18. A rare example of an advertisement with minimalist text, almost entirely visual. For a detailed analysis, see: https://madspace.org/Press/?ID=238.

sented by its agent George McBain, who was responsible for distributing the Bournville Cocoa brand in China.[460] As the advertising landscape evolved, further changes

---

460 Bournville Cocoa (Benwei kekefen), *SB*, January 3, 1924, 16.

were observed in the 1940s. The physical address of the manufacturer, previously common in advertisements, started to fade away, giving way to more modern contact information, such as telephone numbers.

Textual elements like slogans and headlines remained relatively infrequent in Chinese advertising. During the Republican era, only a few advertisements featured a distinct and identifiable slogan, with My Dear and The Rat being exemplary brands, as noted in the manuals.[461] *Shenbao* advertisements reflected the preference for title-names, where headlines merged with the name of the manufacturer, brand, or product. Few advertisements mentioned the selling price, except for cigarettes, show tickets and certain medications. Prior to the First World War, displaying the price was more typical for high-priced items, such as the Jintan medication, a famous Japanese brand, which leveraged its prohibitively high cost to convey a sense of quality and exclusivity. The price served as a social marker for an elite group of consumers seeking refined gifts for New Year celebrations.[462] The social function of price strengthened after the war. In the 1920s, the Doan Ointment brand embraced its elitism by explicitly disparaging cheap competing products.[463] The price effect reversed with the onset of the economic depression in the mid-1930s. Advertisers began playing on the economic argument to attract lower-class consumers. "The cheapest cigarettes" (Jiaqian bi renjia pianyi), proclaimed the Datongnan company regarding its brand The Golf (Gao'erfu). The same argument was used for the Three Stars toothpaste brand (Sanxing yagao) and Wateh electric bulbs (Huade gongchang), although the exact selling price was not clearly indicated in the advertisements.[464]

The Diversification of Visual Devices

Similar to the textual elements, the prescribed visual components from the manuals were not consistently present in advertisements. Figurative images saw progression during the 1920s but later began to fade by the end of the era. In contrast, illustrated scenes gained prominence from the 1930s onwards, gradually replacing packaging reproductions. While the presence of logos experienced a decline in the 1930s, it remained relatively stable, appearing in approximately 10% of advertisements on average. Conversely, other visual elements that were considered second-

461 Su, 39.
462 Jintan, *SB*, January 4, 1914, 9.
463 Doan Ointment, *SB*, January 1, 1934, 17.
464 The Golf (Gao'erfu), *SB*, January 1, 1949, 7; Three Stars (Sanxing yagao), *SB*, January 5, 1934, 2; Wateh (Huade gongchang), *SB*, January 5, 1934, 7.

ary in the normative literature, such as borders, typography, lines and contrasts, gained significance in the *Shenbao* newspaper's advertisements.

Before World War I, illustrations were rare and limited to specific pages of the newspaper, primarily distinguishing multinational tobacco companies like British-American Tobacco (BAT) and pharmaceutical industries such as Sanatogen, Scott & Bowne, or Toa & Company. As advised in the manuals, product reproductions were prevalent, systematically featuring in medical advertisements (e.g., Waterbury Compound), for cigarettes (Three Castles), alcoholic beverages (Hennessy cognac) and the mechanical industry (Carlowitz).[465] Product packaging was depicted widely open to showcase its contents, exemplified by the Three Castles cigarettes seemingly emerging from their pack. The brand name was prominently displayed, often in both languages for foreign brands. Alongside the logo, packaging facilitated product identification and prevented confusion with competing brands. During this period, the logo was synonymous with the trademark, serving as the primary visual element in advertisements for industrial goods (e.g., Onoda cement) and intangible services (e.g., Asia Life insurance). This approach attracted attention at a lower cost compared to the elaborate illustrations used in the pharmaceutical or tobacco industry.[466]

After the war, there was a notable shift towards more central usage of product reproductions in advertisements. Initially limited to medical and cigarette advertisements, this motif expanded to include food products, hygiene items and cosmetics. Illustrated scenes also saw progress, although they were often found on the back pages of newspapers and remained primarily associated with the pharmaceutical industry and cigarettes. Logos continued to be used, but more as reinforcements in already richly illustrated advertisements, such as those for Wateh light bulbs or pharmaceutical products from Great China Dispensary. While composition lines remained regular and somewhat monotonous, commercial artists began to explore typographic resources, experimenting with contrast effects, font size and style. Some borders were elaborately ornamented, but the majority served simply as demarcation lines between neighbouring advertisements.

In the 1930s, logos and packaging took a backseat to situational placements that now occupied the front page of the newspaper and sometimes covered an entire page, as seen in the advertisement for Maskee cigarettes [Figure 16]. In this particular advertisement, borders, contrast effects and typography began to gain prominence. Punctuation, a recent introduction in the Chinese language, was crea-

---

465 Waterbury Coumpound (Huadabaoli yuganyou), *SB*, January 7, 1914, 7; Three Castles (Sanpaotai xiangyan), *SB*, January 7, 1914, 5; Hennessy (Haineisi), *SB*, January 7, 1914, 3; Carlowitz & Company (Chanhe yanghang), *SB*, January 7, 1914, 14.
466 Onoda Dragon brand Portland cement (Longpai shuimenting), *SB*, January 7, 1914, 4; Asia Life Insurance, Everlasting Himalaya, *SB*, January 3, 1924, 16.

tively used by advertisers like the International Savings Society and Taihe Pharmacy to attract attention. Inspired by Italian Futurism, commercial artists began to experiment with composition and image dynamics. Lines curved and deformed to captivate the eye and disrupt the regularity of the pages. Taking advantage of the horizontalisation of Chinese character writing, copywriters explored all possible reading directions, sometimes combining them within a single advertisement, as in the case of Great China Dispensary. The boldest advertisers, like Taihe Pharmacy and the International Dispensary, even adopted diagonal headlines and catchphrases to divert the reader's gaze and add further intrigue to their advertisements.[467]

During the Sino-Japanese War, illustrated scenes persisted in medical advertisements (De Witt Kidney Pills), as well as cigarette (My Dear) and food product ads (Maling Canned Food). In an image-saturated environment, an increasing number of advertisements, such as Doan Backache & Kidney Pills, New Star Research Laboratories and Yiwentai, employed alternative means to stand out from their surroundings.[468] After a brief hiatus, logos made a strong comeback to draw attention to more understated advertisements, such as those of New Star Research Laboratories and Kanyang Canning Factory, or to counter the persistent threat of counterfeits, as in the case of Chi Chong Rubber Factory, Huamao harmonicas and Qinkanghang Cod Liver Oil.[469] In densely populated pages, typography, borders and contrasts were heightened to highlight text-oriented advertisements, including event announcements, financial and educational services, and classified ads. These non-figurative techniques became more widespread after the war. Some advertisers, such as the manufacturer of Hubiao balm or the Eight Immortals' Longevity Elixir (Baguadan), employed *trompe-l'œil* effects to create an illusion of depth in the printed characters.[470]

Variations Across Products

The level of adherence to the visual model in advertising varied depending on the nature of the products. Cigarettes and medicines were among the first to fully em-

---

467 Great China Dispensary (Zhongxi dayaofang), *SB*, January 5, 1934, 5; Taihe Pharmacy, *SB*, January 5, 1934, 10; International Dispensary (Wuzhou dayaofang), *SB*, January 5, 1934, 15.
468 Doan Backache & Kidney Pills (Dou'anshi mizhi baoshen wan), *SB*, February 1, 1941, 6; Yiwentai dancing (Yiwentai wutai), *SB*, February 1, 1941, 8; New Star Research Laboratories (NS) (Xinxing xiyaohang wuxian gongsi), *SB*, February 1, 1941, 10.
469 Qinkanghang Cod Liver Oil, *SB*, January 1, 1949, 2; Huamao, *SB*, January 1, 1949, 9; Chi Chong Rubber Factory (Qichang xiangjiao chang), *SB*, January 1, 1949, 10.
470 *SB*, January 5, 1934, 11.

Figure 16: Advertisement for Huamei Tobacco Company (Huamei yangongsi) and Maskee cigarettes (Hongmai sigan xiangyan), *Shenbao*, January 5, 1934, 1. This serves as an exemplary full-page advertisement, prominently positioned at the front page, encompassing all elements of the ideal copy: the brand name, serving as the title, placed prominently; an emotionally appealing slogan; elaborate typography inspired by the Art Deco movement, employing various directional writings; shades of grey to compensate for the absence of colours; meticulous composition utilising vanishing lines to capture attention; an open package displaying its contents; a festive life scene enlivening the advertisement and signifying the shift towards positive emotional appeals in the 1930s. For a detailed analysis, please refer to: https://madspace.org/Press/?ID=186.

brace the visual ideal before World War I. For instance, in 1914, Three Castles advertisements already featured a realistic reproduction of the packaging, effectively displaying the brand name and its contents. After the war, ads for Hatamen, The Rat and Maskee [Figure 16] enriched their visuals with everyday life scenes to establish a deeper connection with consumers, presenting the products in a context that resonated with their daily lives. In the subsequent decades, other product categories, including food items, cosmetics, cultural goods and entertainment, followed suit and adopted the visual approach.[471]

Pharmaceutical products, hygiene products, cosmetics and food products were also aligned with the visual norm, although they generally included longer texts describing product usage and expected effects. Despite their reliance on text, these advertisements frequently incorporated images to complement the message. For example, in advertisements for Sanatogen, Pond's Cold Cream, Sodozont toothpast and Horlicks Malted Milk, educational illustrations were strategically employed to support product demonstrations and provide visual cues to consumers. These images effectively conveyed the benefits and usage of the products, enhancing the overall persuasive appeal of the advertisements.[472]

While advertisements for theatrical troops continued to allocate a significant amount of space to text, the emergence of the film industry in the 1930s brought about a distinct style of visual advertising [Figure 17]. At the heart of this advertising approach was the prominent display of the screening venue's name, written in white characters against a striking black background, capturing viewers' attention immediately. In the absence of tangible products, the film's title functioned as the brand name in these advertisements. To convey the essence of the movie, the posters were richly illustrated with captivating scenes from the film or close-ups of the actors' faces. As movie theatres became more familiar to urban audiences, the physical address was replaced by a more convenient telephone number. Viewers could now dial the provided number to obtain information or reserve seats for the film.[473]

---

471 Three Castles (cigarette) (Sanpaotai xiangyan), *SB*, January 7, 1914, 5; Hatamen (Hademen), *SB*, January 4, 1924, 2; Maskee (Hong mai si gan xiangyan), *SB*, January 5, 1934, 1; My Dear (Meilipai), *SB*, February 1, 1941, 3; The Rat (Jinshupai), *SB*, January 1, 1949, 10.

472 Sanatogen, *SB*, January 7, 1914, 7; Ever-ready blades (Changbei daopian), *SB*, January 5, 1934, 19; Shanghai Dairy Farm (Shanghai xuzhi niunai gongsi), *SB*, January 5, 1934, 21.

473 Peking Theatre (Beijing daxiyuan), *SB*, January 5, 1934, 26; Nanking Theatre (Nanjing daxiyuan), *SB*, January 5, 1934, 29; Carlton Theatre (Ka'erdeng daxiyuan), *SB*, January 5, 1934, 28; Crystal Theatre (Huangjin daxiyuan), *SB*, January 5, 1934, 29. Grand Theatre (Daguangming daxiyuan), *SB*, January 5, 1934, 26; Cathay Theatre (Guotai daxiyuan), *SB*, January 5, 1934, 29.

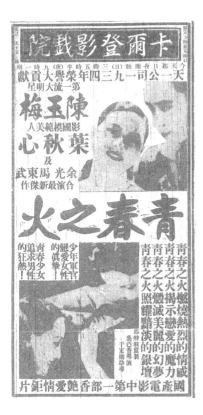

Figure 17: Advertisement for the "Fires of Youth" (Qingchun zhi huo) movie at Carlton Theater (Ka'erdeng daxiyuan), *Shenbao*, January 5, 1934, 28.

Alcohol brands like Lager Beer and Hennessy Cognac, as well as industrial goods such as Carlowitz, Willard Storage Batteries, and Kailing Electric Motor, adopted a more minimalist approach in their advertisements. These ads often focused on straightforward product reproductions or prominently displaying the brand's logo, as exemplified by the Onoda cement advertisement. Similarly, financial services providers like Butterfield & Swire and Asia Life Insurance, lacking tangible products to showcase, relied on their logos as the primary visual element in their advertisements.[474]

In contrast to other industries, educational offerings and classified ads diverged significantly from the visual ideal. Falling under the genre of "announcement" or "notification" (xinwenshi), these advertisements were primarily text-

---

[474] In *Shenbao*, see for instance: Willard Storage Batteries (Huile hongyinpai xudianchi), *SB*, January 5, 1934, 15; Kailing Electric Motor Factory (Kailing mada dianye zhizhaochang), *SB*, January 1, 1949, 3; Lager Beer (Qingdao pijiu), *SB*, January 7, 1914, 3. *SB*, January 7, 1914, 8; *SB*, January 3, 1924, 16.

based. While some classified ads utilised symbols to attract attention and employed borders to distinguish themselves from neighbouring ads, their visual elements were relatively limited compared to other types of advertisements.[475]

Shifting Discourses

In *Shenbao*, the three major discursive registers highlighted in the manuals were prominently represented. Exaggeration dominated before World War I, but in the 1920s rational advertising began to assert itself and became the dominant approach until 1949, constituting around 60% of advertisements. Concurrently, suggestive advertising emerged as a significant force, increasing from 5% in 1914 to 45% in the 1930s (averaging 25% throughout the period). Despite its prevalence, however, rational discourse did not entirely eliminate the use of exaggeration. Similarly, emotions did not replace reason. In practice, advertisers continued to employ a combination of different registers, blending elements of exaggeration, rationality and emotions in their advertisements.

The Metamorphoses of Exaggeration

In the realm of medical advertisements, the influence of charlatans was evident in the abundant use of superlatives, panaceas (buyao, lingyao, shenyao, wanyao) and a lexicon of miracles, particularly in healing narratives. For instance, in 1914, the Holland company claimed their remedy Xudaoyuan could provide instant relief from all ailments.[476] Exaggeration also subtly permeated advertisements for industrial goods (Rose, Downs & Thompson), spirits (Hennessy cognac) and some cigarette brands (President, Conqueror).[477] However, as early as 1914, a shift towards a more rational discourse began to emerge. For example, in an advertisement for Scott's Emulsion, despite the use of superlatives and universal claims,

---

475 Lu, 78. See for example: International Correspondence Schools (ICS), *SB*, January 1, 1924, 29; Beixin Bookstore, SB, January 1, 1934, 6; Parker Pen, *SB*, January 5, 1934, 17; Everlasting Himalaya (Asia Life Insurance), *SB*, January 3, 1924, 16; Commercial Bank of China (Zhongguo tongshang yinhang), *SB*, January 5, 1934, 16. Fenlei guanggao (Classified ads), *SB*, January 5, 1934; February 1, 1941, 12; January 1, 1949, 7.
476 Xudaoyuan wanyao (Holland China Handels Compagnie), *SB*, January 7, 1914, 3.
477 Rose, Downs & Thompson, *SB*, January 7, 1914, 11; Hennessy (Haineisi) cognac, *SB*, January 7, 1914, 3; President (Dazongtong pai), Conqueror (Qiangjunpai xiangyuan), *SB*, January 30, 1914, 14.

the clinical effects of the medicine were described rigorously.[478] After the war, traces of exaggeration persisted in certain brand names, such as the "universal" cod liver oil (diqiupai maijing yuganyou) manufactured by the International Dispensary, or in certain disproportionate representations, such as the giant shoes of Red Star Rubber Factory and Chi Chong Rubber Factory in 1949. Nevertheless, the influence of rational discourse grew, and advertisers started to dilute exaggeration with more evidence-based and factual claims in their advertisements.[479]

The Age of Reason

In *Shenbao*, rational discourse was applied to all products, but it was more commonly associated with medicines, body culture (hygiene, food, cosmetics), "serious" sectors like industry, finance and culture, as well as novel products that required detailed introduction. Following the guidelines of advertising manuals, most advertisements featured accurate reproductions of the product, showcasing its contents. For instance, Chamberlain Pain Balm, Three Castles cigarettes and Ulifans tablets were presented in a manner that allowed easy identification of the brand and manufacturer, especially in highly competitive sectors.[480] In emerging sectors such as hygiene and cosmetics, advertisements often depicted the product being used, such as with Sodozont and Listerine toothpaste brands, or Tiger brand vanishing cream.[481] Some ads preferred to showcase the achieved result, like a dish prepared with Royal Baking Powder. Additionally, medical advertisements, such as De Witt Backache & Kidney Pills, effectively used before-and-after comparisons to visually demonstrate the medication's effectiveness.[482] The use of photography in advertisements remained limited due to high printing costs and potential quality issues. Before World War I, early attempts at using photography were often disappointing, with readers struggling to identify subjects in the images.[483] As a result, drawings were generally used in conjunction with low-quality

---

478 Scott's Emulsion (Sigetuo rubaican yuganyou), *SB*, January 7, 1914, 7.
479 Red Star Rubber Factory (Keda pai), Chi Chong Rubber Factory (Qichang xiangjiao chang), *SB*, January 1, 1949, 3, 10; International Dispensary (Wuzhou dayaofang) (diqiupai maijing yuganyou), *SB*, February 1, 1941, 14.
480 Chamberlain Pain Balm, *SB*, January 3, 1924, 16; Three Castles (Sanpaotai xiangyan), *SB*, January 7, 1914, 5; Ulifans, *SB*, February 1, 1941, 1.
481 Sodozont (Soshudun), *SB*, January 3, 1924, 16; Listerine, *SB*, January 5, 1934, 16; Tiger brand Snow Cream (Hupai bailanshuang), *SB*, January 3, 1924, 9; Hai'er mian, *SB*, January 5, 1934, 5, 13.
482 Sodozont (Soshudun), *SB*, January 3, 1924, 16; Listerine, *SB*, January 5, 1934, 16; Tiger brand Snow Cream (Hupai bailanshuang), *SB*, January 3, 1924, 9; Hai'er mian, *SB*, January 5, 1934, 5, 13.
483 Virol, *SB*, January 6, 1914, 14; Toa & Company (Taogu shuntian guan), *SB*, January 7, 1914, 14.

photographs. However, from the 1930s onwards, film studios began to exploit photography more successfully by incorporating film scenes or portraits of actors in their advertisements [Figure 17].[484]

During the early period, rational texts in advertisements tended to be lengthy, meticulously describing the product's qualities, instructions for use and expected effects, particularly when introducing a new and unfamiliar product.[485] Medical advertisements, such as Kepler, Sanatogen and De Witt, indulged in detailed portrayals of symptoms and ailments experienced by fictional patients, inviting readers to empathise and identify with the sufferers.[486] Testimonials played a crucial role as proof for the efficacy of medicines and cosmetics. In *Shenbao*, two types of testimonials were prevalent. Firstly, ordinary people's confessions provided a rationalised form of miracle narratives, where patients shared their recovery stories after using the remedy, aiming to evoke empathy and gain readers' trust.[487] Advertisements for products like Dr. William's Pink Pills for Pale People, Pinkettes, or Respiroids often featured portraits of presumed witnesses to authenticate the narratives.[488] Secondly, rational advertisements sought to bolster credibility through endorsements from experts or celebrities. For example, Peking opera actor Mei Lanfang was chosen to promote Du Maurier cigarettes, leveraging his fame and status.[489] Cosmetics manufacturers capitalised on the cinema trend by featuring Hollywood stars like Jean Parker endorsing Lux Toilet Soap, accompanied by taglines asserting that nine out of ten celebrities chose the brand.[490] Similarly, food and pharmaceutical products relied on endorsements from scientific experts, with claims of recommendations from doctors and even polar explorers endorsing products like Horlicks Malted Milk. In the 1930s, the appeal to authority frequently came with certificates issued by competent institutions, such as the Ministry of Health or the Shanghai Municipal Health Bureau, further solidifying the credibility of the advertised products.[491]

---

484 Carlton Theatre (Ka'erdeng daxiyuan), *SB*, January 5, 1934, 28; Cathay Theatre (Guotai daxiyuan), *SB*, January 5, 1934, 29.

485 Glaxo (Gelansu naifen), *SB*, January 3, 1924, 20.

486 Kepler, *SB*, January 6, 1914, 14; Sanatogen, *SB*, January 7, 1914, 7; De Witt Long Life Pills (Diweide huli wan), *SB*, January 1924, 8.

487 Xudaoyuan wanyao (Holland China Handels Compagnie), *SB*, January 7, 1914, 3.

488 Dr. William's Pink Pills for Pale People (Weilianshi dayisheng hongsi buwan), *SB*, January 1, 1917, 15; Pinkettes (Hongse qing daowan), *SB*, January 4, 1924, 11; Respiroids (Weilianshi xiju zhikepian), *SB*, January 6, 1934, 13.

489 Du Maurier (Dumanli xiangyan), *SB*, January 5, 1934, 24.

490 Jack Birns, Billboard advertising Lux Toilet Soap (Lishi xiangzao), Photograph, Google LIFE Photo Archive (Shanghai, January 1948), https://madspace.org/Photos/?ID=250.

491 Great Eastern Dispensary (Zhongfa dayaofang), *SB*, January 5, 1934, 13.

During the nationalist regime, rational discourse in advertisements underwent a process of politicisation. Companies sought to align themselves with the nationalist agenda and proudly displayed their national labelling and participation in nationalist events, such as the Year of Women in 1934.[492] Additionally, the imagery of laboratories and scientific equipment was extensively utilised to enhance the perceived scientific nature of production methods. Medical advertisements were adorned with test tubes, chemical formulas, microscope views and anatomical diagrams, while industries and financial institutions used statistics to demonstrate their credibility and accounting transparency.[493]

As emphasised in the textbooks, rational advertisements were not solely cerebral; they incorporated a touch of exaggeration before the war but evolved in the 1920s to adopt a more suggestive tone infused with emotions.

Tapping into Emotions

Between the First World War and the Communist revolution, advertisements in *Shenbao* underwent noteworthy transformations. The emergence of suggestive advertising was marked by illustrated life scenes, a broader sensory appeal and a shift towards more positive emotions. This new style was predominantly applied to products related to appearance and aesthetics (hygiene, cosmetics) and sensory pleasures (food, alcohol, cigarettes). The illustrations employed in suggestive advertisements fell into three main categories. Naive depictions depicted family and everyday life scenes, often featuring children or domestic animals, adding an element of charm and relatability to advertisements for products like Kepler, Taihe and Betavit, as well as Philips and Beixin Bookstore.[494] Seductive scenes centred on elegant and captivating women posing for cosmetic brands (e.g., Two Sisters, Tiger brand Snow Cream), clothing brands (Zhuanghua), or cigarette brands (My Dear), appealing to readers' aspirations and desires.[495] Still-life illustrations accompanied food and edible products, enticing readers' appetites with mouth-

---

492 Zhuanghua Wool Company (Zhanghua maorong fangzhi gongsi), *SB*, January 5, 1934, 22.

493 Dr. Yao Juyan, *SB*, February 1, 1941, 9; Sine Laboratory (Xinyi huaxue zhiyaochang), *SB*, January 5, 1934, 11, February 1, 1941, 3; Ulifans, *SB*, February 1, 1941, 1. Chinese Engineering and Mining Co. (Kaiping kangwu youxian gongsi), *SB*, January 3, 1924, 20.

494 Kepler, *SB*, January 1, 1934, 24; February 1, 1941, 7; Taihe cough syrup (Taihe baifeijiang), *SB*, February 1, 1941, 13; Betavit (Bitafei), *SB*, February 5, 1941, 4. Philips (Feilipu), *SB*, January 3, 1924, 16; Beixin Bookstore (Beixin shuju), *SB*, January 1, 1934, 6.

495 Two Sisters (Shuangmei) Face Powder, *SB*, January 7, 1914, 14; Tiger brand Snow Cream (Hupai bailanshuang), *SB*, January 3, 1924, 9; Zhuanghua Wool Company (Zhanghua maorong fangzhi gongsi), *SB*, January 5, 1934, 22; My Dear (Meilipai), *SB*, January 6, 1934, 1.

watering depictions of products like Royal Baking Powder and Maling canned goods. In the case of cigarette brands such as Red Kores, these illustrations aimed to evoke a smoker's reverie, creating an alluring and sensory experience.[496]

Suggestive advertising brought about a rich lexicon of senses and emotions, moving beyond the reliance on sight to explore neglected senses such as taste, smell and touch. This approach catered to specific products. For cigarettes and food products, the emphasis shifted to taste as early as 1914 with BAT advertisements evoking the subtle aromas of tobacco. In the 1920s, food and alcoholic beverage advertisements (e.g., Bournville Cocoa, Royal Baking Powder, Peter Dawson Scotch Whisky) presented alluring scenes to stimulate readers' taste buds. Cosmetics and hygiene products focused on the senses of smell and touch. Advertisements for perfumes, deodorants, soaps and scented creams addressed concerns about unpleasant body odours and sought to evoke enticing fragrances. Carl Crow noted that, in Chinese culture, women associated beauty with fragrance, making it essential to mention the scent in such advertisements.[497] To engage readers on multiple sensory levels, the manufacturer of Hai'ermian cream skilfully employed a refined vocabulary, evoking touch (zhidi, qing, jiao, hua, run, bainen, youguang, han, xi), smell (xiang, fenfang, han), hearing (yun) and sight (seze, yan, meihua, chi, hui'an).[498] In later years, advertisements for products like Pond's Cold Cream and Richard Hudnut (Three Flowers, Sanhua xiangshuang) continued to focus on the sense of touch and smell, emphasising the perfume and texture of the skin rather than just its appearance.[499]

After World War I, emotions in advertising underwent a significant transformation. Initially, emotions were neutral or even negative in tone. However, from the 1920s onwards, there was a shift towards more positive and uplifting emotions, particularly in advertisements for food products and cigarettes like Hatamen, Maskee and My Dear.[500] These advertisements aimed to create a festive and warm atmosphere to appeal to consumers' emotions. Despite this shift, certain medical advertisements continued to employ fear, threat, or pain as emotional triggers to elicit a response from the reader. Examples of such advertisements can be seen in Doan Backache & Kidney Pills or Santal Midy. Until the 1920s, ad-

---

496 Royal Baking Powder (Baitang xiaobing), Maling Canned Food (Meili fanqing guantou shipin), *SB*, February 1, 1941, 7; Red Kores (Hong gao lian), *SB*, January 1, 1949, 5.
497 Crow, "Advertising and Merchandising", 195.
498 Hai'er mian, *SB*, January 5, 1934, 5, 13.
499 Pond's Cold Cream (Pangshi baiyujiang), *SB*, January 5, 1934, 13; Richard Hudnut, *Three Flowers Vanishing Cream* (Sanhua xiangshuang), *SB*, February 1, 1941, 7.
500 Hatamen (Hademen), *SB*, January 4, 1924, 2; Maskee (Hongmaisi ganxiangyan), *SB*, January 5, 1934, 1; My Dear (Meilipai), *SB*, February 1, 1941, 3.

vertisements remained relatively austere, often featuring serious or concerned faces, as in the cases of Jintan and Sanatogen.[501] However, there were exceptions to this solemn trend. The Anglo-Chinese Dispensary introduced mischievous little elves in their advertisements, challenging the guidelines that prohibited comedic elements in subjects related to health and illness. The atmosphere began to lighten after the war, and by the mid-1930s childlike characters like Mickey Mouse, Snow White and Santa Claus started to appear in advertisements for products such as Listerine toothbrushes, Brandy cigarettes, Children Young Companion magazine and the nutritional supplement Covimalton.[502] The comic genre also gained popularity during this period, featuring in advertisements for hygiene and food products like Kolynos toothpaste and Quaker Oats cereal.[503]

The Renewal of Appeals

In response to, and in conjunction with, rational advertisements centred on health and safety, suggestive advertisements increasingly emphasised taste and beauty from the 1930s onward.

From Health to Taste: The Case of Food Products

With the transition from reason to suggestion, advertisements increasingly emphasised sensory pleasure over health concerns. The use of taste appeal, previously uncommon before World War I, gained prominence under the influence of the food industry. The health appeal, however, did not entirely disappear. In the *Shenbao*, both appeals coexisted, following distinct developments based on the products they were associated with. While the health appeal remained prevalent in medications, it also extended to unexpected items like cigarettes, alcoholic beverages and food products. On the other hand, the taste appeal gradually found its

---

501 Jintan (Rendan), *SB*, January 4, 1914, 9; Toa & Company (Taogu shuntian guan), *SB*, January 7, 1914, 14; Sanatogen, *SB*, January 7,1914, 7.

502 Sanatogen, Bournville Cocoa (Benwei kekefen), *SB*, January 3, 1924, 24; Hatamen (Hademen), *SB*, January 4, 1924, 2; Listerine, *SB*, January 5, 1934, 16; Children Young Companion Company (Ertong liangyou she), *SB*, January 1, 1949, 6; Covimalton (Kangfu maiju jing), *SB*, January 1, 1949, 12; The Brandy (Bailandi), *SB*, January 5, 1949, 1.

503 Quaker Oats (Guige maipian), *SB*, January 1, 1934, 16; Kolynos (Gulingyu yagao), January 5, 1934, 19.

way into medical products, where not only efficacy but also the enjoyable taste of medications became significant.

At the turn of the twentieth century, cigarettes were introduced to China as a substitute for opium and a remedy for addiction.[504] Before World War I, advertisements for brands like President (Dazongtong) and Conqueror (Qiangjun) boldly claimed the health benefits of tobacco. From 1914 onwards, however, the focus of cigarette ads shifted towards pleasure rather than health. Following the tobacco industry's lead, beverages also shed their medicinal attributes and embraced gustatory pleasure. Before the war, the alcohol sector showcased a duality of taste and health, exemplified by Hennessy Cognac's emphasis on its curative virtues and Lager Beer's lean towards sensory pleasure and refinement. The shift in focus towards pleasure occurred gradually in the mid-1920s. Examples like Dupont Cognac illustrate this transition, combining health appeal with taste in their advertisements in January 1924, emphasising the seasonality of a beverage that warmed during the winter months.[505]

The shift occurred around the same time for non-alcoholic beverages, though with variations depending on the products and brands. In 1924, Bournville cocoa continued to combine both appeals, asserting in its advertisements that hot chocolate was not only good for health but also pleasant in taste.[506] While powdered milk had been marketed for its curative properties until the 1920s, from the 1930s onwards, producers of pasteurised milk increasingly emphasised its taste qualities.[507] A 1934 advertisement for Horlick's Malted Milk suggested using it for cereal preparation or as a coffee substitute, relying on both appeals. Horlick's was presented as both a pleasurable beverage and a remedy requiring a medical prescription.[508]

Food products embraced the taste appeal at a later stage. Brands like Royal Baking Powder utilised still-life images to tantalise the reader's appetite, while Maling Canned Goods evoked the enticing colour of tomatoes to suggest their flavour and texture.[509] Some advertisements offered culinary advice and even provided readers with recipe books upon request.[510] In the 1930s, culinary guides became a prominent advertising material, exemplified by A.C. Row's campaign

---

504 Benedict, 215–16.

505 Dupont Cognac, *SB*, January 3, 1924, 17.

506 Bournville Cocoa (Benwei kekefen), *SB*, January 3, 1924, 16.

507 Liberty Dairy (Ziyou nongchang), Shanghai Dairy Farm (Shanghai xuzhi niunai gongsi), *SB*, January 5, 1934, 21.

508 Horlicks Malted Milk (Haolike maijing niurufen), *SB*, January 5, 1934, 12.

509 Maling Canned Food (Meili fanqing guantou shipin), Royal Baking Powder (Baitang xiaobing), *SB*, February 1, 1941, 7.

510 R. Calder-Marshall and P.L. Bryant, *The Anglo-Chinese Cook Book* (Shanghai: Commercial Press, 1916).

for Crescent Manufacturing Company.[511] In a similar vein, Carl Crow organised a playful baking contest to introduce the California brand of Sun-Maid raisins, which turned out to be a great success with numerous enthusiastic participants. Overwhelmed by the responses, the American publicist had to rely on the gluttony of his coolies to select the winners.[512]

To enhance their message and widen their market, copywriters often employed a combination of appeals. Sun-Maid Raisins advertisements, for instance, integrated three key arguments. Firstly, they underscored the natural richness of grapes in iron, promoting the health benefits of consuming raisins. Secondly, they leveraged the Chinese preference for snacking, positioning raisins as delightful treats to enjoy between meals. Lastly, in a bid to democratise a food once linked to luxury, the ads emphasised the reasonable selling price of individual packs, tailored to the average budget of Chinese consumers.[513]

From Health to Beauty: The Cases of Medicines and Cosmetics

In advertisements related to the culture of appearances encompassing hygiene, fashion and cosmetics, the suggestive discourse experienced a shift from health to beauty. In *Shenbao*, the beauty appeal prevailed consistently throughout the period, with health references appearing only once or twice a day on average. However, both appeals experienced a noticeable increase in the 1930s. During the Sino-Japanese War, advertisements frequently combined both beauty and health elements. By 1949, the beauty appeal had triumphed, while health completely disappeared from advertisements for cosmetics.

Until the Sino-Japanese War, advertisements for cosmetics invoked both beauty and health. While these appeals were closely intertwined in the 1920s, they gradually separated as the cosmetics industry distanced itself from the pharmaceutical sector. By the 1930s, commercial discourses became more specialised, and cosmetics were exclusively marketed as beauty products.[514] Hygiene products, on the

---

511 Letter from Albert C. Row Company (Marketing & Sales Promotion) to Alonzo Bland Calder, Shanghai, June 4, 1931, Alonzo Bland Calder Papers, 1911–1956, Hoover Institution Archives, Stanford, Calif., Box 45.

512 Crow, *Four Hundred Million Customers*, 214–15.

513 Crow, 214–15. About Sun-Maid Raisin, see previous chapters (4 to 9) and Cécile Armand, "The Grapes of Happiness: Selling Sun-Maid Raisins to the Chinese in the 1920s-1930s", *Asia Pacific Perspectives* XIII, n° 2 (Fall/Winter 2015).

514 Tzu-Hsuan Sung, "Cosmétiques, beauté et genre en Chine. Une analyse de la presse et des publicités (Fin des Qing – 1930)" (Doctoral dissertation, Lyon, ENS Lyon, 2015).

other hand, wavered between health and beauty, occasionally combining both elements, as in 1949. The history of companies partly explains the discursive links between health and appearance. Until World War I, many pharmaceutical firms manufactured medicines, hygiene products and cosmetics concurrently. The British company Burroughs Wellcome, for instance, offered at least three different products to *Shenbao* readers, including a medication (Kepler Cod Liver Oil) and two cosmetic brands (Hazeline Snow and Hazeline Rose Frost).[515] In 1934, the International Dispensary (Wuzhou dayaofang) marketed both cod liver oil (Wuzhou rubai yuganyou) and scented soaps (Rose Soap), positioning them under the dual sign of health and beauty. Towards the end of the period, the Chinese company Great China Dispensary, which had been manufacturing medicines since the 1920s, began selling creams and scented soaps relying exclusively on the beauty appeal.[516]

Implementation in Outdoor Spaces

Practitioners encountered challenges in coping with the limited space allocated to outdoor advertising in textbooks. While they could rely on the instructions provided for press advertisements, transposing these guidelines into the cityscape demanded ingenuity and capacity for adaptation. For historians studying urban advertisements, the available documentation presents its own set of limitations. Municipal archives typically prioritised the physical aspects of billboards rather than delving into the design and content of the posters. Consequently, information on the visual aspects and messaging of outdoor advertisements may be scarce or incomplete. The reliance on amateur photographs, although occasionally capturing advertisements, often resulted in images with inadequate clarity for thorough composition and content analysis. Furthermore, the compiled photographic corpus may present challenges in drawing comprehensive conclusions and tracking long-term changes in outdoor advertising practices. The heterogeneous and fragmented nature of the photographs gathered during research may hinder historians' ability to discern consistent patterns and trends in outdoor advertising over time.

Despite the challenges in documenting outdoor advertisements, a thorough examination of preserved photographs reveals a significant adherence to the guidelines outlined in advertising manuals. During the 1920s, billboards predomi-

---

515 Kepler Cod Liver Oil, *SB*, January 6, 1914, 14; Hazeline Rose Frost, *SB*, January 8, 1914, 11; Hazeline Snow, *SB*, January 12, 1914, 14.
516 Long life pills (Bailingji), *SB*, January 3, 1924, 10; Great China Dispensary (Zhongxi daoyaofang), *SB*, February 1, 1941, 1.

nantly featured enlarged reproductions depicting items like coal stoves and soap bars on Nanking Road, Asahi beer cans and Castillon champagne on the outer roads of the concessions and packs of Three Castles cigarettes along the Tianjin-Beijing railway line [Figure 13].[517] These illustrations tended to be simple and realistic, but occasionally came to life through the inclusion of characters and everyday scenes, such as an elegant Chinese woman enjoying Bournville cocoa, a young couple admiring their new "Keds" shoes, or a family embarking on a vacation in a Morris automobile. Amidst this visual focus, outdoor advertisements displayed a minimalist approach to text. Occasionally, catchy slogans like "Morris for Happiness" for Morris automobiles reinforced the basic elements of the advertisement. Due to limited space, outdoor ads relied more heavily on concise and attention-grabbing phrases than their press counterparts.

In the 1930s, outdoor advertising anticipated trends similar to those observed in *Shenbao*. The text was condensed to reduce display costs and adapt to the limited attention span of urban dwellers. The font size increased proportionally to remain legible from a distance, as seen in advertisements for Elgin cigarettes (Ai'erjin) and Darkie toothpaste (Heiren yagao).[518] Illustrated scenes multiplied and characters were placed in situations to humanise and energise previously cold and static posters. Tones appeared less dull, although it is challenging to appreciate contrast effects and colours from black and white photographs. In the aftermath of the Sino-Japanese War, poster designers focused more on the arrangement of the text and composition lines to create a sense of movement, as seen in Horse Shoe (Matipai) and The Brandy (Bailandi) brands.[519] More aggressive punctuation, using question marks and exclamation marks, engaged passers-by, as exemplified by Red Kores cigarettes (Honggaole) or Dog Head lingerie (Goutou laopai).[520] In Jack Birns' photographs, some billboards experimented with

---

517 J. Sanger, Painted sign along railway, near Tientsin, Photograph (Tianjin, 1921), 77; C.A. Bacon, "China to be 'wet'? Light beers on the two sideboards outshine "Castillon" in the centre 2-1", Photograph (Shanghai, 1929), 758; Sikh Guard on duty (Advertising for Lux Toilet Soap), Photograph, Virtual Shanghai (Shanghai, ca 1912), https://www.virtualshanghai.net/Photos/Images?ID=34159.

518 Advertisement for Elgin (Ai'erjin) cigarettes, Shanghai, January 1948 (https://madspace.org/Photos/?ID=34264); Advertisement for Darkie toothpaste (Heiren yagao), Shanghai, January 1948 (https://madspace.org/Photos/?ID=34278). From Jack Birns, Google LIFE Photo Archive.

519 Advertisement for Horse Shoe (Matipai) cigarettes, Shanghai, January 1948 (https://madspace.org/Photos/?ID=34258); Advertisement for The Brandy (Bailandi) cigarettes, Shanghai, January 1948 (https://madspace.org/Photos/?ID=34265). From Jack Birns, Google LIFE Photo Archive.

520 Advertisement for Red Kores (Honggaole) cigarettes on the Great World, Shanghai, January 1948 (https://madspace.org/Photos/?ID=34270); Advertisement for Dog Head (Goutou laopai) lingerie, Shanghai, January 1949 (https://madspace.org/Photos/?ID=34270). From Harrison Forman Collection box L10, Forman 1340, University of Wisconsin-Milwaukee Libraries, Gift of Sandra Carlyle Forman, 1987.

new typographic styles, while others took on animal forms, such as geese for the Goose cotton brand (E mianmao shan) pecking around the racecourse [Figure 18].

Figure 18: Goose-shape advertisement for the "Goose" cotton brand (E mianmao shan), Shanghai, January 1948. Jack Birns, Google LIFE Photo Archive.

The emotional discourse triumphed in outdoor spaces, as it was deemed more suitable for less educated urban audiences. On the billboards lining the streets of Shanghai, women stroke suggestive poses to attract the attention of smokers. Some posters used provocative imagery, like a pair of legs in the air, which captured attention even more than the lingerie they were meant to promote.[521] On the rooftops of buildings, Hollywood stars lent their names and faces to various cigarette and cosmetics brands, such as Elgin (Ai'erjin) and Lux Toilet Soap.[522] Amidst the turbulence of the civil war (1945–49), The Brandy (Bailandi) cigarettes brand aimed to bring humour to the streets of Shanghai, seeking to brighten the daily lives of city dwellers.[523]

---

521 Advertisement for Dog Head.
522 Advertisements for Lux Toilet Soap and Elgin cigarettes (Jack Birns).
523 Advertisements for The Brandy cigarettes (Jack Birns).

Conclusion

The advertisements featured in the Chinese press, taking *Shenbao* as an example, demonstrated a substantial alignment with the standards advocated in the text-books. Notably, a pronounced shift towards visual communication occurred from the 1920s onwards. Textual content gradually receded in prominence, giving way to an increasing emphasis on illustrations, logos, borders and typographic designs. The previously prevalent exaggerated style in early advertisements waned, supplanted by the ascendancy of rational and suggestive advertising approaches. Simultaneously, the health appeal witnessed a decline in prominence within medical, food and cosmetic advertisements, with taste and beauty emerging as primary focal points. Aiming to captivate a broader audience characterised by limited attention spans, outdoor advertisements strategically leaned towards emotive imagery, effectively overshadowing the role of text and reflective messaging.

While visual advertising gained prominence in sectors like medications, cigarettes and new consumer goods, it did not uniformly dominate all industries and products. Text continued to play a significant role in certain domains, notably in financial advertisements and school announcements. Headlines and slogans, though progressing steadily, did not fully embrace the visual shift. Moreover, subtle exaggeration persisted in brand names and product representations, subtly influencing consumer perceptions. Throughout both print and street advertisements, a pure and singular form was rarely observed. Instead, practitioners wisely adhered to the advice provided in the textbooks, skilfully combining different styles and appeals to optimise impact and expand their market reach.

Chapter 9
In Search of the Four Hundred Million Customers

Since the era of reforms following Mao Zedong's death in 1976, research on consumption in China has witnessed an unexpected surge. With the country's rapid economic growth in recent decades, scholars have come to recognise the emergence of a distinct consumer society in China worthy of dedicated study. This new paradigm, known as the "consumer revolution", has gradually overshadowed the long-standing political approach centred on the Communist revolution.[524] The wave of cultural studies has played a pivotal role in shaping historians' interest in material culture, consumption practices, consumer imaginaries and consumer politics.[525] However, many of these studies have adopted a teleological perspective, portraying the consumer society as a self-evident phenomenon, retroactively inevitable in its development. As a result, they tend to overlook the historical actors and conditions that intricately shaped its evolution. An alternative historical approach to advertising prompts us to critically deconstruct the notion of the consumer society. By understanding it as a social construct that first took root in the late Qing Empire and flourished after the First World War, we gain valuable insights into its

---

524 Deborah Davis, *The Consumer Revolution in Urban China* (Berkeley: University of California Press, 2000).

525 On the subject of consumer imaginaries, see: Barbara Mittler, "Imagined Communities Divided: Reading Visual Regimes in Shanghai's Newspaper Advertising (1860s–1910s)", in *Visualising China, 1845–1965: Moving and Still Images in Historical Narratives*, ed. Christian Henriot and Wen-hsin Yeh (Leiden: Brill, 2013), 267–378, Laikwan Pang, *The distorting mirror: visual modernity in China* (University of Hawaii Press, 2007), 102–30; Weipin Tsai, *Reading Shenbao: Nationalism, Consumerism and Individuality in China, 1919–37* (Houndmills, Basingstoke: Palgrave Macmillan, 2008); Ping Xin et Xiao Feng, "20 shiji 30 niandai shanghairen de xiaofei guan – yi 'shenbao' jiantao wei zhongxin (Consumerism in 1930s Shanghai – A Perspective from *Shenbao* Advertisements)", *Shanghai daxue xuebao*, n° 3 (2012); Yulong Tang, "Jindai Shanghai xiaofei wenhua shi yu xia Shenbao guanggao de fazhan (*Shenbao* advertisements and the development of consumer culture in modern Shanghai)", *Wenhua yuekan*, n° 6 (2017). On the subject of material culture and consumptions practices, from a *longue-durée* perspective, see: Frank Dikötter, *Things Modern: Material Culture and Everyday Life in China* (London: C. Hurst & Co. (Pub.) Ltd., 2007); Frank Dikötter, *Exotic Commodities: Modern Objects and Everyday Life in China* (New York: Columbia University Press, 2006). Regarding consumer politics, boycotts and the National Products Movement, see: Karl Gerth, *China Made: Consumer Culture and the Creation of the Nation* (Cambridge: Harvard University Press, 2003); David Embrey Fraser, "Smoking out the Enemy: The National Goods Movement and the Advertising of Nationalism in China, 1880–1937" (Doctoral dissertation, Berkeley, University of California, 1999); Min Wang, "Jindai guo huoyun dong zhongdi yanghuo xiaofei shishang" (The National Products Movements and the crave for foreign goods), *Lantai shijie*, n° 3 (2013).

https://doi.org/10.1515/9783111390000-010

historical context and complexities. Such an approach allows us to unravel the multifaceted forces that contributed to the rise of consumerism in China, shedding light on the dynamic interactions between individuals, institutions and societal norms that have driven the transformation of consumption patterns over time. Embracing this historical perspective enables a more nuanced understanding of the consumer society, avoiding the pitfalls of over-simplification and acknowledging the intricate web of historical circumstances that underpin its development.

The convergence of the emergence of the advertising profession and the birth of a consumer society in China is not a mere coincidence; rather, it reflects the pivotal role played by advertising pioneers in shaping this transformative development. Unlike studies that focus primarily on consumer imaginaries, this final chapter delves into the discursive strategies employed by advertising experts to craft and mould the image of the Chinese consumer, laying the very foundations of consumer culture in the country. Central to this investigation is an exploration of how market professionals perceived Chinese consumers and how these perceptions influenced their practices. What facts and fantasies informed their work, and how did these elements permeate their advertising campaigns? To facilitate this examination, this chapter commences with a critical assessment of the available sources that shed light on the formation of consumer society in China. It then proceeds to analyse and deconstruct the three key themes – poverty, ignorance and the weight of traditions – which collectively contributed to shaping the prevailing myth of the "four hundred million customers".

Issues with Sources

The question of who the consumers were in pre-communist China encompasses three distinct aspects: who the advertisers targeted, who purchased the products and who ultimately used them. However, the available sources, particularly advertisements, provide uneven answers to these questions, making their interpretation a delicate task. While a combined analysis of texts and images can offer hypotheses regarding the intended audience and end users of products, these conjectures remain unverifiable without access to company archives, particularly campaign plans that would explicitly outline the advertisers' intentions. As a result, historians are compelled to rely on alternative sources.

The first market studies, which emerged in Europe and the United States in the early twentieth century, proved challenging to implement in China. Local experts mentioned the difficulties they faced due to the vastness of the territory, language barriers, low levels of education and the population's distrust.[526] Unlike sociologists who participated in the social survey movement (shehui diaocha), market professionals lacked the means and expertise to conduct surveys among the lower classes. Furthermore, their objectives differed. Market experts found the middle and upper classes of the population more accessible and economically interesting to study.[527] A press article published in the *North China Herald* in 1921 reveals that the major department stores in Shanghai maintained customer registries containing their names, professions, addresses and purchasing preferences.[528] Some large companies, such as the Shanghai Bank of China, conducted detailed surveys of their staff, collecting information on income levels, family and medical status, expenses, leisure activities and consumption habits.[529] However, such surveys are exceptional and have often disappeared with the company archives.

As a result, the pioneers in advertising relied essentially on intuitive understandings of consumers, drawing from random observations gathered during their travels. Their "market surveys" lacked the methodological rigor of contemporary sociological research and were less systematic than the marketing studies that emerged in the West after World War II, a period when China was transitioning to communism.[530] These early marketing pioneers were sometimes biased by their ethnocentric perspectives, leading to fanciful conclusions. For example, Carl Crow conducted a study on soap sales, where he observed that people in northern China took daily baths even in sub-zero temperatures and consumed more meat, while the predominantly Buddhist population in the south followed a vegetarian diet and washed less frequently. Correlating religion, hygiene and diet, Crow concluded that to increase soap sales it would be necessary to persuade Buddhists to consume meat and bathe more frequently.[531]

---

526 Crow, *Four Hundred Million Customers*, 257.

527 The first social surveys in China were conducted in urban areas by missionaries and foreign sociologists such as Sidney Gamble and John Burgess in Beijing, or Herbert Lamson in Shanghai. From the 1930s onwards, Chinese sociologists such as Chen Da, Cao Yucong and Feng Rui took the lead in this movement and shifted the focus of study from cities to rural areas. Tong Lam, *A passion for facts: social surveys and the construction of the Chinese nation state, 1900–1949* (Berkeley: University of California Press, 2011), 32–38.

528 "The cost of life in Shanghai", *North China Herald*, April 16, 1921, 196.

529 Brett Sheehan, "Middling Elites: Middle Managers at the Shanghai Bank of China on the Eve of the Communist Revolution", in *Knowledge, Power, and Networks: Elites in Transition in Modern China*, ed. Cécile Armand, Christian Henriot and Huei-min Sun (Leiden: Brill, 2022), 83–112.

530 Crow, *Four Hundred Million Customers*, 257.

531 Crow, 140–41.

In the absence of corporate archives, the professional literature and local press become valuable sources for understanding how market professionals perceived consumers and shaped their social image in pre-communist China. While these sources may provide an impressionistic picture, they offer valuable insights into the evolving developments and diverse perspectives that animated professional circles during the Republican period.

Envisioning the Mass Market

The turn of the twentieth century marked a significant shift in the approach of advertisers, moving from a focus solely on their merchandise to paying greater attention to the recipients of their products. This transformation was evident in advertisements through the increasing portrayal of characters and scenes from everyday life, as explored in previous chapters. Until World War I, European and Japanese pioneers in China primarily targeted a niche market, with foreign imports catering mainly to expatriates. However, by the late 1890s, some trading houses began showing interest in the Chinese elites seeking social distinction.[532] During the war, the second wave of Chinese industrialisation led to the emergence of local substitutes for foreign imports. These Chinese-made products were more affordable, making them accessible to new population segments. The combination of decreased selling prices and increased purchasing power contributed to the development of an urban middle class and increased rural consumption.[533] After the war, a new generation of vernacular entrepreneurs and American multinational corporations began to look beyond the narrow circle of urban elites residing in treaty ports and envisioned a mass market encompassing the "four hundred million consumers". This newfound interest in the broader consumer base prompted a desire to better understand them in order to tailor products and commercial messages specifically for their needs and preferences.

In the 1920s, market professionals in China classified society into three hierarchically organised groups based on social status and education level. In his 1921 survey, trade commissioner Sanger briefly mentioned the 150,000 foreign nationals and focused more extensively on the indigenous society. At the top, he explained, power rested in the hands of mandarins and scholar-officials. Although a minority (a few tens of thousands), these educated elites had significant purchas-

---

532 Sanger, 58; Gerth, *China Made*, 53, 68–72.

533 Gerth, *China Made*, 52–66; Thomas G Rawski, *Economic Growth in Prewar China* (Berkeley: University of California Press, 1989), 208–9; Marie-Claire Bergère, *L'âge d'or de la bourgeoisie chinoise, 1911–1937* (Paris: Flammarion, 1986).

ing power. The second group comprised merchants, businessmen and intellectual elites. Although less affluent, they were more numerous and had a greater influence on consumption practices. At the bottom were millions of peasants and coolies, mostly illiterate, living near the poverty line. Sanger emphasised that their inability to read advertisements and access the offered products posed a significant constraint from a commercial perspective.[534] In his 1929 report, journalist Bacon adopted a similar classification, placing greater emphasis on the cultural profile of consumers. The top group consisted of expatriates and Westernised Chinese elites who regularly read the foreign press. Just below them were educated but non-English-speaking Chinese who engaged with the vernacular press. At the lowest rung of the social ladder, illiterate individuals constituted 90% of the population, making outdoor advertising the most effective means to reach them.[535]

The myth of the "four hundred million" gradually took shape towards the end of the Qing dynasty, initially devoid of any commercial connotation. Instead, the figure symbolised the vast potential and fears evoked by the immense Chinese population. After World War I, the metaphor evolved to be applied to the market, gaining prominence with Carl Crow's eponymous bestseller, *Four Hundred Million Customers*. However, the figure remained ambivalent, carrying different meanings and competing points of view. For American exporters, China seemed like an Eldorado capable of absorbing surplus goods that their domestic market could not accommodate.[536] On the other hand, Chinese nationalist elites saw the development of domestic consumption as vital for strengthening the nation and emancipating it from imperialist powers.[537] Despite the allure of this myth, numerous challenges emerged, tempering the pioneers' enthusiasm. By the 1920s, on-the-ground publicists warned distant clients enchanted by this statistical mirage of potential pitfalls. By the time Crow's novel was published, the metaphor of the "four hundred million" had lost its dream-like quality and gave way to a more realistic understanding of the challenges and complexities of the Chinese market.

---

534 Sanger, 55–56.
535 Bacon, 764. These alarmist figures must be approached with caution, lacking systematic investigation to support them. Recent research has established that in the early years of the Republic, approximately 30% of the Chinese population was able to read a simple text. With the development of mass primary education during the Republican period, historians have calculated that the number of students increased six-fold within a generation, from 2.8 million in 1930 to 11 million, and then to 17 million in 1945. See: Xavier Paulès, *La République de Chine: histoire générale de la Chine: 1912–1949* (Paris: Belles-Lettres, 2019), 308–9.
536 Michael H. Hunt, "Americans in the China Market: Economic Opportunities and Economic Nationalism, 1890s-1931," *The Business History Review* 51, n° 3 (October 1, 1977): 277–307.
537 Kuo, "Foreign Trade and Advertising", 27–28; Tong, "Newspapers as an Advertising Medium in China", 29–32.

During the Republican period in China, the formation of a mass market faced significant challenges. The vastness of the territory, internal customs and inadequate transportation networks hindered the free movement of goods and the integration of a national market. Despite efforts to promote a national vernacular language, the divide between the classical culture inherited from the imperial era and the diverse range of local dialects persisted until 1949. As a result, communication and advertising campaigns remained largely localised due to the absence of nationwide coverage media.[538] The lack of reliable data on the Chinese population further complicated the work of market professionals. While there were gradual improvements in purchasing power and education levels, certain habits and cultural norms hindered the adoption of foreign consumer goods. Variations in dietary habits, medical culture and gender relations were often cited as serious impediments in professional literature. However, these portrayals of Chinese society, partially based on reality and partly fantastical, require critical examination.

Three Tropes in Professional Literature

Illiteracy and Visuality

During the Republican era, the prevailing theme of widespread illiteracy was a significant concern among Chinese reformers and foreign observers alike. The lack of education was seen as a major problem in Chinese society, and it became a recurrent topic in professional literature. To address this issue, market professionals often depicted illiteracy through three distinct social archetypes, each associated with specific media: rumours for peasants, colourful posters for coolies and illustrated magazines for housewives. While they highlighted the need for choosing the most suitable medium to reach the target audience effectively, they also recognised that the vernacular press remained the most effective channel for reaching the entire territory.[539]

In addition to utilising the press, advertisers in China showed a keen interest in exploring other forms of printed media. An intriguing observation by U.S. trade commissioner Sanger revealed a certain fascination with the written language among the less educated Chinese. Notably, it was not uncommon for them to retain freely distributed advertising brochures they encountered on the streets and seek the assistance of more educated neighbours to read the content. In rural areas,

---

538 Tong.
539 Crow, "Advertising and Merchandising", 196; Bacon, 763–64; Sanger, 65–66; Tong, 32.

word-of-mouth communication remained an effective method to introduce new brands and propagate them from one village to another. Market professionals observed that multinational corporations, such as British-American Tobacco and Morishita, adeptly incorporated elements of traditional folkloric practices such as processions, itinerant storytellers, and fly-kite displays, to effectively introduce their products in the most remote provinces. However, these methods inspired by popular culture mainly proved efficient within small rural communities. Their effectiveness waned among urban populations who demanded more sophisticated methods.[540]

Outdoor advertising in republican China was primarily perceived as a complement to the press, serving as a means to enhance its reach and effectiveness. However, its impact was more localised and challenging to quantify.[541] In socially diverse treaty ports like Shanghai, advertisers carefully selected their medium based on both social and spatial considerations. Newspapers and billboards were indispensable for those aiming to engage the entire urban population, while colourful and illuminated advertisements were specifically tailored to target the lower classes. To maximise its popularity and visibility, British-American Tobacco ingeniously erected a luminous clock displaying its brand at a bustling intersection in Shanghai, strategically capturing the attention of a vast audience passing through the area. Combining light and movement, this spectacle featured minimalist text, making the message easily comprehensible and memorable.[542] However, such elaborate installations were exceptional, as they incurred substantial costs for construction and maintenance. Similarly, sound advertising was a rare venture, as only a minority of professionals experimented with it. For instance, in the 1930s, Millington contemplated parking radio trucks outside stadiums and factories, but these devices faced strict regulations and were generally prohibited in the already noisy and congested streets of Shanghai.[543] Advertisers, seeking to expand their audience, also recognised the potential of urban transportation. However, it was not until 1928 that commercial advertising was permitted on the exteriors of trams and buses in the International Settlement of Shanghai.[544]

---

540 Sanger, 77–81.
541 Crow, "Advertising and Merchandising", 198; Bacon, 764; "The Advertiser's Dilemma: Another Chinese Puzzle", *NCH*, June 1929.
542 Bacon, 764; Wu and Zhu, 288.
543 F.C. Millington, Suggested Revenue from Advertising on Trams, Buses, Lorries, etc. (August 1928); Tramway Company, Advertising on Exterior of Trams (November–December 1928), SMA (SMC), U1-3-1284.
544 Sanger, 79.

During the New Year period, some advertisers sought to capitalise on the popularity of commercial calendars, which were not only functional timekeeping devices but also aesthetically pleasing interior decorations for households. Their aim was to introduce their brands into the intimacy of people's homes and establish a lasting presence in their daily lives. However, the use of commercial calendars as an advertising medium did not enjoy unanimous support within professional circles. Carl Crow observed that the most refined calendars remained out of reach for the less affluent, and he questioned whether the initial investment justified their limited impact on sales.[545] Similarly, Crow advised against the use of coupons and free samples as promotional tools. While these offers often generated a significant response, the majority of respondents did not necessarily translate into a viable market. Moreover, such promotions could occasionally backfire on the advertiser. Crow recounted an incident where a newspaper delivery person, having learned about a special offer before its launch, collected all the coupons and resold them before the morning edition was published. On another occasion, the offer attracted such a large crowd in front of the store that it led to a disturbance, resulting in the advertiser having to pay a fine.[546] However, these uncertainties in the effectiveness of certain advertising strategies seemed to be better managed in the 1930s. As seen in previous chapters, specialised agencies like the Consolidated Coupon Company contributed to the widespread adoption of coupon practices within Chinese society.

The Power of the Pocket

The depiction of massive poverty, often symbolised by the figure of the coolie, was a recurring theme in professional literature during the Republican era. However, it is essential to approach this portrayal with caution, considering the various factors influencing its presentation. Foreign observers, operating within the framework of the "unequal treaties" regime, tended to exaggerate the issue of poverty, influenced by prevailing colonialist ideologies. Many expatriates and missionaries, convinced of their own cultural superiority, sought to justify their presence in China through such portrayals. Similarly, Chinese reformers, driven by a comparative obsession with Western societies, were also prone to evaluating their country's performance through this lens. Despite the political instability and recurring crises of the time,

---

545 Sanger, 81–82. Crow, "Advertising and Merchandising", 200. On the making of calendars, see: Ellen Johnston Laing, *Selling Happiness: Calendar Posters and Visual Culture in Early Twentieth-Century Shanghai* (Honolulu: University of Hawai'i Press, 2004).
546 Crow, "Advertising and Merchandising", 200; *Four Hundred Million* Customers, 52–55.

the overall poverty level in China tended to decline during the Republican era. The boundaries between luxury and necessity were shifting, exemplified by products like cigarettes, once considered luxury items before World War I, becoming more accessible in the following decades. The development of the Chinese industry, enabling mass production of affordable substitutes, played a decisive role in broadening the social scope of consumption. This transformation allowed previously unattainable goods to reach a broader segment of the population, contributing to the gradual improvement in living standards and expanding consumer possibilities.[547]

The degree of accessibility to various products in China during the Republican era indeed varied significantly. While items like cigarettes, cosmetics and food products experienced a gradual increase in popularity and affordability in the 1920s, automobiles remained luxury items until 1949. Among these products, cigarettes stood out as one of the fastest growing and widely adopted mass consumer goods. Introduced to China in the late nineteenth century, cigarettes witnessed a remarkable surge in sales from 300,000 in 1902 to 88 million in 1933 for British-American Tobacco alone. Journalist Bacon noted that by the late 1920s, cigarettes had emerged as the true mass product in China, surpassing all others, especially when considering outdoor publicity.[548] However, despite their widespread popularity, the tobacco market remained highly segmented. Many smokers opted for generic and more affordable products. To cater to consumers with different budgets, manufacturers employed various pricing strategies based on quantity sold. For instance, British-American Tobacco offered cigarettes in packs of ten or 50, accommodating different consumer preferences. Morishita similarly provided two different sizes for its famous Jintan medicine brand to meet varying needs. Sun-Maid Raisin adapted to local living standards by reducing the size of its packages compared to those sold in the United States, significantly lowering the unit selling price. These pricing adjustments aimed to expand the consumer base and cater to a wider audience, particularly the emerging urban middle class and rural consumers.

Indeed, price was not the sole decisive factor influencing purchasing decisions in the Chinese consumer market during the Republican era. Market professionals discovered that several less quantifiable parameters significantly impacted consumer behaviour. Individual preferences and brand loyalty played a crucial role in shaping choices, as consumers developed affinities for specific products and brands over time. Moreover, the recycling culture in China had a notable influence on consumer choices and product packaging. Local experts observed that the Chinese pop-

---

547 Margherita Zanasi, *Saving the Nation: Economic Modernity in Republican China* (Chicago: University of Chicago Press, 2006).
548 Bacon, 756, 764.

ulation was adept at repurposing packaging materials, leading to a heightened focus on the utility value of product packaging. For instance, metal cans found new life as small household stoves, while colourful packaging was ingeniously transformed into decorative objects. Not only did consumers find creative uses for packaging, but they also engaged in resale practices, where certain packaging items were resold for considerably higher prices than their initial purchase price.[549]

Cultural Barriers to Consumption

The question of what products could be successfully sold to the Chinese market during the Republican era was a complex one, influenced by various cultural and social factors. While some products, like cigarettes, medications and food items, gained popularity and widespread acceptance, others faced cultural barriers that impeded their adoption. Foreign observers and market professionals were divided on the universality of consumption practices in China. Trade commissioner Sanger believed that Chinese ways of living and thinking were so different that they challenged the notion of a universal human nature. He pointed out various singularities in Chinese society, such as social divisions based on education and wealth, dress codes, etiquette rules and ancestor worship. Dietary habits were another significant cultural barrier, as seen in the failure of a condensed milk brand campaign that portrayed Chinese consumers pouring milk into their tea or coffee, unaware that the Chinese disliked coffee and drank their tea plain. This canonical example, echoed by commercial attaché Julean Arnold, highlights the potential consequences of overlooking cultural nuances in advertising. The fact that no advertisements in the *Shenbao* reproduced this "error" indicates a level of cultural awareness among foreign advertisers who increasingly recognised the importance of aligning their messages with the preferences and habits of their audience.[550] Sanger's observations revealed other intriguing disparities in body culture. While talcum powder and tooth powder enjoyed considerable success, shampoos faced resistance among Chinese women who preferred dry hair washing. This preference was evident in the *Shenbao*'s advertising landscape, which prominently featured powders and toothpaste ads but noticeably lacked any shampoo promotions.[551] Carl Crow, on the other hand, took a more cosmopolitan approach, emphasising the universality of needs shared by Chinese and Ameri-

---

549 Crow, *Four Hundred Million* Customers, 51–52, 56–57, 212.
550 Crow, "Advertising and Merchandising", 195.
551 In the examined samples of *Shenbao*, we have found only one instance of shampoo advertisement: Qushi dayaofang (Sanmei paisheng fayou), *SB*, January 7, 1914, 8.

cans. He believed that differences between cultures primarily lay in minor details like colours, materials, or textures, while the fundamental desires and needs were the same.[552]

Foreign observers held contrasting views regarding the universal appeal of certain needs in Chinese society, particularly regarding food and clothing. Bacon believed that food products circulated easily due to the absolute necessity of eating, while clothing culture faced challenges in export due to varied tastes and fashion preferences between countries. However, there were exceptions; rare commodities like mangoes found success in Shanghai, and Californian oranges could compete with local varieties due to their larger size, better taste and improved preservation. In contrast, Carl Crow emphasised that dietary habits in China were vastly different, making it challenging for foreign foods to find a place in Chinese cuisine, except for rare instances among Westernised elites who consumed imported items like raisins.[553] However, he saw fashion as an easily circulated cultural element. As a witness to cultural changes after the 1911 revolution, Crow noted how the adoption of skirts had liberated Chinese women's fashion, and as a publisher of the first fashion catalogue in the vernacular language, he believed that advertising had the transformative power to influence clothing practices.[554]

As the 1920s unfolded, cultural practices in China underwent rapid changes, leading to some intriguing anomalies in consumption patterns. Notably, foreign observers like Bacon were surprised by the success of seemingly "superfluous" novelties such as phonographs and radios in the Chinese market.[555] The boundary between universality and diversity in consumer preferences was not fixed and shifts in cultural barriers varied depending on the products and social groups involved. Within a span of less than ten years after Sanger's survey, certain cultural barriers began to shift, revealing a dynamic and evolving consumer landscape. However, while novelties found acceptance, some traditional practices persisted alongside modern ones. For instance, despite the widespread adoption of ciga-

---

552 Crow, *Four Hundred Million Customers*, 39–40. In his thesis on the American community in Shanghai, James Huskey makes a distinction between "cosmopolitan" Americans, who felt a certain sympathy towards the local population, and those marked by a "parochial" mindset, who held disdain for the Chinese and kept themselves apart. Carl Crow's ambivalent attitude suggests that these two categories were not mutually exclusive. James Layton Huskey. "Americans in Shanghai: Community Formation and Response to Revolution, 1919–1928" (Doctoral Dissertation, University of North Carolina, 1985).
553 Crow, 215–16.
554 Crow, 29–32.
555 Bacon, 763.

rettes, they did not entirely replace older practices like water pipes.[556] Similarly, while health remained a universally pursued goal, medical practices continued to be culturally differentiated. Chinese consumers remained attached to their family doctors and continued the use of self-medication, often favouring traditional remedies over new and more expensive pharmaceutical products. These deeply entrenched preferences, however, did not deter advertisers from attempting to influence habits. Advertisements for products like Scott's Emulsion, for instance, sought to promote new practices, encouraging readers to take early action in treating symptoms and even adopting preventive measures.[557]

Foreign food products found a place in local diets without causing significant disruptions. Grapes had been known in China since ancient times but were cultivated in small quantities. It was the introduction of raisins by the Californian company Sun-Maid that popularised their consumption as snacks between meals or desserts at banquets. Similarly, Bournville cocoa gained popularity as a remedy for indigestion and chronic insomnia caused by excessive tea consumption, as observed by Carl Crow. Other products like Quaker Oats and Horlicks Malted Milk became popular due to their resemblance to congee, a nutritious rice porridge appreciated in Chinese culture.[558] Only the consumption of milk itself represented a true revolution, although it was limited to urban elites until the Sino-Japanese War.[559] On the other hand, some foods, like cheese, failed to establish themselves in China, primarily due to issues with its smell and an unfortunate translation.

Conclusion

While the mass market remained an elusive concept during the Republican era, the three decades between the First World War and the Communist revolution marked an unprecedented attempt to broaden the consumer social base in China. Starting in the 1920s, advertising professionals cultivated the myth of the "four hundred million" to express the fantasy of a market with staggering potential, while not denying the obstacles that hindered its development – poverty, illiteracy and cultural preferences. In fact, acknowledging these challenges became an

---

556 Benedict, *Golden-Silk Smoke*, 136–39, 149–62.
557 *SB*, January 7, 1914, 7.
558 Crow, 216.
559 Susan Glosser, *Chinese Visions of Family and State, 1915–1953* (Berkeley: University of California Press, 2003); Jia-Chen Fu, *The Other Milk Reinventing Soy in Republican China* (Seattle: University of Washington Press, 2018).

integral part of their legitimisation strategy. By exaggerating difficulties, these professionals sought to underscore the value and importance of their work. Advertising, with its persuasive power, promised to mitigate the constraints of limited purchasing power. Through visual imagery, it could transcend educational limitations, and through its didactic approach, it aimed to reform consumer habits. The impact on actual sales and consumers was not as crucial as the professionals' ability to construct a credible representation of society, convincing clients to employ their services. Ultimately, the success of advertising hinged on constructing a compelling portrayal of the market's potential and their expertise in navigating its complexities.

Assessing the power of advertising during the early twentieth century in China was a challenging task, and the professional literature acknowledged the difficulty of measuring its impact on sales and consumer behaviour. While the effectiveness of newspaper advertising could be evaluated to some extent through returned coupons, providing evidence that the advertisement had been read, assessing the impact of outdoor advertising was more elusive. Newspapers occasionally reported on the public's reactions to outdoor advertisements, such as the fascination with the first electric advertisements or the scandal caused by provocative movie posters. Concerns about the visual impact on residential areas were also documented. However, the focus was often on the most spectacular or controversial artifacts, and little attention was given to the daily influence of more mundane advertisements. To gain insights into the ordinary experiences of city-dwellers and newspaper readers, historians would need to delve into municipal archives and carefully examine photographs. These sources may reveal the subtle and indirect ways that advertising shaped consumer attitudes and behaviours, going beyond the sensationalised stories highlighted in the press.

Conclusion

Hong Kong, December 11, 2018, Lai Chi Kok metro (Kowloon). A young Chinese man in a suit and tie is waiting for me at the top of the stairs to take me to the Adling advertising agency's headquarters. I have been waiting for this moment for months. Heir to the China Commercial Advertising Agency (CCAA) founded in 1926, Adling is the only pre-communist agency that has survived to this day. A year earlier, I had tracked down the founder's grandson on the social network LinkedIn. The Lin family was now living in Vancouver, but a meeting had been arranged with the head of the agency in Hong Kong. Was I at last about to get my hands on those precious archives I had been searching for in vain since the beginning of my research? From the subway station, we walked a few minutes to reach the agency. Far from the Admiral Square and the business centre, Lai Chi Kok is an uninspiring district where the working classes and small businesses live for the sake of cheap rents. Arriving at the foot of an unassuming building, we climb several floors. At the end of a corridor, my host stops in front of a door on which a small plate simply indicates Adling (Holding) Ltd. The young manager invites us to enter. Behind the door there is a narrow office full of files, shared by the agency's sole two employees. What a shock! Imbued with U.S. television series, I had imagined that a Chinese Don Draper would receive me in a huge glass office overlooking the bay. Sadness followed disappointment. Was this all that was left of the Chinese J. Walter Thompson of the 1930s?[560]

Because they disappeared without leaving archives, professional agencies like CCAA remained in the shadows of history for a long time. Historians have focused on commercial calendars, illustrated advertisements in the press, iconic brands like Jintan, or massive campaigns by multinational corporations like the British-American Tobacco Company. Despite the wealth of these works, our knowledge was limited to the margins and the surface of the advertising industry, while its main protagonists remained hidden behind the scenes of history. For the first time, this work has attempted to bring them into the light. In the aftermath of World War I, the first self-proclaimed professionals made efforts to distance themselves

---

560 Don Draper is the main protagonist of the television series *Mad Men*, which is set in a New York advertising agency in the late 1950s. Founded in 1864, the J. Walter Thompson Company is one of the oldest and most important American advertising agencies. It has left an exceptionally rich archive, held at Duke University, Durham, North Carolina (John Hartman Center for Sales, Advertising & Marketing History, David M. Rubenstein Rare Book & Manuscript Library). On this subject, see: Cécile Armand, "J. Walter Thompson Newsletters (1910–2005) – A Journey", blog post, *Advertising History* (blog), consulted on July 29, 2022, https://advertisinghistory.hypothe ses.org/1284.

https://doi.org/10.1515/9783111390000-011

from brokers and so-called "charlatans" that could harm their reputation. Claiming professionalism, independence and service to the public, drawing references from the arts and sciences, as well as antiquity and progress, they succeeded in making advertising a respectable and ultimately indispensable activity from the 1930s onwards. Unlike well-known professions such as lawyers and doctors, strictly regulated by the state and cemented by nationalism, the advertising profession asserted itself as a relatively open and multinational interprofessional group, functioning on the basis of self-regulation. While associations allowed pioneers to gather and organise themselves, it was independent agencies that, from the 1920s onwards, implemented the professional ideal. Although they did not eliminate amateurism, these specialised agencies contributed to making advertising a full-fledged industry. While foreigners initially dominated after World War I, vernacular agencies multiplied under the Nanjing regime (1927–37) and eventually came to prominence after the Sino-Japanese War (1937–45), sometimes forming true conglomerates, such as the Lianhe agency. Reflecting the central role that advertising occupied in the group's strategy, the Lianhe agency was the focal point within the constellation of companies controlled by its partners, covering sectors as diverse as the press, textile industry, tobacco, finance and food products.

Chinese advertising was shaped by the pace of global history while following its own trajectory. The two world wars had a decisive impact on its development. The end of World War I facilitated the birth of the first independent agencies, founded by American journalists like Carl Crow and by Chinese professionals educated in the United States, such as Lin Zhenbin, Lu Meiseng and Wang Yingbin. The nationalist regime was conducive to the formation of vernacular agencies, although many were short-lived and did not survive the Nanjing decade euphoria. The Sino-Japanese War ultimately eliminated all foreign competition, both in the advertising industry and in the production of consumer goods. It provided conglomerates like Lianhe with the opportunity to increase their prestige through their contribution to the war effort and post-war reconstruction. In this regard, World War II played a legitimising role for Chinese agencies similar to the one played by World War I for American agencies in the United States.[561] The available documentation suggests that during the Republican period advertising agencies were not solely utilised by private businesses but were also sought after by public institutions. Instances such as Millington's involvement in the launch of the first national radio station and Lin Zhenbin's campaigns promoting athletic

---

561 Regarding the impact of World War I on advertising agencies in the United States, see: Cécile Armand, "JWT et la guerre (WWI)", Blogpost, *Advertising History*, consulted July 28, 2022, https:// advertisinghistory.hypotheses.org/1679.

games and road construction indicate that advertising techniques and expertise were not limited to commercial enterprises but also extended to the public sector. The political applications of advertising during this period warrant further investigation, although it falls beyond the scope of the current study. Such an examination should focus on understanding how advertising techniques were recycled and adapted between the public and private sectors and across different regimes. By delving into this area, scholars can gain insights into how the advertising industry's development during the Republican era laid the groundwork for propaganda strategies used by subsequent regimes.

Mobile and versatile, advertising professionals were emblematic of the new class of cultural entrepreneurs that emerged during the Republican era, navigating between journalism, industry, philanthropy, arts and academia. The individual trajectories examined in this book reveal that, during this incubation period, there were not just one but multiple routes to entering the advertising profession, although the curricula became more standardised in the 1930s. While Carl Crow and Francis Millington, coming from journalism and scouting, incidentally found themselves in advertising, for Lin Zhenbin, Lu Meiseng and Wang Yingbing, acquiring a high-level academic education from top American universities was part of a long-term entrepreneurial strategy. While the war brought an end to the careers of expatriates in China, it was the Communist revolution in 1949 that interrupted or redirected the paths of Chinese advertisers. Some, like Lin Zhenbin or Millington, chose to continue their activities in Hong Kong, Europe and the United States. Others, like the Lianhe's artisans, remained in China and briefly benefited from the restructuring of the industry before being swept away by the wave of nationalisations imposed in the mid-1950s. The fate of these leaders and their personnel remains an area of interest for further research. Additionally, exploring the transfer of skills from the Republican to the Communist regime is crucial in understanding how the talents and expertise inherited from the former period were assimilated by the latter. Bridging the gap between the historiographies of these two regimes would provide valuable insights into the transition and continuity between them.

This extensive research offers a valuable complement to previous monographic studies, shedding light on the crucial role that the professionalisation of advertising during the Republican era played in scaling up Chinese capitalism and diversifying its markets. Prior to the emergence of independent agencies, only industry giants in the pharmaceutical and tobacco sectors, such as British-American Tobacco, Nanyang Brothers and the International Dispensary, heavily engaged in advertising using their in-house services. Independent agencies did not replace these internal services but they expanded the reach of advertising to a broader range of products and allowed smaller advertisers to access advertising opportunities. These professional agencies became instrumental in driving the boom of consumer industries, which, in turn, became their primary clients after World War I. One of the most notable effects of this development was the widespread creation of commercial brands, previously reserved for multinational corporations like BAT and vernacular industrialists such as Huang Chujiu or Chen Dexian, who successfully established cultural brands like Rendan and Butterfly (Wudipai), respectively. In addition to traditional trademarks, these cultural brands aimed at filling gaps in industrial protection and sought to establish an emotional connection with product users. This approach facilitated the emergence of new consumer categories, particularly women and children, who were central to the debates in the natalist climate of the interwar period and were key targets of social "regeneration" programs pursued by the nationalist regime.

The 1920s witnessed the emergence of professional literature that provided advertising with a theoretical framework and better codified its practices. While the initial writings were the work of foreign experts or translated from American manuals, Chinese professionals quickly broke free from Western norms and began producing their own literature by the late 1920s. While embracing the ideal of simplicity advocated by foreigners, Chinese authors gave it a distinct significance. Influenced by the New Culture and the May Fourth Movement (1919), they linked simplicity to the project of creating a vernacular language (baihua) in reaction to the classical *literati* culture inherited from the imperial period. The call for simplicity also aligned with the efforts of vernacular industrialists like Chen Dexian, who focused on producing popular knowledge (changshi). However, as the period progressed, authors of advertising manuals introduced an abundance of neologisms and adopted more technical vocabulary, drawing from new cognitive and social sciences. This move distinguished their literature from the popular magazines of vernacular industrialists, which targeted a broad audience of amateurs and enthusiasts. The advertising manuals, on the other hand, were aimed at an elite group of practitioners and students eager to learn about the state of the art in their field. By emphasising their professionalism and the scientific nature of their knowledge, the new professionals sought to distance themselves from the perceived discredit that hung over the advertising profession, which was often associated with "amateurs" and "charlatans". During the Republican era, the adoption of images in advertising, initially advocated by foreigners to address the perceived illiteracy of the Chinese population, was also embraced by Chinese professionals. However, they ascribed new functions to images, appreciating their educational qualities and their ability to evoke emotions. As a result, visual advertising steadily gained prominence in the Chinese press. While the production of fully illustrated advertisements remained a luxury during this period, Chinese copywriters were innovative in finding ways to enhance the appeal of their ads. They employed various techniques, such as strategic composition, creative borders, impactful typography and leveraging the visual properties of Chinese characters, to capture the attention of their audience and effectively convey their messages.

Ultimately, this book provides a nuanced perspective on the narrative of "Westernisation" in Chinese society, a prevalent theme in the historiography of the Republican era since the works of scholars like John Fairbank and Marie-Claire Bergère.[562] While the paradigm of modernisation gained prominence after Mao Zedong's death and the Reform era in China (1978–), replacing the focus on revolution, the more recent sino-centric perspective has replaced the "response to the West" approach, which previously suggested that foreign intrusion stimulated Chinese modernisation. In contrast, this research navigates a middle ground, highlighting the contributions of various actors, including vernacular industrialists, Chinese professionals educated in the United States and foreign experts active in China, to the development of the advertising industry, each with their distinct objectives. Interactions among these groups are evident from available information, including personnel mobility and joint participation in professional organisations. Due to the lack of access to their archives, however, the specifics of these contacts remain elusive. It is conceivable that rising competition in the 1920s and 1930s may have led to concerns about intellectual property, fear of counterfeiting and a focus on maintaining professional secrecy, which could have potentially hindered exchanges among these groups.

More than two decades ago, Sherman Cochran pondered the origins of advertising in modern China, considering whether it was imported from outside or locally invented.[563] This vast question has sparked diverse and sometimes contradictory answers within the historiography of modern China and its relationship with the West, ranging from ideas of imitation and adaptation to appropriation and hybridisation. In my research, rather than seeking the cultural origins of Chinese advertising, I chose to focus on tracing the journey of the social actors who played a pivotal role in its development. By delving into the experiences of U.S.-trained professionals, I uncovered the crucial role they played in introducing American advertising methods to China. Through their writings, teachings and agency management, these pioneers were eager to share the knowledge gained during their studies while adapting it to

---

562 John King Fairbank and Ssu-yü Teng, *China's Response to the West: A Documentary Survey, 1839–1923* (Cambridge: Harvard University Press, 1954); Paul A Cohen, *Discovering History in China: American Historical Writing on the Recent Chinese Past* (New York: Columbia University Press, 1984); Bergère, *L'âge d'or de la bourgeoisie chinoise, 1911–1937.*
563 Sherman Cochran, ed. *Inventing Nanjing Road: Commercial Culture in Shanghai, 1900–1945* (Ithaca, NY: Cornell University Press, 1999), 3–18.

local conditions and concerns. While foreign pioneers like Carl Crow grappled with translating texts and sinicising imagery for multinational brands, their Chinese counterparts were dedicated to expanding the consumer base and tailoring advertising messages to the nuanced differences of gender, age and social class that shaped Chinese society. Their efforts led to the gradual acceptance of once unthinkable representations and practices, such as orientalist motifs, domestic animals, dairy products and the use of coupons to incentivise purchases – a technique that the Lianhe agency excelled at. Over time, certain taboos surrounding colours, symbols and products waned, largely due to the work of these vernacular professionals. The amalgamation of cultural diversity in treaty ports and the widespread distribution of newspapers further facilitated the acceptance of these evolving representations and practices within Chinese consumer culture.

Exchanges in the field of advertising were not one-sided. In addition to numerous young Chinese students traveling abroad to gain new knowledge, professionals from around the world flocked to Shanghai to study local agencies and explore the potential of the multimillion-dollar market. After the First World War, American-educated experts contemplated the idea of a mass market in China, while acknowledging the obstacles in its realisation. Amidst the discourse, the metaphor of the "four hundred million consumers" emerged as a cautionary tale and a justification for the uncertain impact of advertising. Poverty, illiteracy and cultural barriers were often cited, but foreign observers and Chinese reformers differed in their perspectives. The former displayed condescension and sympathy without earnestly seeking change, while the latter viewed these challenges as hindrances to their country's modernisation, actively working to overcome them. As social surveys and vernacular sociology emerged, Chinese market professionals shifted their focus from cultural differences between nations, which preoccupied the pioneers, to the social disparities within Chinese society. Their main concern was to mitigate the impact of recurring crises that plagued the young Republic. Advocates of gradual change rather than radical revolution, these enlightened capitalists engaged in philanthropic activism and occasional political involvement. For instance, the Lianhe agency utilised advertising resources to raise funds, assist refugees, establish hospitals and finance scholarships. Their patriotism went beyond nationalism, as they redirected efforts towards resisting Japan after the invasion of Manchuria in 1931, demonstrating a more tolerant outlook towards Western imperialism.

After a three-decade hiatus during the Maoist regime, the myth of the "four hundred million" has experienced a resurgence with the advent of Deng Xiaoping's reforms (1978–). Now surpassing a billion people and propelled by rapid economic growth, the mass market has far exceeded the predictions of pioneers from the previous century, although in the past decade the rise of inequality and increasing environmental concerns have begun to reveal the market's inherent limitations.

During the Republican era, advertising exerted a profound influence on Chinese society, extending well beyond the confines of professional circles. It left a significant impact on the daily lives of urban dwellers and newspaper readers. As the absence of company archives necessitated alternative research methods, we have uncovered previously unexplored facets of Chinese advertising. How did advertisements shape the reading experience of newspapers and their economic models during the Republican era? How did they transform urban landscapes and the spatial dynamics of Chinese cities? What challenges did they present to municipal administrations in terms of urban planning? How did city dwellers react to the increasing influence of advertising on their daily lives? These lesser-known aspects form the core of a separate research endeavour, which readers will encounter in the second book that constitutes the second part of this comprehensive study.

Appendices

Table 1: Advertising agencies in Shanghai (1896–1956).

Name (English)	Vernacular	Pinyin	Start Year	End Year
A.A. Art Service Studio	愛愛美術印刷靈?社	Ai'ai meishu yinshua ling? she	1938	
Acme Advertising Agency	愛克美廣告公司	Aikemei guanggao gongsi	1923	1943
Advertisers' Guild (Shanghai branch)	上海特別市廣告同業公會	Shanghai tebieshi guanggao tongye gonghui	1930	1930
Advertising Art Studio			1942	1943
Advertising Service	維利廣告公司	Weili guanggao gongsi	1941	1941
Aerial Advertising Company (P. Boorlin & Company)			1921	1921
Aiming Advertising Service Incorporated	一敏廣告社	Yimin guanggao she	1930	
Arrow Advertising Agency	愛羅廣告公司	Ailuo guanggao gongsi	1926	1927
Art and Drawing Studio	聯揮書社, 聯揮美術社	Lianhui shushe, Lianhui meishu she	1935	1941
Art Picture Advertising Company	星發洋行	Xingfa yanghang	1928	1929
Asahi Advertising Company			1931	
Asahi Donchu Kokokusha			1943	
Asia Advertising Company	亞西亞廣告公司	Ya xiya guanggao gongsi	1940	1941
Asia Decorating & Advertising Company	亞洲圖畫廣告公司	Yazhou tuhua guanggao gongsi	1928	1937
Associated Advertisers, Federal Incorporated	普益廣告公司	Puyi guanggao gongsi	1932	1936
Atrax Company, Illuminated Advertising	明華公司	Minghua gongsi	1930	1941
Baiji yishu guanggao gongsi	百吉藝術廣告公司	Baiji yishu guanggao gongsi	1948	
Bangda yishu guanggao she	邦達藝術廣告社	Bangda yishu guanggao she	1947	

https://doi.org/10.1515/9783111390000-012

Table 1 (continued)

Name (English)	Vernacular	Pinyin	Start Year	End Year
Begdon & Nobbins			1928	1928
Begdon & Read			1929	
Belge-Neonlite Company, Limited			1929	1930
Bercott's Advertising Agency (International Advertising Corporation)	柏高廣告社	Baigao guanggao she	1930	1935
Berlin Transparent Advertising Company			1939	1939
Big Ben Advertising Agency	大鵬廣告公司	Dapeng guanggao gongsi	1935	
Bozallo Engineering Company	?士羅管造建築公司	? Shiluo guanzao jianzhu gongsi	1922	1922
Bruno Perme	貝美廣告公司	Beimei guanggao gongsi	1933	1943
Carl Crow, Incorporated	克勞廣告公司	Kelao guanggao gongsi	1923	1948
Cathay Advertising Company	國泰廣告公司	Guotai guanggao gongsi	1940	1941
Central Advertising Agency	中央廣告社	Zhongyang guanggao she	1929	
Chee Fah Advertising Service, C.F. Lin & Company (General Advertising Contractors)	其發廣告(推銷)社	Qifa guanggao (tuixiao) she	1931	1940
Chester Cowen Company	哲斯德	Zheside	1916	
China Advertising Agency	中華廣告社	Zhonghua guanggao she	1922	1941
China Advertising Company, The	立發	Lifa	1908	1921
China Advertising Service, Incorporated	中國廣告公司	Zhongguo guanggao gongsi	1925	1932
China Art Publishing Company (Advertising Department)			1928	1928
China Automatic Advertising Company, Limited			1929	
China Bill Board Advertising Agency (Cheng Tai Sing Advertising Agency)	陳泰興廣告公司	Chentaixing guanggao gongsi	1927	1943

Table 1 (continued)

Name (English)	Vernacular	Pinyin	Start Year	End Year
China Commercial Advertising Agency	華商廣告公司	Huashang guanggao gongsi	1926	1948
China Film Service Bureau	電影服務社	Dianying fuwu she	1935	
China Publicity Company	中國商務廣告公司	Zhongguo shangwu guanggao gongsi	1914	1941
China Ricksah Advertising Company, Limited	柏高廣告股份有限公司	Baigao guanggao gufenyouxian gongsi	1931	1931
China/Chinese Advertising Company, The	鳴藝廣告公司	Mingyi guanggao gongsi	1925	1939
Chinese Advertising Letters	中華信益廣告公司	Zhonghua xinyi guanggao gongsi	1926	
Chisolm and Keifer	啓森凱發	Qisen kaifa	1933	1935
Chun Mei News Agency	中美通信社	Zhongmei tongxinshe	1918	1919
Claude Neon Lights, Fed. Inc, U.S.A.	麗安電氣有限公司	Li'an gongqi youxiangongsi	1929	1942
Commercial Advertising Company	商業廣告公司	Shangye guanggao gongsi	1930	
Communicatus Advertising Company	交通廣告公司	Jiaotong guanggao gongsi	1931	1935
Consolidated National Advertising Company	聯合廣告公司	Lianhe guanggao gongsi	1928	1948
Consolidated National Advertising Company	聯合廣告公司	Lianhe guanggao gongsi	1933	1941
Continental Advertisers, Union Advertising Company	聯華廣告(股份有限)公司	Lianhua guanggao (gufen youxian) gongsi	1935	1941
Continental Advertising Company (Dah Loh Advertising Company)	大陸廣告公司	Dalu guanggao gongsi	1938	1943
Continental Trading Company (Advertising Department)			1929	1931
Cosmos Trading Company			1929	1929
Dadong guanggao gongsi	大東廣告公司	Dadong guanggao gongsi	1930	1948

Table 1 (continued)

Name (English)	Vernacular	Pinyin	Start Year	End Year
Dafa guanggao she	大發廣告社	Dafa guanggao she	1935	
Dagong guanggao gongsi	大公廣告公司	Dagong guanggao gongsi	1928	1929
Dah Lai Commercial Service	大來華行	Dalaihuahang	1935	
Dah Loh Advertising Agency			1934	
Dah Lung Neon Light Company	大來氣光燈行	Dalai qiguang denghang	1938	1942
Dah Sin Advertising Agency	大新廣告公司	Daxin guanggao gongsi	1937	1956
Dah Wah Advertising Company	大華廣告公司	Dahua guanggao gongsi		
Daitung Advertising Agency			1936	
David & Company, Samuel	合盛	Hecheng	1924	1941
De Luxe Neon Light Company			1935	1942
Dianzhong guanggao gongsi	電鍾廣告公司	Dianzhong guanggao gongsi	1946	
Direct Mail Advertising Agency	捷運廣告公司	Jieyun guanggao gongsi	1935	1936
Dittman, S.			1917	1931
Dollar Advertising Company, Limited			1932	
E.H. McMichael			1935	1938
Eastern Advertisers	大美廣告公司	Da mei guanggao gongsi	1937	1941
Eastern Advertising Agency	東方廣告公司	Dongfang guanggao gongsi	1914	1943
Eastern China Advertising Company (Wa-Tong)	華東廣告社	Huadong guanggao she	1931	1933
Eastern Neon Light Company	東方年紅電光公司	Dongfang nianhong dianguang gongsi	1930	1942
Echo Advertising Agency			1930	1930

Table 1 (continued)

Name (English)	Vernacular	Pinyin	Start Year	End Year
Electric Lamp Advertisement Company, Limited			1926	
Electro Advertising Corporation			1938	1938
Faguo dianguang guanggao gongsi	法國電光廣告公司	Faguo dianguang guanggao gongsi	1928	1929
Far Eastern Advertising Company Limited			1919	1931
Far Eastern Commercial Advertising Company	遠東商務廣告公司	Yuandong shangwu guanggao gongsi	1934	1937
Faxing guanggao gongsi	法興廣告公司	Faxing guanggao gongsi	1924	1929
Fine Art Studio	精藝照相館	Jingyi zhaoxiang guan	1939	1939
Floydson Neon Light Company			1934	
Foo Lay Sun Neon Light Company			1941	1942
General Neon Light Company			1932	1934
Globe Advertising Agency	天球廣告公司	Tianqiu guanggao gongsi	1929	1929
Gold Dragon Advertising Company	金圓廣告公司	Jin yuan guanggao gongsi	1927	1927
Golden Neon Light Company			1938	1942
Gongyi guanggao gongsi	公益廣告公司	Gongyi guanggao gongsi	1948	
Grant Advertising, Incorporated			1936	
Great China Publicity Company Limited	中華廣告股份有限公司	Zhonghua guanggao gufenyouxiangongsi	1935	
Great Eastern Neon Light Company			1936	1938
Guojin guanggao she	國際廣告社	Guojin guanggao she	1930	
Guotai boyin guanggao gongsi	國泰播音廣告公司	Guotai boyin guanggao gongsi	1947	
Hampson, C.W.	海姆生	Haimusheng	1932	1935

Table 1 (continued)

Name (English)	Vernacular	Pinyin	Start Year	End Year
Han Yang Advertising Company/Agency	漢洋廣告公司/社	Hanyang guanggao gongsi / she	1938	1943
Harvey's Advertising & Billposting Agency	哈維告白經理	Hawei gaobai jingli	1911	1928
Hau Kee & Company			1935	
Hengyu guanggao gongsi	恒裕廣告公司	Hengyu guanggao gongsi	1948	
Holodovich, N.V.			1935	
Holy Eagle Advertising Company			1930	
Honest Advertising	誠信廣告服務社	Chengxin guanggao fuwushe	1935	
Hong Chang (or Chong) Advertising Company (Fou Hong Gneu)	鴻昌廣告營造公司	Hongchang guanggao yingzao gongsi	1930	1939
Hong Dah Advertising Company			1940	1940
Howe's Advertising Company	好華廣告公司	Haohua guanggao gongsi	1919	1924
Hsu, Smin	徐世民	Xushimin	1933	1935
Hu Yi-chi (Woo Yih Kee) Advertising Agency	胡一記廣告公司	Huyiji guanggao gongsi	1930	1935
Hua'an guanggao gongsi	華安廣告公司	Hua'an guanggao gongsi	1949	
Huafu guanggao gongsi	華孚廣告公司	Huafu guanggao gongsi	1933	
Huamuxinghuagao guanggao she	華木行華高廣告社	Huamuxinghuagao guanggao she	1945	1948
Huanan guanggao she	華南廣告社	Huanan guanggao she	1947	1949
Huaxing guanggao gongsi	華星廣告公司	Huaxing guanggao gongsi	1949	
Huazhong guanggao she	華衆廣告社	Huazhong guanggao she	1946	

Table 1 (continued)

Name (English)	Vernacular	Pinyin	Start Year	End Year
Hwa May Advertising Company	華美廣告公司	Huamei guanggao gongsi	1935	1939
Hwa Sung Advertising Company			1943	
Illuminated Advertising Company	照明廣告行	Zhaoming guanggao hang	1926	1929
Incorporated Advertising Consultant			1927	
International Advertising Agency	國際廣告公司	Guoji guanggao gongsi	1947?	
International Advertising Corporation (Bercott's Advertising Agency)	美國廣告公司	Meiguo guanggao gongsi	1930	1943
International Trade Advertisers	萬國廣告公司	Wanguo guanggao gongsi	1924	1946
Isida Service Association, Isida Associations (Isida-Hwei-Za) (Chung-Pu)	億捷達會社 (總部)	Yijieda huishe (zongbu)	1932	1932
Jansen Cinema, W.H., A.S.C.			1935	1935
Jh Dah Advertising Company	一大廣告公司	Yida guanggao gongsi		
Jianguo guanggao gongsi	建國廣告公司	Jianguo guanggao gongsi	1948	
Jiedeng guanggao she	捷登廣告社	Jiedeng guanggao she		
Jimmy Advertising (Zeh Mei Advertising Agency)	集美廣告公司	Jimei guanggao she	1936	1943
Jincheng guanggao gongsi	訴金城廣告公司	Jincheng guanggao gongsi	1946	
Jinyi guanggao she	晉益廣告社	Jinyi guanggao she	1948	
Kawakita Electric Company			1941	1942
Kee (Koo) Zung Mow Advertising Company			1943	
Keenad, Inc	金亞廣告公司	Jinya guanggao gongsi	1934	1941
King-Degaw International			1935	

Table 1 (continued)

Name (English)	Vernacular	Pinyin	Start Year	End Year
Kokumin Sefu Advertisers			1941	1941
Kong Tai Advertising Company	康泰廣告公司	Kangtai guanggao gongsi	1929	1943
Kongque guanggao she	孔雀廣告社	Kongque guanggao she	1947	1955
Kow How Advertising Company	國華廣告印刷社	Guohua guanggao yinshua she	1934	
Kwang Ming Neon Light Company	光明霓虹公司	Guangmingnihong gongsi	1934	1942
Liancheng guanggao she	聯成廣告社	Liancheng guanggao she	1946	1947
Lianhui guanggao meishu she	聯揮廣告美術社	Lianhui guanggao meishu she		
Lingchege guanggao gongsi	令飭各廣告公司	Lingchege guanggao gongsi	1931	
Liuhe guanggao gongsi	六合廣告公司	Liuhe guanggao gongsi	1948	
Luminous Advertising Company	露明電光廣告公司	Luming dianguang guanggao gongsi	1921	1925
Martynow & Company, B.	天?洋行	Tian ? yanghang	1923	1923
Mason Company, Limited	美新公司	Meixin gongsi	1926	1927
McMichael's Agency			1938	
Metropole Neon Light Company	大上海霓虹氣電公司	Dashanghai nihongqidian gongsi	1935	1935
Metropolitan Advertisement Company			1931	1931
Millington, Limited	美靈登(廣告有限公司)	Meilingdeng (guanggao youxian gongsi)	1927	1941
Mingming dianlihuoli guanggao she	明明電力活力廣告社	Mingming dianlihuoli guanggao she	1933	1934
Mingming guanggao gongsi	明明廣告公司	Mingming guanggao gongsi	1933	

Table 1 (continued)

Name (English)	Vernacular	Pinyin	Start Year	End Year
Mingtai guanggao she	明泰廣告社	Mingtai guanggao she	1910	
Modern Art Services	摩登美術廣告書社	Modeng meishu guanggao shushe	1935	
Modern Neon Light Company	美登霓虹燈氣電公司	Meideng nihongdeng qidian gongsi	1934	1947
Modern Publicity Company			1932	
Mutual Advertisers Limited	益衆廣告公司	Yizhong guanggao gongsi	1933	1935
Nanyang Advertising Company	南洋廣告公司	Nanyang guanggao gongsi	1931	1935
National Advertising Agency (N.A.A.)	國民廣告公司	Guomin guanggao gongsi	1927	1928
National Advertising Agency & Publishers	國民廣告圖書公司	Guomin guanggao tushu gongsi	1929	1935
National Neon Light Company, Inc.			1933	1934
Night Glory Neon Light Company			1938	1942
Nihon Dempo Tsushin Sha	日本電報通信社	Riben dianbao tongxinshe	1922	1935
North China Advertising Bureau, The	惠見告白代理處	Hui jian gaobai daili chu	1911	1911
North China Advertising Company	中國北方告白公司	Zhongguo beifang gaobai gongsi	1930	
Novelty Advertising Company (ex Shanghai Public Motorcars Advertising Company)	新?廣告公司	Xin? guanggao gongsi	1941	1941
Oriental Advertising Agency (Company), The	法興廣告公司	Faxing guanggao gongsi	1914	1930
Oriental Cinematographic Advertising Company	東方電光廣告公司	Dongfang dianguang guanggao gongsi	1922	1923
Oriental Cinematographic Advertising Company	華大廣告社	Huada guanggao she	1936	1943
Oriental Neon Light Company			1931	1935

Table 1 (continued)

Name (English)	Vernacular	Pinyin	Start Year	End Year
Oriental Press, The [La Presse Orientale]	法興印書館, 法新匯	Faxing yinshuguan, Faxinhui	1899	1934
Outdoor Publicity Company			1923	1924
Parlin (Pah Ling) Advertising Company			1940	1943
Pax Publicity	太平廣告公司, 太平廣告社	Taiping guanggao gonsi, Taiping guanggao she	1943	1948
Publikans				
Qinfeng boyin guanggao gongsi	慶豐播音廣告公司	Qinfeng boyin guanggao gongsi	1948	
Qixin guanggao gongsi	企新廣告公司	Qixin guanggao gongsi	1936	
Roaming Advertising Company	途行廣告公司	Tuhang guanggao gongsi	1923	
Zung Chong Ziang Advertising Company, Limited	榮昌祥廣告公司	Rongchangxiang guanggao gongsi	1939	1956
Runmao guanggao gongsi	潤茂廣告公司	Runmao guanggao gongsi	1931	1937
Screen Advertising Service			1940	1940
Shanghai Advertising & Bill Posting Company	明得綠貼洋行	Mingdei lütie yanghang	1906	
Shanghai Advertising Company	上海廣告公司	Shanghai guanggao gongsi	1937	1937
Shanghai Mainichi Shimbun Limited	上海每日新聞社	Shanghai meirixinwen she	1925	1941
Shanghai meishu	上海美術	Shanghai meishu	1934	
Shanghai Neon Light Company, Limited (Strand Neon Light Company)	上海新光公司	Shanghai xinguang gongsi	1930	1934
Shanghai Nippo, The Sha	上海日報社	Shanghai ribao she	1913	1939

Table 1 (continued)

Name (English)	Vernacular	Pinyin	Start Year	End Year
Shanghai Public Motorcars Advertising Company (Novelty Auto Advertising Company)	公共汽車廣告公司	Gonggong qiche guanggao gongsi	1933	1935
Shanghai Ricsha Advertising Company, Limited	人力廣告公司	Renli guanggao gongsi	1930	1930
Shanghai Service Corporation			1935	1935
Shanghai Tramway Advertising Company	上海電車招帖公司	Shanghai dianche zhao tie gongsi	1909	1911
Shanghai xinxin guanggao gongsi	上海新新廣告公司	Shanghai xinxin guanggao gongsi	1947	
Shenguang guanggao gongsi	申光廣告公司	Shenguang guanggao gongsi	1947	
Shijie guanggao gongsi	世界廣告公司	Shijie guanggao gongsi	1936	1948
Shijie meishu guanggao she	世界美術廣告社	Shijie meishu guanggao she	1936	1937
Silver Star Advertising Agency	銀星廣告	Yinxing guanggao gongsi	1956	
Sin(g) Sin(g) Advertising Company			1939	1943
Sing Kwang Company			1935	
Sing Poo Advertising Company			1943	
Sing Sen News Agency	新生通訊社	Xinshen tongxunshe	1913	1935
Singer Paunzen Advertising Studio			1939	
Société / Compagnie Française de Réclames Lumineuses	上海法商電燈電車公司	Shanghai fashang diandeng dianche gongsi	1908	1934
Star Advertising Agency			1938	1939
Strand Neon Light Company (formerly Shanghai Neon Light Company)	新光霓虹公司	Xinguangnihong gongsi	1934	1936
Strother's Advertising Service Agency			1926	1931
Sung Wei Kee Advertising Company			1943	

Table 1 (continued)

Name (English)	Vernacular	Pinyin	Start Year	End Year
Sunmay Advertiser	生煤廣告社	Shengmei guanggao she	1935	
Suzhou Advertisement & Company, Limited	蘇州廣告股份有限公司	Suzhou guanggao gu fen youxian gongsi	1946	
Tanaka, M.	田中實	Tianzhong shi	1932	1936
Tokyo Neon Light Company			1941	1942
Transmutograph (Far East)			1928	1931
Truck Cab Advertising Company			1934	1934
Tseng Ching Advertising Company			1939	
Tsong Wei Advertising Company			1938	1939
Tung Ming Hsiang Chi Neon Light Company	通明汽電無限公司	Tongming qidian wuxian gongsi	1936	1936
Union Advertising Agency	發聯廣告公司	Fa lian guanggao gongsi	1928	1929
Union Advertising and Publishing Company			1930	1931
Union Press Company	聯合印刷公司	Lianhe yinshua gongsi	1933	1935
United Advertising Advicers, Incoporated			1927	1930
Universal Neon Light Company			1936	
Universal Press Co.	中南印務報	Zhongnan yinwubao	1935	
Van Lee Advertising	萬利廣告社	Wanli guanggao she	1935	
Vee Loo Advertising Company	維羅廣告公司	Weiluo guanggao gongsi	1922	1943
Vee Sing Advertising Company			1941	1941
Vio Neon Light Company	紫光電器廣告製造廠	Ziguang dianqi guanggao zhizaochang	1930	1942
Wei Kee Advertising Company			1938	1939
Weixin guanggao gongsi	維新廣告公司	Weixin guanggao gongsi	1949	

Table 1 (continued)

Name (English)	Vernacular	Pinyin	Start Year	End Year
Wha Teh Electric Light Company			1931	
Wushida, S.			1942	1943
Xiangmeideng guanggao she	向美登廣告社	Xiangmeideng guanggao she	1927	1954
Xiehe guanggao gongsi	協和廣告公司	Xiehe guanggao gongsi	1936	
Xingye guanggao gongsi	興業廣告公司	Xingye guanggao gongsi	1946	
Xinshen guanggao she	新申廣告社	Xinshen guanggao she	1948	
Yanggao guanggao she	楊高廣告社	Yanggao guanggao she	1931	
Yao Nan Advertising Company	耀南廣告社	Yaonan guanggao she	1920	1930
Yaxiya guanggao gongsi	亞西亞廣告公司	Yaxiya guanggao gongsi	1934	1948
Yifeng Advertising Company	于益豐廣告公司	Yifeng guanggao gongsi	1956	
Yilian guanggao sheji gufenyouxian gongsi	藝聯廣告設計股份有限公司	Yilian guanggao sheji gufenyouxian gongsi		
Yindu guanggao gongsi	銀都廣告公司	Yindu guanggao gongsi	1940	1941
Yong'an guanggao gongsi	永安廣告公司	Yong'an guanggao gongsi	1936	
Youxin guanggao she	又新廣告社	Youxin guanggao she	1943	
Yu Hsin Advertising Company	中國又新廣告公司	Zhongguo youxin guanggao gongsi	1922	1923
Yuanhe guanggao gongsi	元合廣告公司	Yuanhe guanggao gongsi	1949	
Yuanyan guanggao gongsi ?	園隒廣告公司	Yuanyan guanggao gongsi	1948	

Table 1 (continued)

Name (English)	Vernacular	Pinyin	Start Year	End Year
Yuen Chong Advertising & Broadcasting Station	原廠廣告公司及廣播電台	Yuanchang guanggao gongsi ji guangbo diantai	1935	
Yuen Yuen Advertising Company	源源廣告公司	Yuenyuen guanggao gongsi	1934	1935
Yung Chong Ziang Advertising Company			1938	1943
Yung Sung Neon Light Company			1938	1942
Zhengda guanggao she	正大廣告社	Zhengda guanggao she	1936	
Zhenhua guanggao gongsi	振華廣告公司	Zhenhua guanggao gongsi	1934	
Zhisheng guanggao gongsi	訴氏生廣告公司	Zhisheng guanggao gongsi	1947	
Zhongguo feihang guanggao gongsi	中國飛行廣告公司	Zhongguo feihang guanggao gongsi	1935	
Zhongguo gongshang guanggao she	中國工商廣告社	Zhongguo gongshang guanggao she	1947	
Zhongguo leidian guanggao she	中國雷電廣告社	Zhongguo leidian guanggao she	1946	
Zhongxing guanggao she	中興廣告社	Zhongxing guanggao she	1929	1930
Zhongyi guanggao gongsi	中藝廣告公司	Zhongyi guanggao gongsi	1948	
Zimmerman & Company, W.I.	上海齊美洋行	Shanghai Qimei yanghang	1896	1929

This list was compiled from various sources, including the 1935 directory of the Bankers' Cooperative Credit Service (Zhongguo zhengxinsuo), the 1941 Shanghai telephone directory (honglist) and various files held at the Shanghai Municipal Archives. The table indicates the names of the agencies, in the vernacular and their transliterations, and, as far as possible, the date of their establishment and termination. While the level of information may vary across different agencies, this compilation represents the most comprehensive and up-to-date list currently accessible. This list is also available at: https://madspace.org/cooked/Tables?ID=110
(last consulted on April 24, 2020).

Table 2: Advertising textbooks published in China between 1918 and 1948.

Author(s)		Title			Publisher			Year of publication	Place
Ding Xinbo	丁馨伯	Guanggaoxue	廣告學	Advertising Studies	立信會計圖書用品社	Lixin kuaiji tushu yongpin she	Lixin Accounting Books and Supplies Co., Ltd.	1944	Shanghai
Feng Hongxin	馮鴻鑫	Guanggaoxue	廣告學	Advertising Studies	中華書局	Zhonghua shuju	Chung Hwa Bookstore	1946	Shanghai
Feng Hongxin	馮鴻鑫	Guanggaoxue	廣告學	Advertising Studies	中華書局	Zhonghua shuju	Chung Hwa Bookstore	1948	Shanghai
Gan Yonglong	甘永龍	Guanggao xuzhi	廣告須知	Advertising Principles	商務印書館	Shangwu yinhshuguan	Commercial Press	1927	Shanghai
Gan Yonglong	甘永龍	Guanggao xuzhi	廣告須知	Advertising Principles	商務印書館	Shangwu yinhshuguan	Commercial Press	1933	Shanghai
Gan Yonglong	甘永龍	Guanggao xuzhi	廣告須知	Advertising Principles	商務印書館	Shangwu yinhshuguan	Commercial Press	1935	Shanghai
Gan Yonglong	甘永龍	Guanggao xuzhi	廣告須知	Advertising Principles	商務印書館	Shangwu yinhshuguan	Commercial Press	1939	Shanghai
Gao Boshi	高伯時	Guanggao qianshuo	廣告淺說	Introduction to Advertising	中華書局	Zhonghua shuju	Chung Hwa Bookstore	1930	Shanghai
Gao Boshi	高伯時	Guanggao qianshuo	廣告淺說	Introduction to Advertising	中華書局	Zhonghua shuju	Chung Hwa Bookstore	1932	Shanghai

(continued)

Table 2 (continued)

Author(s)		Title			Publisher		Year of publication	Place
Iseki Jiro	井關十三郎	Guanggao xinlixue	廣告心理學	Psychology of Advertising	Shangwu yinhshuguan	商務印書館	1925	Shanghai
Iseki Jiro	井關十三郎	Guanggao xinlixue	廣告心理學	Psychology of Advertising	Shangwu yinhshuguan	商務印書館	1931	Shanghai
Kuai Shixun	蒯世勳	Guanggao ABC	廣告學ABC	The ABC of Advertising	Shijie shuju	世界書局	1928	Shanghai
Kuai Shixun	蒯世勳	Guanggao ABC	廣告學ABC	The ABC of Advertising	Shijie shuju	世界書局	1929	Shanghai
Liu Baoru	劉葆儒	Guanggaoxue	廣告學	Advertising Studies	Zhonghua shuju	中華書局	1930	Shanghai
Liu Baoru	劉葆儒	Guanggaoxue	廣告學	Advertising Studies	Zhonghua shuju	中華書局	1932	Shanghai
Liu Baoru	劉葆儒	Guanggaoxue	廣告學	Advertising Studies	Zhonghua shuju	中華書局	1936	Shanghai
Lu Meiseng	陸梅僧	Guanggao	廣告	Advertising	Shangwu yinhshuguan	商務印書館	1940	Shanghai

Author	Pinyin title	Chinese title	English title	Chinese publisher	Pinyin publisher	English publisher	Year	City
Lu Meiseng	陸梅僧	Guanggao	廣告	Advertising	商務印書館	Shangwu yinhshuguan	Commercial Press	1947	Shanghai
Su Shangda	蘇上達	Guanggaoxue gangyao	廣告學綱要	The Essentials of Advertising	商務印書館	Shangwu yinhshuguan	Commercial Press	1930	Shanghai
Su Shangda	蘇上達	Guanggaoxue gailun	廣告學概論	The fundamentals of Advertising	商務印書館	Shangwu yinhshuguan	Commercial Press	1934	Shanghai
Sun Xiaojun	孫孝鈞	Guanggao jingjixue	廣告經濟學	The Economics of Advertising	南京書店	Nanjing shudian	Nanking Bookstore	1930	Nanjing
Wang Gongsan	王貢三	Guanggaoxue	廣告學	Advertising Studies	世界書局	Shijie shuju	World Bookstore	1933	Shanghai
Wu Tiesheng, Zhu Shengyu	吳鐵聲, 朱勝馀	Guanggaoxue	廣告學	Advertising Studies	中華書局	Zhonghua shuju	Chung Hwa Bookstore	1946	Shanghai
The system company (Xisidun gongsi)	哲斯敦公司	Guanggao xuzhi	廣告須知	Advertising Principles	商務印書館	Shangwu yinhshuguan	Commercial Press	1918	Shanghai
The system company (Xisidun gongsi)	哲斯敦公司	Guanggao xuzhi	廣告須知	Advertising Principles	商務印書館	Shangwu yinhshuguan	Commercial Press	1933	Shanghai
Ye Xinfo	葉心佛	Guanggao shishixue	廣告實施學	Advertising in Practice	中國廣告學社	Zhongguo guanggao xueshe	China Advertising Society	1935	Shanghai

References

Primary Sources

Archives

Carl Crow Papers (1913–1945), State Historical Society of Missouri, Columbia, Missouri.
Hoover Institution Archives, Stanford University, Stanford, California.
J. Walter Thompson Company Archives, John Hartman Center for Sales, Advertising & Marketing
History, David M. Rubenstein Rare Book & Manuscript Library, Duke University, Durham, North
Carolina.
Shanghai Municipal Archives (SMA), Shanghai.
National Archives and Records Administration (NARA), Washington, D.C.

Periodicals

China Press
China Monthly Review
China Weekly Review
Chinese Economic Monthly
Millard's Review of the Far East
North China Herald and Daily News
Shenbao
South China Morning Post

Second-hand Literature

Alford, William P. *To Steal a Book Is an Elegant Offense: Intellectual Property Law in Chinese Civilization*.
Stanford: Stanford University Press, 1995.
Allman, Norwood F. *Handbook on the Protection of Trade-Marks, Patents, Copyrights, and Trade-Names in
China*. Shanghai: Kelly & Walsh, Ltd., 1924.
Allman, Norwood F. "Transliteration of 'Coca-Cola' Trade-Mark to Chinese Characters". *The
New Yorker*, February 1959, 61–62.
"An Analytical Study of Advertisements in Chinese Newspapers". *Chinese Economic Monthly* 3, n° 4
(April 1926): 139–43.
Apple, Rima D. *Vitamania: Vitamins in American Culture*. New Brunswick, N.J.: Rutgers University
Press, 1996.
Araujo, Luis, John Finch, and Hans Kjellberg. *Reconnecting Marketing to Markets*. Oxford: Oxford
University Press, 2010.

https://doi.org/10.1515/9783111390000-013

Armand, Cécile. "Foreign Clubs with Chinese Flavor: The Rotary Club of Shanghai and the Politics of Language". In *Knowledge, Power, and Networks: Elites in Transition in Modern China*, edited by Cécile Armand, Christian Henriot and Huei-min Sun, 233–59. Leiden: Brill, 2022.

Armand, Cécile. "MADSpace: a Janus-faced digital companion to a PhD dissertation in Chinese history". In *Shaping the Digital Dissertation: Knowledge Production in the Arts and Humanities*, edited by Virginia Kuhn and Anke Finger, 119–28. Open Book Publishers, 2021. https://doi.org/10.11647/OBP.0239.08.

Armand, Cécile. "The Grapes of Happiness: Selling Sun-Maid Raisins to the Chinese in the 1920s-1930s". *Asia Pacific Perspectives* XIII, n° 2 (Fall/Winter 2015).

Arnett, Jeffrey Jensen. *Emerging Adulthood the Winding Road from the Late Teens through the Twenties*. New York; Oxford: Oxford University Press, 2004.

Bacon, C.A. "Advertising in China". *Chinese Economic Journal and Bulletin* 5, n° 3 (September 1929): 754–67.

Bailey, Paul J. *Gender and Education in China: Gender Discourses and Women's Schooling in the Early Twentieth Century*. Routledge, 2007.

Bankers' Cooperative Credit Service (Zhongguo zhengxinsuo), Credit Men's Business Directory of Shanghai (Zhengxin gongshang hang minglu, Shanghai zhibu). Shanghai: Bankers' Cooperative Credit Service, 1935.

Baranowski, Shelley, Castillo Greg, Victoria de Grazia, Pamela E. Swett, S. Jonathan Wiesen, and Jonathan R. Zatlin. *Selling Modernity: Advertising in Twentieth-Century Germany*. Durham: Duke University Press, 2007.

Barlow, Tani. "Advertising Ephemera and the Angel of History". *Positions: East Asia Cultures Critique* 20, n° 1 (2012): 111–58.

Barthes, Roland. "Rhétorique de l'image". *Communications* 4 (1964): 41–42.

Bastid, Marianne, and Chien Chang. *Educational Reform in Early Twentieth Century China*. Ann Arbor: Center for Chinese Studies, University of Michigan, 1985.

Baum, Emily. "Health and the Bottle: The Dr. William's Medicine Company and the Commodification of Well-Being in Liangyou". In *Liangyou: Kaleidoscopic Modernity and the Shanghai Global Metropolis, 1926–1945*, edited by Paul Pickowicz, 71–94. Leiden: Brill, 2013.

Becker, C.H. *Reorganisation of Education In China*. Paris: League of Nations' Institute of Intellectual Cooperation, 1932.

Belk, Russell W., and Xin Zhao. "Advertising Consumer Culture in 1930s Shanghai: Globalization and Localization in Yuefenpai". *Journal of Advertising* 37, n° 2 (2008): 45–56.

Benedict, Carol. *Golden-Silk Smoke*: *A History of Tobacco in China, 1550–2010*. Berkeley: University of California Press, 2011.

Bergère, Marie-Claire. *L'âge d'or de la bourgeoisie chinoise, 1911–1937*. Paris: Flammarion, 1986.

Berghoff, Hartmut, Philip Scranton, and Uwe Spiekermann. *The Rise of Marketing and Market Research*. New York: Palgrave Macmillan, 2011.

Bickers, Robert. "Shanghailanders: The Formation and Identity of the British Settler Community in Shanghai 1843–1937". *Past & Present*, n° 159 (1998): 161–211.

Bickers, Robert A., and Christian Henriot, eds. *New Frontiers: Imperialism's New Communities in East Asia, 1842–1953*. Manchester; New York: Manchester University Press, 2000.

Bickers, Robert A., and Isabella Jackson, eds. *Treaty Ports in Modern China: Law, Land, and Power*. Routledge, 2016.

Bieler, Stacey. *"Patriots" or "Traitors"?: A History of American-Educated Chinese Students*. New York: Routledge, 2003.

Black, Ernest J. "Advertising in Shanghai". Consular Trade Report. General records of the Department of State, RG59, Box 948. Washington, D.C.: National Archives and Records Administration (NARA), 1932.

Brasó Broggi, Carles. *Trade and Technology Networks in the Chinese Textile Industry: Opening Up Before the Reform*. New York: Palgrave Macmillan: Palgrave Macmillan, 2015.

Brown, Margaret E. "Advertising to the Elite: The Role of Innovation of Fine Art in Advertising in the Development of the Advertising Industry". M.A. Department of History, Indiana University-Purdue University, 2015.

Büchsel, Ulrike. "Lifestyles, Gender Roles and Nationalism in the Representation of Women in Cigarette Advertisements from the Republican Period". Doctoral Dissertation, University of Heidelberg, 2009.

Calder-Marshall, R., and P.L. Bryant. *The Anglo-Chinese Cook Book*. Shanghai: Commercial Press, 1916.

Callon, Michel. *The Laws of the Markets*. Oxford: Blackwell, 2011.

Callon, Michel, Yuval Millo and Fabian Muniesa, eds. *Market Devices*. Malden, Mass.: Blackwell, 2008.

Carl Crow, Inc. *Newspaper Directory of China (Including Hongkong)*. Shanghai: Carl Crow, Inc., 1931.

Chan, Wellington K.K. "Personal Styles, Cultural Values and Management: The Sincere and Wing on Companies in Shanghai and Hong Kong, 1900–1941". *Business History Review* 70, n° 2 (July 1996): 141–66.

Chen, Deming. *Yuanqu de huihuang: "Shenbao" (1929–1949) haipai guanggao meishu zitu ji* (Distant Glory: Haipai-style advertising art in *Shenbao*, 1929–1949). Shanghai: Shanghai daxue chubanshe, 2019.

Chen, Janet Y. *Guilty of Indigence: The Urban Poor in China, 1900–1953*. Princeton: Princeton University Press, 2013.

Cheng Chaonan, and Feng Yiyou, eds. *Lao guanggao* (Old advertising). Shanghai: Shanghai huabao chubanshe, 1998.

Cheng, Linsun. *Banking in Modern China: Entrepreneurs, Professional Managers, and the Development of Chinese Banks, 1897–1937*. Cambridge; New York: Cambridge University Press, 2006.

Chessel, Marie-Emmanuelle. *La publicité: naissance d'une profession, 1900–1940*. Paris: CNRS Éditions, 1998.

Chessel, Marie-Emmanuelle. "Une méthode publicitaire américaine ? Cadum dans la France de l'entre-deux-guerres". *Entreprises et Histoire*, n° 11 (1996): 61–76.

Chessel, Marie-Emmanuelle, and Sophie Dubuisson-Quellier. "The Making of the Consumer: Historical and Sociological Perspectives". In *The SAGE Handbook of Consumer Culture*, edited by Olga Kravets, Pauline Maclaran, Steve Miles and Alladi Venkatesh, 43–60. London: Sage, 2018.

Clark, J.D. *Sketches in and around Shanghai*. Shanghai: "Shanghai Mercury" and "Celestial Empire" Offices, 1894.

Cochoy, Franck. *Une histoire du marketing: discipliner l'économie de marché*. Paris: La Découverte, 1999.

Cochoy, Frank, and Sophie Dubuisson-Quellier. "The sociology of market work". *Economic Sociology – the European Electronic Newsletter* 15, n° 1 (2013): 4–11.

Cochran, Sherman. *Big Business in China: Sino-Foreign Rivalry in the Cigarette Industry, 1890–1930*. Cambridge, Mass.; London: Harvard University Press, 1980.

Cochran, Sherman. *Encountering Chinese Networks: Western, Japanese, and Chinese Corporations in China, 1880–1937*. Berkeley, Calif.: University of California Press, 2000.

Cochran, Sherman, ed. *Inventing Nanjing Road: Commercial Culture in Shanghai, 1900–1945*. Ithaca, NY: Cornell University Press, 1999.

Cochran, Sherman. "Marketing Medicine and Advertising Dreams in China, 1900–1950". In *Becoming Chinese: Passages to Modernity and Beyond*, edited by Wen-Hsin Yeh, 62–97. Berkeley: University of California Press, 2000.

Cohen, Paul A. *Discovering History in China: American Historical Writing on the Recent Chinese Past*. New York: Columbia University Press, 1984.

Conrad, Christoph, and Patrick Fridenson. "Observer les consommateurs. Études de marché and histoire de la consommation en Allemagne, des années 1930 aux années 1960". *Mouvement Social*, n° 206 (June 2004): 17–39.

Corbin, Alain. *La pluie, le soleil and le vent: une histoire de la sensibilité au temps qu'il fait*. Paris: Aubier, 2013.

Crawford, Robert. "Opening for Business: A Comparison of J. Walter Thompson and McCann Erickson's Entries into the Australian Market". *Journal of Historical Research in Marketing* 8, n° 3 (2016): 452–72.

Crawford, Robert, and Jacqueline Dickenson. *Behind Glass Doors: The World of Australian Advertising Agencies, 1959–1989*, Crawley, W.A.: University of Western Australia, 2016.

Crow, Carl. *The Travelers' Handbook for China*. San Francisco, Calif.: San Francisco News Co., 1913.

Crow, Carl. *Four Hundred Million Customers; the Experiences – Some Happy, Some Sad, of an American in China, and What They Taught Him*. New York; London: Harper, 1937.

Crow, Carl. "Advertising and Merchandising". In *China. A Commercial and Industrial Handbook*, edited by Julean Herbert Arnold, 191 Crow, Carl 200. Washington: Govt. Print. Off., 1926.

Crow, Carl. "When You Advertise to Orientals". *Printers' Ink Monthly*, December 1927, 39–40, 116–23.

Crow, Carl. "Advertising Meets War and Survives". *Printers' Ink Monthly*, April 1937.

Crow, Carl. *China Takes Her Place*. New York; London: Harper & Bros., 1944.

Crow, Carl, and Esther Brock Bird, eds. *Foreign Devils in the Flowery Kingdom*. New York; London: Harper & Bros., 1940.

Crow, Carl. *The Long Road Back to China: Along the Burma Road to China's Wartime Capital in 1939*. Hong Kong: Earnshaw Books, 2009.

Curran, Thomas D. *Educational Reform in Republican China: The Failure of Educators to Create a Modern Nation*. Lewiston, NY: Mellen, 2005.

Davis, Deborah. *The Consumer Revolution in Urban China*. Berkeley: University of California Press, 2000.

De Grazia, Victoria. *Irresistible Empire: America's Advance through Twentieth-Century Europe*. Cambridge, Mass.: Belknap Press of Harvard University Press, 2005.

De Iulio, Simona, and Carlo Vinti. "The Americanization of Italian Advertising during the 1950s and the 1960s Mediations, Conflicts, and Appropriations". *Journal of Historical Research in Marketing* 1, n° 2 (2009): 270–94.

Delacroix, Christian. "Linguistic turn". In *Historiographies: concepts and débats*, edited by Christian Delacroix, Patrick Garcia and Nicolas Offenstadt, 1: 476–90. Paris: Gallimard, 2010.

Dickenson, Jacqueline. *Australian Women in Advertising in the Twentieth Century*. 2015.

Dikötter, Frank. *Exotic Commodities: Modern Objects and Everyday Life in China*. New York: Columbia University Press, 2006.

Dikötter, Frank. *Things Modern: Material Culture and Everyday Life in China*. London: C. Hurst & Co. (Pub.) Ltd., 2007.

Drège, Jean Pierre. *La Commercial Press de Shanghai (1897–1949)*. Paris: PUF, 1978.

Effosse, Sabine, Hervé Joly and Marc de Ferrière Le Vayer, éd. *Les entreprises de biens de consommation sous l'Occupation*. Traduit par Arlerte Stroumza. Perspectives Historiques. Tours: Presses universitaires François-Rabelais, 2013.

Elman, Benjamin A. *Civil Examinations and Meritocracy in Late Imperial China*. Harvard University Press, 2013.

Fairbank, John King, and Ssu-yü Teng. *China's Response to the West: A Documentary Survey, 1839–1923*. Cambridge: Harvard University Press, 1954.

Fass, Paula S. *The Routledge History of Childhood in the Western World*. London: Routledge, 2012.

Faure, David, ed. *China and Capitalism: Business Enterprise in Modern China*. Hong Kong: Division of Humanities, Hong Kong University of Science and Technology, 1994.

Feng, Xiaocai. *Zhengshang Zhongguo: Yu Qiaqing yu ta de shidai* (Political merchants in China: Yu Qiaqing and his times). Beijing: Shehui kexue wenxian chubanshe, 2013.

Fernsebner, Susan. "A People's Playthings: Toys, Childhood, and Chinese Identity, 1909–1933". *Postcolonial Studies* 6, n° 3 (2003): 269–93.

Field, Andrew. *Shanghai's dancing world: cabaret culture and urban politics, 1919–1954*. Hong Kong: Chinese University Press, 2010.

Fraser, David Embrey. "Smoking out the Enemy: The National Goods Movement and the Advertising of Nationalism in China, 1880–1937". Doctoral Dissertation, University of California, 1999.

French, Paul. *Carl Crow, a tough old China hand: the life, times and adventures of an American in Shanghai*. Hong Kong: Hong Kong University Press, 2006.

Fu, Jia-Chen. *The Other Milk: Reinventing Soy in Republican China*. Seattle: University of Washington Press, 2018.

Galy, Laurent. "Yishibao (Social Welfare)". In *Encyclopédie des historiographies: Afriques, Amériques, Asies: Volume 1: sources and genres historiques (Tome 1 and Tome 2)*, edited by Nathalie Kouamé, Éric P. Meyer and Anne Viguier, 1975–87. TransAireS. Paris: Presses de l'Inalco, 2020.

Gan, Yonglong. *Guanggao xinglixue* (Psychology of Advertising). Shanghai: Commercial Press, 1927.

Ge, Gongzhen. *Zhonguo baoxue shi* (History of Journalism in Chine). Shanghai: Commercial Press, 1927.

Gerth, Karl. *China Made: Consumer Culture and the Creation of the Nation*. Cambridge: Harvard University Press, 2003.

Goodman, Bryna. *Native Place, City, and Nation Regional Networks and Identities in Shanghai, 1853–1937*. Berkeley: University of California Press, 1995.

Gudis, Catherine. *Buyways: Billboards, Automobiles, and the American Landscape*. New York: Routledge, 2004.

Hamilton, John Maxwell. "The Missouri News Monopoly and American Altruism in China: Thomas F.F. Millard, J. B. Powell, and Edgar Snow". *Pacific Historical Review* 55, n° 1 (1986): 27–48.

Hamilton, Peter E. "The American-Returned Students: Educational Networks and New Forms of Business in Early Republican China". In *Knowledge, Power, and Networks. Elites in Transition in Modern China*, edited by Cécile Armand, Christian Henriot, and Huei-min Sun, 258–88. Leiden: Brill, 2022.

Henriot, Christian. "Shanghai and the Experience of War: The Fate of Refugees". *European Journal of East Asian Studies* 5, n° 2 (2006): 215-45.

Henriot, Christian, Lu Shi and Charlotte Aubrun. *The Population of Shanghai (1865–1953): A Sourcebook*. Leiden; Boston: Brill, 2019.

Ho, Ping-ti. *The Ladder of Success in Imperial China: Aspects of Social Mobility, 1368–1911*. New York: Columbia University Press, 1962.

Huang, Kewu. "Cong Shenbao yiyao guanggao kan minchu Shanghai de yiliao wenhua yu shehui shenghuo, 1912~1926 (Medical culture and social life seen through *Shenbao* advertisements, 1912–1926)". *Zhongyang yanjiu yuan Jindai shi yanjiu suo jikan* 17 (1988): 141–94.

Hunt, Michael H. "Americans in the China Market: Economic Opportunities and Economic Nationalism, 1890s-1931". *The Business History Review* 51, n° 3 (October 1, 1977): 277–307.

Hunt, Michael H. "The American Remission of the Boxer Indemnity: A Reappraisal". *The Journal of Asian Studies* 31, n° 3 (1972): 539–59.

Huskey, James Layton. "Americans in Shanghai: Community Formation and Response to Revolution, 1919–1928". Doctoral Dissertation, Durham: University of North Carolina, 1985.

International Textbook Company. *Engraving and printing methods, advertisement illustration, technical- and trade-paper advertising, street-car advertising, outdoor advertising, house publications.* Scranton, PA: Smithsonian Libraries, 1909.

Iseki Jiro. *Guanggao xinglixue* (Psychology of Advertising). Shanghai: Commercial Press, 1925.

Kaske, Elisabeth. *The Politics of Language in Chinese Education, 1895–1919*. Vol. 82. Sinica Leidensia. Leiden: Brill, 2007.

Kerlan-Stephens, Anne, and Christian Delage. *Hollywood à Shanghai: l'épopée des studios Lianhua, 1930–1948*. Rennes: Presses universitaires de Rennes, 2015.

Köll, Elisabeth. *Railroads and the Transformation of China*. Hardcover. Harvard University Press, 2019.

Kuai, Shixun. *Guanggao ABC* (Advertising ABC). Shanghai: Shijie shudian, 1928.

Kuisel, Richard F. *Seducing the French: The Dilemma of Americanization*. Berkeley: University of California Press, 1997.

Kuo, P.W. "Foreign Trade and Advertising". *China Press*, 1 September 1936, 27–28.

Laing, Ellen Johnston. *Selling Happiness: Calendar Posters and Visual Culture in Early Twentieth-Century Shanghai*. Honolulu: University of Hawai'i Press, 2004.

Lam, Tong. *A passion for facts: social surveys and the construction of the Chinese nation state, 1900–1949*. Berkeley: University of California Press, 2011.

Lean, Eugenia. *Vernacular industrialism in China: Local Innovation and translated technologies in the making of a cosmetics empire, 1900–1940* (New York: Columbia University Press, 2020).

Lean, Eugenia. "The Modern Elixir: Medicine as a Consumer Item in the Early Twentieth-Century Chinese Press". *UCLA Historical Journal* 15 (1995): 65–92.

Liang Chen, Ren Yunzhu and Li Zhongqing, eds. *Qi shanlin zhe: Zhongguo xiandai zhishi jieceng de xingcheng 1912–1952*. Beijing: Beijing shehuikexue wenxian chubanshe, 2023.

Lien, Ling-ling. *Dazao xiaofei tiantang: baihuogongsi yu jindai Shanghai chengshi wenhua* (Creating a Consumer Paradise: Department Stores and Modern Urban Culture in Shanghai). Beijing: Shehui kexue wenxian chuban she, 2017.

Lin, Shengdong. *Zhongguo jin xiandai jingdian guanggao chuangyi pingxi: "Shenbao" qishi qinian* (Analysis of modern advertising in China, through 70 years of *Shenbao*). Nanjing: Dongnan daxue chubanshe, 2005.

Liu, Li. *Zhongguo jindai baoye caifang shilun: yi shenbao wei zhongxin de kaocha* (History of newspapers interviews in modern China: a study centered on *Shenbao*). Hefei: Anhui daxue chubanshe, 2014.

Lu, Meiseng. *Guanggao* (Advertising). Shanghai: Commercial Press, 1940.

Ma, Guoliang. *Liangyou yijiu: yijia huabao yu yige shidai* (Remembering *Liangyou*: an illustrated journal and its times). Beijing: Sanlian shudian, 2002.

Marchand, Roland. *Advertising the American Dream: Making Way for Modernity, 1920–1940*. Berkeley: University of California Press, 1985.

Martin, Marc. *Trois siècles de publicité en France*. Paris: Éditions Odile Jacob, 1992.

Merkel, Ina, and Christine Grosse. "Au bonheur des petites gens. Publicité, étude des besoins and consommation au quotidien en RDA". *Mouvement Social*, n° 206 (June 2004): 41–57.

Mittler, Barbara. *A newspaper for China? Power, identity, and change in Shanghai's news media, 1872–1912*. Cambridge: Harvard University Press, 2004.

Mittler, Barbara. "Gendered Advertising in China: What History Do Images Tell?" *European Journal of East Asian Studies* 6, n° 1 (2007): 13–41.

Mittler, Barbara. "Imagined Communities Divided: Reading Visual Regimes in Shanghai's Newspaper Advertising (1860s–1910s)". In *Visualising China, 1845–1965: Moving and Still Images in Historical Narratives*, ed. Christian Henriot and Wen-hsin Yeh, 267–378. Leiden: Brill, 2013.

Mo, Yajun. *Touring China: A History of Travel Culture, 1912–1949*. Ithaca: Cornell University Press, 2021.

Morgan, Stephen L. "Economic growth and the biological standard of living in China, 1880–1930". *Economics & Human Biology* 2, n° 2 (1 June 2004): 197–218.

Mullaney T.S. "Quote Unquote Language Reform: New-Style Punctuation and the Horizontalization of Chinese". *Modern Chinese Literature and Culture* 29, n° 2 (2017): 206–50.

Nakajima, Chieko. *Body, Society, and Nation: The Creation of Public Health and Urban Culture in Shanghai*. Cambridge: Harvard University Press, 2018.

Narramore, Terry. "Making the News in Shanghai: *Shen Bao* and the Politics of Newspaper Journalism, 1912–1937". Doctoral Dissertation, Australian National University, 1989.

Nellist, George F.M. *Men of Shanghai and North China. A Standard Biographical Reference Work*. Shanghai: The Oriental Press, 1933.

Nixon, Sean. "Apostles of Americanization? J. Walter Thompson Company Ltd, Advertising and Anglo-American Relations 1945–67". *Contemporary British History* 22, n° 4 (December 2008): 477–99.

Pan, Junxiang. *Zhongguo jindai guohuo yundong* (The National Products Movement in modern China). Beijing: Zhongguo wenshi, 1995.

Pang, Ju'ai. *Kuawenhua guanggao yu shimin wenhua de bianqian: 1910–1930 nian "Shenbao" kuawenhua guanggao yanjiu* (Transcultural advertising and the transformation of popular culture: a study of transcultural advertisements in *Shenbao* in the 1910–1930s). Shanghai: Jiaotong daxue chubanshe, 2011.

Pang, Laikwan. *The Distorting Mirror: Visual Modernity in China*. Honolulu: University of Hawaii Press, 2007.

Paulès, Xavier, and Damien Chaussende. *La République de Chine: histoire générale de la Chine: 1912–1949*. Paris: Belles-Lettres, 2019.

Peng, Hsiao-yen, and Isabelle Rabut, eds. *Modern China and the West: Translation and Cultural Mediation*. Brill, 2014.

Pouillard, Véronique. "American Advertising Agencies in Europe: J. Walter Thompson's Belgian Business in the Inter-War Years". *Business History* 47, n° 1 (January 2005): 44–58.

Pouillard, Véronique. *La publicité en Belgique, 1850–1975: des courtiers aux agences internationales*. Bruxelles: Académie Royale de Belgique, 2005.

Powell, John Benjamin. *Who's Who in China*. Shanghai: China Weekly Review, 1936.

Rawski, Thomas G. *Economic Growth in Prewar China*. Berkeley: University of California Press, 1989.

Rea, Christopher G. "Enter the Cultural Entrepreneur". In *The Business of Culture: Cultural Entrepreneurs in China and Southeast Asia, 1900–65*, ed. Nicolai Volland and Christopher G Rea, 9–34. Vancouver: University of British Columbia Press, 2014.

Reinhardt, Anne. *Navigating Semi-Colonialism: Shipping, Sovereignty, and Nation-Building in China, 1860–1937*. Harvard University Press, 2018.

Roche, Daniel. *La culture des apparences: une histoire du vêtement (XVIIe-XVIIIe siècle)*, 1989.

Rorty, Richard. *The Linguistic Turn: Recent Essays in Philosophical Method*. Chicago: University of Chicago Press, 1967.

Sanger, J. *Advertising methods in Japan, China, and the Philippines*. Washington: Govt. Print. Office, 1921.

Schneider, Helen M. *Keeping the Nation's House Domestic Management and the Making of Modern China*. Vancouver: UBC Press, 2011.

Schwartz, Thomas A. "Coca-Cola and Pax Americana: The limits of americanization in postwar Europe". *Contemporary Austrian Studies* 3 (January 1995): 262–72.

Scott, Walter Dill. *The Psychology of Advertising: A Simple Exposition of the Principles of Psychology in Their Relation to Successful Advertising*. Boston: Small, Maynard & Co., 1908.

Shanghai gongshangren minglu (Shanghai Business directory). Shanghai: Meihua shuju, 1936.

Shanghai gongshang renwu zhi (Chronicles of Shanghai Businessmen). Shanghai: Quanguo geda shuju, 1948.

Shanghaishi renzhi (Chronicles of Shanghai Industrialists). Shanghai: Zhanwang chubanshe, 1947.

Sheehan, Brett. *Trust in Troubled Times: Money, Banks, and State-Society Relations in Republican Tianjin*. Cambridge, MA: Harvard University Press, 2003.

Sheehan, Brett. "Middling Elites: Middle Managers at the Shanghai Bank of China on the Eve of the Communist Revolution". In *Knowledge, Power, and Networks: Elites in Transition in Modern China*, edited by Cécile Armand, Christian Henriot and Huei-min Sun, 83–112. Leiden: Brill, 2022.

Song, Jialin. *Lao yuefenpai* (Old calendar posters), 11. Shanghai: Shanghai huabao chubanshe, 1997.

Song Shuqiang, Yin Zhaolu and Zhao Feifei, eds. *"Shenbao" baodao yu pinlgun* (Surveys and commentaries in Shenbao). Nanjing: Nanjing daxue chubanshe, 2019.

Spiegel, Gabrielle. *Practicing History: New Directions in Historical Writing after the Linguistic Turn*. Taylor & Francis, 2005.

Starch, Daniel. *Advertising: Its principles, practice, and technique*. Chicago; New York: Scott, Foresman and Company, 1914.

Su, Shangda. *Guanggaoxue gailun* (The Fundamentals of Advertising). Shanghai: Commercial Press, 1929.

Sun, Shunhua. *Zhongguo guanggao shi* (History of Advertising in China). Jinan: Shandong daxue chuban she, 2007.

Sung, Tzu-Hsuan. "Cosmétiques, beauté and genre en Chine. Une analyse de la presse and des publicités (Fin des Qing – 1930)". Doctoral Dissertation, Ecole Normale Supérieure de Lyon, 2015.

Susan Glosser. *Chinese Visions of Family and State, 1915–1953*. Berkeley: University of California Press, 2003.

Tang, Yulong. "Jindai Shanghai xiaofei wenhua shi yu xia shenbao guanggao de fazhan (Shenbao advertisements and the rise of consumerism in Shanghai)". *Wenhua yuekan*, n° 6 (2017).

Tillman, Margaret. *Raising China's Revolutionaries: Modernizing Childhood for Cosmopolitan Nationalists and Liberated Comrades, 1920s-1950s*. Columbia University Press, 2018.

Trentmann, Frank. *The Empire of Things: How We Became a World of Consumers, from the Fifteenth Century to the Twenty-First*, 2016.

Trentmann, Frank. *The Making of the Consumer: Knowledge, Power and Identity in the Modern World*. Oxford: Berg, 2006.

Tsai, Weipin. *Reading Shenbao: Nationalism, Consumerism and Individuality in China, 1919–37*. Houndmills, Basingstoke: Palgrave Macmillan, 2008.

Vittinghoff, Natascha, and Michael Lackner, eds. *Mapping Meanings the Field of New Learning in Late Qing China*. Leiden; Boston: Brill, 2004.

Wagner, Rudolf G. "The Role of the Foreign Community in the Chinese Public Sphere". *The China Quarterly*, n° 142 (June 1995): 423–43.

Wang, Fei-Hsien. *Pirates and Publishers: A Social History of Copyright in Modern China*. Princeton, New Jersey: Princeton University Press, 2019.

Wang, Min. "Jindai guo huoyun dong zhongdi yanghuo xiaofei shishang (The National Products Movements and the crave for foreign goods)". *Lantai shijie*, n° 3 (2013).

Wang, Pengcheng, ed. *Shanghai shiyanjiu* (Studies in Shanghai history). Shanghai, 1984.

Wang, Runian. *Yuwang de xiangxiang: 1920–1930 niandai "Shenbao" guanggao de wenhua shi yanjiu* (The imaginary of desire: a cultural study of *Shenbao* advertisements in the 1920–1930s). Shanghai: Shanghai renmin chubanshe, 2007.

Wang, Y.C. *Chinese intellectuals and the West, 1872–1949*. Chapel Hill: University of North Carolina Press, 1966.

Wang, Zhenzhu. "Popular Magazines and the Making of a Nation: The Healthy Baby Contest Organized by The Young Companion in 1926–27". *Frontiers of History in China* 6, n° 4 (2011): 525–37.

Ward, Douglas B. "Tracking the Culture of Consumption: Curtis Publishing Company, Charles Coolidge Parlin, and the Origins of Market Research, 1911–1930". 1996.

Weinbaum, Alys Eve, and Tani Barlow, eds. *The Modern Girl around the World Consumption, Modernity, and Globalization*. Durham, N.C.: Duke University Press, 2008.

Wen Chunying, and Zhu Chen. "Zhong-Xi ronghe: jindai yiyao guanggao de 'shen' yu 'nao' – yi Shanghai *Xinbao, Shenbao* weili (1862–1915) (Liver and brain in the medical ads of *Xinbao* and *Shenbao*)". *Guanggao daguan* (2012): 84–88.

White, Percival. *Market Analysis, Its Principles and Methods*. New York: McGraw-Hill, 1921.

Who's Who in China. Shanghai: China Weekly Review, 1940.

Wong, Katrine. "Wang Xiaolai (1887–1967): A Biography". Doctoral Dissertation, University of Lyon 2, 2019.

Woodard, James P. "Marketing Modernity: The J. Walter Thompson Company and North American Advertising in Brazil, 1929–1939". *Hispanic American Historical Review* 82, n° 2 (May 2002): 257.

Wu Shenyuan. *Shanghai zui zao de zhongchong* (The earliest species of Shanghai). Shanghai: Huadong shifan daxue chubanshe, 1989.

Wu Tiesheng, and Zhu Shengyu. *Guanggaoxue* (Advertising Studies). Shanghai: Zhonghua shuju, 1946.

Xin, Ping, and Xiao Feng. "20 shiji 30 niandai shanghairen de xiaofei guan – yi 'shenbao' jiantao wei zhongxin (Consumerism in 1930s Shanghai – A Perspective from *Shenbao* Advertisements)". *Shanghai daxue xuebao*, n° 3 (2012).

Xu, Xiaoqun. *Chinese Professionals and the Republican State: The Rise of Professional Associations in Shanghai, 1912–1937*. Cambridge: Cambridge University Press, 2009.

Xu Yin, and Xiaoqun Xu. "Becoming Professional: Chinese Accountants in Early 20th Century Shanghai". *Accounting Historians Journal* 30, n° 1 (June 2003): 129–53.

Yang, Tsui-hua. *Patronage of Science: The China Foundation for the Promotion of Education and Culture*. Taipei: Institute of Modern History, Academia Sinica, 1991.

Ye, Weili. *Seeking Modernity in China's Name: Chinese Students in the United States, 1900–1927*. Stanford: Stanford Univ. Press, 2001.

Yeh, Wen-Hsin. *Shanghai Splendor: Economic Sentiments and the Making of Modern China, 1843–1949*. Berkeley: University of California Press, 2007.

Yeh, Wen-Hsin. *The Alienated Academy: Culture and Politics in Republican China, 1919–1937*. Cambridge, Mass.; London: Council on East Asian studies, Harvard University, 1990.

Zanasi, Margherita. *Saving the Nation: Economic Modernity in Republican China*. Chicago: University of Chicago Press, 2006.

Zhang, Jing. *Zhongguo Taiping Yang guoji xuehui yanjiu, 1925–1945* (Research on the China Institute of Pacific Relations, 1925–1945). Beijing: Shehui kexue wenxian chubanshe, 2012.

Zuo Xuchu. *Zhongguo jindai shangbiao jianshi* (A brief history of modern trademarks in China). Shanghai: Xuelin chubanshe, 2003.

Digital Resources

"Advertising History". https://advertisinghistory.hypotheses.org/
"Historical Photographs of China". https://www.hpcbristol.net/
"MADSpace". https://madspace.org/
"Virtual Shanghai Project". https://www.virtualshanghai.net/

Brand Names

https://doi.org/10.1515/9783111390000-014

Concepts

https://doi.org/10.1515/9783111390000-015

Organisations

https://doi.org/10.1515/9783111390000-016

Persons

https://doi.org/10.1515/9783111390000-017